BLACKSTONE GRIDDLE COOKBOOK

Prepare a Feast for Your Taste Buds with 350+ Simple, Delicious, Recipes – Top Secret Cooking Tips to Effortlessly Become Your Family's Favorite Chef

WILLIAM HENRY CAMERON

TABLE OF CONTENTS

Introduction

Grilled food is as delicious as it is healthy. The best part is, grilling is a relatively simple cooking technique that everyone can master, even the inexperienced, amateur chefs. But, if cooking on the griddle is so simple, why is the home-grilled meat tough, we can't achieve the perfect finish, the fish breaks, and the vegetable are raw or burnt? Because there are few secret techniques everyone keeps for themselves, but this book is about lay it all out!

Are you a greedy caravan? Do you like to do a back door before the big game? Do you like to cook at friends' houses? Well, Blackstone Griddle gives you maximum flexibility, allowing you to take your baking sheet with you wherever you need to go. With minimal effort, you can remove the flat top, safely fold and store the legs, and remove the propane tank. Best of all, the skillet comes with industrial-grade wheels so you can roll the pan where you need it.

Made from industrial grade materials, your Blackstone iron will be a versatile device for years to come. The frame of the pan is made of extremely durable powder-coated steel. The burners are made from restaurant grade stainless steel and are guaranteed to produce perfectly even and strong heat for years to come. After spending time with the Blackstone grill, you might even consider ditching the more conventional gas or charcoal grills.

Say goodbye to dirty embers and fit forever. Charcoal is dirty, expensive, and bad for your health, so why do you keep using it? The Blackstone griddle uses a standard refillable propane tank that fits easily in the skillet. And thanks to the simple power button, turning the pan on is as easy as pressing a button. This cookbook is intended to assist the user of a Blackstone griddle to produce recipes that are simple and easy to make, while producing attractive and delicious results. We have attempted to provide a broad range of tasty recipes that are appropriate for a wide variety of tastes. You will also find some recipes for food that can be cooked on a Blackstone griddle over a big open fire as well. We hope you will enjoy using this cookbook as much as we enjoyed writing it.

We hope you will enjoy using this cookbook as much as we enjoyed writing it.

CHAPTER 1
Blackstone Flat Top Griddle

The Blackstone Flat Top Griddle provides 720 inches of professional grade griddle for your back yard or really anywhere you go. Now you can prepare professional quality meals and get the same results that professional chefs get every time you cook. Make teppanyaki-style food pancakes, quesadillas, grilled cheese, steak, eggs, potatoes, and more. The Blackstone Flat Top griddle is designed to generate perfectly even and adjustable heat across four different cooking zones so you can always have the exact temperature you need right away.

The Blackstone Flat Top griddle is made from professional grade materials, This means that you can carefully control everything you cook with individual controls for each zone. Eggs do not cook properly to the same temperature as a steak and the Blackstone Griddle allows you to cook both perfectly at the same time.

Who is it Good For?

Because the Blackstone Griddle is large enough to cook all the parts of a complete meal at the same time, it is perfect for families who love perfectly Prepared backyard favorites like burgers, steaks, and veggies, but it's also perfect for families who love to make big breakfasts. Prepared are eggs, bacon, hashbrowns, and pancakes for everyone at the same time.

Do you love to cook big meals on the go? The Blackstone Griddle is perfect for camping and tailgating because of how easy it is to transport and set up. Pack it up for your next camping trip and set it up when you want to make an amazing outdoor meal. The Griddle is also perfect for anyone who loves making fresh Griddle food for a professional tailgate party. Since the Griddle easily fits in the trunk of a car, you can take it with you to the game and set it up in minutes. Impress the whole parking lot with the amazing food you make for your fellow fans.

Who is it NOT Good For?

Everyone loves food cooked in the open air, but if you don't have a large enough outdoor space in which to use the Griddle, this may not be for you. A good rule of thumb is that you can use the griddle anywhere you would use a conventional gas or charcoal griddle.

A Few Cautions

Always make sure all connection points are clean and free of debris. When attaching the hose to the tank, make sure the valve is completely tight before allowing gas to flow to the griddle.

The Blackstone Griddle's cold rolled steel flat top produces amazing results, but because it gets very hot, you should make sure children are always supervised when near the griddle.

What Are its Health Benefits?

Charcoal griddleing has been the standard for many years, but it carries a whole host of risks. First of all, charcoal fires increase the risk of fires in your yard. That's pretty bad, but did you know that cooking with charcoal also increases your risk of cancer? The combination of charcoal, lighter fluid, and dripping fats causes a variety of compounds that are considered carcinogenic. And you're not just breathing these chemicals when you cook. They're actually coating your food! Charcoal griddles also contribute to air pollution by releasing large amounts of carbon monoxide and carbon dioxide into the atmosphere. The Blackstone Griddle, on the other hand, uses no charcoal and is much safer to use.

A Brief History of Griddleing

You may not be surprised to hear that griddleing food is a pretty old technique. In fact, it goes back over a half a million years. Early humans found that meat cooked over fire was actually more nutritious than raw meat. The reason? Bioavailability. In short, cooking meat changes the structure of proteins and fats allowing them to be more efficiently digested and absorbed by the body. Until the 1940s griddleing was mostly something that people did around campfires, but after World War II and the expansion of suburbs, the popularity of backyard griddleing skyrocketed. By the 1950s the back yard BBQ was a staple of family entertaining, and it remains this way today.

Better Than Conventional Griddles?

Since the invention of the burger, the debate has raged over whether a griddle or a flat top griddle does the best job. While it's true that griddles offer burgers a smokier flavor, does that really result in a better burger? After years of research burger experts reached the conclusion that the flat top griddle is actually superior to the griddle for one simple reason: It allows the burger to cook in its own juices rather that have all of those juices fall through the grate and into the fire. The end result is a more evenly cooked, juicier, more flavorful burger.

CHAPTER 2
How To Use The Blackstone Flat Top Griddle

Setting up the Griddle

Once you have removed the Blackstone Griddle from its packaging, be sure to consult the user manual to ensure you have all of the included parts and fasteners. Follow the step-by-step instructions to assemble the griddle, and makes sure to place it on a level surface so that it cannot roll.

Learning the controls

The Blackstone Griddle has easy to use controls that will have you cooking in no time.

1. Ignition button: The battery controlled ignition button lights your griddle. Simply press, hold, and the left most burner will light.
2. Left Burner Knob: Turn clockwise to control the heat on the left burner.
3. Left-Center Burner Knob: Turn clockwise to increase the heat on the left-center burner.
4. Right-Center Burner Knob: Turn clockwise to increase the heat on the right-center burner.
5. Right Burner Knob: Turn clockwise to increase the heat on the right burner.

The griddleing process

Thanks to the Blackstone Griddle you can make almost anything with amazing results. Because the griddle has four independent zones, you are free to cook different foods at different temperatures at the same time. Unlike conventional griddles, this gives you far greater flexibility with one appliance.

Since the Blackstone Griddle features a heavy cold rolled steel cooking surface, you will need to wait a few minutes for the burners to heat the surface properly. To prevent your food from sticking, you should take the time to season your griddle before use. We'll cover the seasoning process in the Pro Tips section. Once you have finished cooking, turn the burners off one by one, and be sure to turn off the valve on the propane tank.

Workarounds

The Blackstone Griddle features an easy to use ignition system, but if you find that the ignition burner is not lighting there are several possible causes. First, check to see if the battery in the ignitor has enough power. If that is not the problem. Another problem may be a clogged burner or gas jet. Because food or other debris can fall into the burners, they may become clogged over time. If this is the case, remove the cooking surface and use a damp sponge to clean out the burners or gas jets.

Some users have noticed that the grease drain can allow grease to drip out of the trough and down the leg of the griddle, which can cause grease to pool on the ground. In order to combat this, make sure the grease trough and the catch can are properly aligned. Misalignment can cause leaks. Also, make sure to monitor the grease level so that it does not overflow or overwhelm the grease drain. Be mindful of bits of food that may fall into the grease trough as these may also cause the grease drain to become clogged.

If you find that food sticks to the surface of the griddle, there are several causes with simple solutions. First, you may not have properly seasoned the griddle. Because the griddle does not come pre-seasoned you should be sure to do this before using. Your food may also stick because you are adding it to the griddle too soon. Since the heavy cooking surface needs a little time to heat up, make sure that it is at the proper temperature before adding food. You can do this by touching a corner or small piece of food to the griddle. If it immediately sticks, wait another few minutes. Another common cause of food sticking to the griddle, is not giving it enough time to cook. Great chefs know that you shouldn't be in a hurry to flip your food. This is because most foods undergo a chemical reaction called the Maillard reaction which creates a charred layer on the food by raising it to a certain temperature. This reaction is also responsible for what is commonly known as a "sear." Giving your food enough time to sear before flipping will ensure it does not stick.

CHAPTER 3
Pro Tips

Season the Cooking Surface

Like most high quality cooking appliances, the cold rolled steel cooking surface of your Blackstone Griddle needs to be properly seasoned to ensure optimal cooking results. So you may be asking, "what is seasoning?" Before non-stick coatings existed, there was only one way to make sure food didn't stick to the cooking surface. By creating a layer of burnt on oil, you will not only achieve a perfect non-stick surface, you will also protect the cooking surface from scratches and oxidation. Let's get started. First, use soap and water to wash the cooking surface thoroughly. Use a cloth to dry the surface. Next, apply a small amount of oil to the cooking surface. The best oils to use are those with a high smoke point like vegetable or canola. Use a paper towel to spread the oil evenly across the cooking surface. Turn on all four burners and set the temperature to 275°F. Wait until the oil begins to smoke and the surface begins to darken. Once it is smoking, turn off the burners and allow the griddle to cool. Repeat this process two to three more times until the entire surface is evenly dark. Now your griddle is naturally non-stick and protected from damage and rust.

Keep your Griddle Working from Season to Season

Because you are most likely going to keep your griddle outside, you will need to make sure to do a few things before you store it and before you use it again after being stored. Before you store, make sure to disconnect the gas tank and store away from the griddle with a cap on the valve. You can also purchase a cover for the griddle to keep out insects and dust. When you are ready to start using your griddle again, make sure to check the burner area for spider webs. Webs are flammable and can cause flare ups if you do not clean them out before cooking. Check the level in your gas tank to make sure you have enough fuel to start cooking. Once the tank is attached and you are ready to cook, it's a good idea to perform a new season on the cooking surface. Simply follow the instructions above and your griddle will be good as new.

The Best Way to Clean Your Griddle

After each use you will want to clean your griddle, but your griddle should not be cleaned like regular pots and pans. Since you want to build up a nice coating of seasoning to protect your griddle and get the best possible results, you need to make sure not to use things like dish soap to clean the cooking surface. Most detergents have a grease cutting ingredient and this will eat right through your layer of seasoning. The best way to clean your griddle is the way the pros do in restaurants: with a griddle scraper and hot water. You can purchase a griddle scraper which is designed to get rid of any bits of food left behind without sacrificing the seasoning layer you've achieved. To remove things like fat or sauces, a wash with very hot water will dissolve most things, which you can then scrape away. While you don't have to season your griddle after every cleaning, continuous seasoning will ensure that your griddle stays dark and shiny.

Invest in the Proper Tools

Since the Blackstone Griddle is a professional grade piece of equipment, you should have professional grade cooking tools to get the most out of it. While you may have an array of spatulas in the kitchen, to get the best out of your griddle, we recommend buying two long metal spatulas. These spatulas are not only durable, they allow you to transport and flip a large amount of food at the same time. They are also thin and flexible so you can scoop up things like a whole hashbrown without dropping anything. Also recommended are at least one pair of long handled metal tongs which will allow you to reach anywhere on the griddle without worrying about getting burned.

Try Different Cooking Fats

Unlike a traditional griddle which allows any cooking fat to fall onto the coals or gas jets, the Blackstone Griddle keeps your cooking fat right where you want it: on your food! Because of this, you can experiment with different flavors of cooking fat to optimize your results. Different oils impart different flavors, but they also work differently from each other. Olive oil imparts a robust and sometimes spicy black pepper flavor that gives an extra richness to food. The problem with olive oil, however, is that is has a pretty low smoke point, which means that over a certain temperature, the oil will start to taste burned. Use olive oil for foods you are cooking at lower to medium temperature, but avoid it for foods cooked over high heat. If you're looking for oil for high heat cooking, try canola or regular vegetable oil. They will allow you to cook to high heats without that unpleasant burnt taste. And of course, butter packs more flavor than almost anything, but it also has a tendency to burn; so use butter for low heat cooking or for foods you plan to cook quickly.

The Ultimate Burger

For centuries, humanity has quested after the perfect burger. Since its invention, burger chefs have argued about the best way to grind it; the best way to form the patties; and of course… the best way to cook it. Some say you have to use fancy waygu beef imported from Japan, some say the best method is high heat over charcoal. Well, we're going to put the debate to rest once and for all. The first key to the best burger you've ever had is fat content. If you go to your local supermarket you usually have a choice between 20 percent fat or 10 percent fat. For the perfect burger, this will not do. The perfect burger has between 25 and 30 percent fat, and the best way to achieve this is to grind it yourself using a combination of chuck and short rib. If you don't feel like doing this at home, talk to your local butcher and tell them that you need ground beef with a higher fat content. Also, but sure to always use freshly ground beef. The longer it's sitting in packaging the more compressed it's getting, and compressed beef is the enemy of the perfect burger.

Once you have the right beef, form it into loose balls about 1/3 of a pound. Don't work it too much, and don't press it together, as you want the balls just barely to hold together. Light your griddle and turn the burners to medium heat. You might think that burgers cook best at high heat, but this is wrong. You want to give your burgers time to let their fat render and develop a nice flavorful sear. If you cook too fast you'll end up with overcooked burgers that are chewy inside. Drizzle a little vegetable oil on the griddle and place the ball on the griddle. Using a griddle weight, press down to "smash" the burger as flat as you'd like. Don't reshape it, just let it press onto the griddle and sprinkle with salt. Use your thumb to make an indentation in the center of the burger so that it stays flat. When the first side has developed a nice sear, flip, season with salt and cook for an equal amount of time. This way your burger will have the time to render it's fat and reabsorb it as it cooks. When you've reached the temperature you prefer, remove it from the griddle and allow it to rest for five minutes. Top it however you'd like and enjoy what will be the best burger you've ever had.

CHAPTER 4
Breakfasts Recipes

Fried Pickles

Preparation Time: 10 minutes
Cooking Time: 10 minutes
Servings: 4
Ingredients:

- 20 dill pickle slices
- 1/4 cup all-purpose flour
- 1/8 tsp. baking powder
- 3 tbsps. beer or seltzer water
- 1/8 tsp. sea salt
- 2 tbsps. water, plus more if needed
- 2 tbsps. cornstarch
- 1-1/2 cups panko bread crumbs
- 1 tsp. paprika
- 1 tsp. garlic powder
- 1/4 tsp. cayenne pepper
- 2 tbsps. canola oil, divided

Directions:

1. Preheat the griddle to medium-high.
2. Pat the pickle slices dry, and place them on a dry plate in the freezer.
3. In a medium bowl, stir together the flour, baking powder, beer, salt, and water. The batter should be the consistency of cake batter. If it is too thick, add more water, 1 teaspoon at a time.
4. Place the cornstarch in a small shallow bowl.
5. In a separate large shallow bowl, combine the bread crumbs, paprika, garlic powder, and cayenne pepper.
6. Remove the pickles from the freezer. Dredge each one in cornstarch.
7. Tap off any excess, then coat in the batter. Lastly, coat evenly with the bread crumb mixture.
8. Set on the griddle top and gently brush the breaded pickles with 1 tablespoon of oil. Cook for 5 minutes.
9. After 5 minutes, turn and gently brush the pickles with the remaining 1 tablespoon of oil and resume cooking.
10. When cooking is complete, serve immediately.

Nutrition:
Calories: 296kcal; Fat: 10g; Carbs: 44g; Protein: 7g

Grilled Fruit Salad with Honey-Lime Glaze

Preparation Time: 10 minutes
Cooking Time: 4 minutes
Servings: 4
Ingredients:

- 1/2 pound strawberries, washed, hulled and halved
- 1 (9 oz.) can pineapple chunks, drained, juice reserved
- 2 peaches, pitted and sliced
- 6 tbsps. honey, divided
- 1 tbsp. freshly squeezed lime juice

Directions:

1. Preheat your griddle to medium high.
2. While the unit is preheating, combine the strawberries, pineapple, and peaches in a large bowl with 3 tablespoons of honey. Toss to coat evenly.

3. Place the fruit on the grill top. Gently press the fruit down to maximize grill marks. Grill for 4 minutes without flipping.
4. Meanwhile, in a small bowl, combine the remaining 3 tablespoons of honey, lime juice, and 1 tablespoon of reserved pineapple juice.
5. When cooking is complete, place the fruit in a large bowl and toss with the honey mixture. Serve immediately.

Nutrition:
Calories: 178kcal; fat: 1g; Carbs: 47g; Protein: 2g

Onion, Pepper, and Mushroom Frittata

Preparation Time: 10 minutes
Cooking Time: 10 minutes
Servings: 4 slices
Ingredients:

- 4 large eggs
- 1/4 cup whole milk
- Sea salt
- Freshly ground black pepper
- 1/2 bell pepper, seeded and diced
- 1/2 onion, chopped
- 4 cremini mushrooms, sliced
- 1/2 cup shredded Cheddar cheese

Directions:

1. Preheat the griddle to medium high.
2. In a medium bowl, whisk together the eggs and milk. Season with the salt and pepper. Add the bell pepper, onion, mushrooms, and cheese. Mix until well combined.
3. Pour the egg mixture into the Ninja Multi-Purpose Pan or baking pan, spreading evenly.
4. Place the pan directly to the grill and cook for 10 minutes, or until lightly golden.

Nutrition:
Calories: 153kcal; Fat: 10g; Carbs: 5g; Protein: 11g

Classic Buttermilk Pancakes

Preparation time: 5 minutes
Cooking Time: 10 minutes
Servings: 4
Ingredients:

- 2 cup all-purpose flour
- 3 tbsps. sugar
- 1-1/2 tsps. baking powder
- 1-1/2 tsps. baking soda
- 1-1/4 tsps. salt
- 2-1/2 cup buttermilk
- 2 eggs
- 3 tbsps. unsalted butter, melted
- 2 tbsps. vegetable oil

Directions:

1. In a large bowl, combine the flour, sugar, baking soda, baking powder, and salt.
2. Stir in the buttermilk, eggs, and butter, and mix until combined but not totally smooth.
3. Heat your griddle to medium heat and add a small amount of oil. Using a paper towel, spread the oil over the griddle in a very thin layer.
4. Use a ladle to pour the batter onto the griddle allowing a few inches between pancakes.

5. When the surface of the pancakes is bubbly, flip and cook a few additional minutes. Remove the pancakes from the griddle and serve immediately with butter and maple syrup.

Nutrition:
Calories: 432kcal, Fat: 12.8.g, Carbs: 65.1g, Protein: 14.4g

Fluffy Blueberry Pancakes

Preparation time: 10 minutes
Cooking Time: 10 minutes Servings: 2
Ingredients:

- 1 cup flour
- 3/4 cup milk
- 2 tbsps. white vinegar
- 2 tbsps. sugar
- 1 tsp. baking powder
- 1/2 tsp. baking soda
- 1/2 tsp. salt
- 1 egg
- 2 tbsps. butter, melted
- 1cup fresh blueberries
- butter for cooking

Directions:

1. In a bowl, combine the milk and vinegar. Set aside for two minutes.
2. In a large bowl, combine the flour, sugar, baking powder, baking soda, and salt. Stir in the milk, egg, blueberries, and melted butter. Mix until combined but not totally smooth.
3. Heat your griddle to medium heat and add a little butter. Pour the pancakes onto the griddle and cook until one side is golden brown.
4. Flip the pancakes and cook until the other side is golden.
5. Remove the pancakes from the griddle and serve with warm maple syrup.

Nutrition:
Calories: 499kcal, Fat: 16.5.g, Carbs: 76.2g, Protein: 12.9g

Grilled Pizza with Eggs and Greens

Preparation Time: 10 minutes
Cooking Time: 8 minutes
Servings: 2 slices
Ingredients:

- 2 tbsps. all-purpose flour, plus more as needed
- 1/2 store-bought pizza dough (about 8 ounces)
- 1 tbsp. canola oil, divided
- 1 cup fresh ricotta cheese
- 4 large eggs
- Sea salt
- Freshly ground black pepper
- 4 cups arugula, torn
- 1 tbsp. extra-virgin olive oil
- 1 tsp. freshly squeezed lemon juice
- 2 tbsps. grated Parmesan cheese

Directions:

1. Preheat the griddle to medium high.
2. Dust a clean work surface with flour. Place the dough on the floured surface, and roll it into a 9-inch round of even thickness. Dust your rolling pin and work surface with additional flour, as needed, to ensure the dough does not stick.

3. Brush the surface of the rolled-out dough evenly with 1/2 tablespoon of canola oil. Flip the dough over and brush with the remaining 1/2 tablespoon oil. Poke the dough with a fork 5 or 6 times across its surface to prevent air pockets from forming during cooking.
4. Place the dough to the grill and cook for 4 minutes.
5. After 4 minutes, flip the dough, then spoon teaspoons of ricotta cheese across the surface of the dough, leaving a 1-inch border around the edges.
6. Crack one egg into a ramekin or small bowl. This way you can easily remove any shell that may break into the egg and keep the yolk intact. Imagine the dough is split into four quadrants. Pour one egg into each. Repeat with the remaining 3 eggs. Season the pizza with salt and pepper.
7. Continue cooking for the remaining 3 to 4 minutes, until the egg whites are firm.
8. Meanwhile, in a medium bowl, toss together the arugula, oil, and lemon juice, and season with salt and pepper. Transfer the pizza to a cutting board and let it cool. Top it with the arugula mixture, drizzle with olive oil, if desired, and sprinkle with Parmesan cheese.
9. Cut into pieces and serve.

Nutrition:
Calories: 788kcal; Fat: 46g; Carbs: 58g; Protein: 34g

Bacon and Gruyere Omelet

Preparation time: 5 minutes
Cooking Time: 15 minutes
Servings: 2
Ingredients:

- 6 eggs, beaten
- 6 strips bacon
- 1/4 pound gruyere, shredded
- 1 tsp. black pepper
- 1 tsp. salt
- 1 tbsp. chives, finely chopped
- vegetable oil

Directions:

1. Add salt to the beaten eggs and set aside for 10 minutes.
2. Heat your griddle to medium heat and add the bacon strips. Cook until most of the fat has rendered, but bacon is still flexible. Remove the bacon from the griddle and place on paper towels.
3. Once the bacon has drained, chop into small pieces.
4. Add the eggs to the griddle in two even pools. Cook until the bottom of the eggs starts to firm up. Add the gruyere to the eggs and cook until the cheese has started to melt and the eggs are just starting to brown.
5. Add the bacon pieces and use a spatula to turn one half of the omelet onto the other half.
6. Remove from the griddle, season with pepper and chives and serve.

Nutrition:
Calories: 734kcal, Fat: 55.3.g, Carbs: 2.8g, Protein: 54.8g

Grilled Cinnamon Toast with Berries and Whipped Cream

Preparation Time: 15 minutes
Cooking Time: 10 minutes
Servings: 4 slices
Ingredients:

1 (15-ounce) can full-fat coconut milk, refrigerated overnight
1/2 tablespoon powdered sugar
1-1/2 teaspoons vanilla extract, divided
1 cup halved strawberries
1 tablespoon maple syrup, plus more for garnish
1 tablespoon brown sugar, divided
3/4 cup lite coconut milk
2 large eggs
1/2 teaspoon ground cinnamon
2 tablespoons unsalted butter, at room temperature
4 slices challah bread

Directions:

1. Turn the chilled can of full-fat coconut milk upside down (do not shake the can), open the bottom, and pour out the liquid coconut water. Scoop the remaining solid coconut cream into a medium bowl. Using an electric hand mixer, whip the cream for 3 to 5 minutes, until soft peaks form.
2. Add the powdered sugar and 1/2 teaspoon of the vanilla to the coconut cream, and whip it again until creamy. Place the bowl in the refrigerator.
3. Preheat the griddle to medium high. While the unit is preheating, combine the strawberries with the maple syrup and toss to coat evenly.
4. Sprinkle evenly with ½ tablespoon of the brown sugar.
5. In a large shallow bowl, whisk together the lite coconut milk, eggs, the remaining 1 teaspoon of vanilla, and cinnamon.
6. Place the strawberries on the grill top. Gently press the fruit down to maximize grill marks. Grill for 4 minutes without flipping.
7. Meanwhile, butter each slice of bread on both sides. Place one slice in the egg mixture and let it soak for 1 minute. Flip the slice over and soak it for another minute. Repeat with the remaining bread slices. Sprinkle each side of the toast with the remaining 1/2 tablespoon of brown sugar.
8. After 4 minutes, remove the strawberries from the grill and set aside. Decrease the temperature to medium low. Place the bread on the Grill and cook for 4 to 6 minutes, until golden and caramelized. Check often to ensure desired doneness.
9. Place the toast on a plate and top with the strawberries and whipped coconut cream.
10. Drizzle with maple syrup, if desired.

Nutrition:
Calories: 386kcal; Fat: 19g; Carbs: 49g; Protein: 7g

Classic French Toast

Servings: 4 Preparation time: 5 minutes
Cooking Time: 10 minutes Ingredients:

- 6 eggs, beaten
- 1/4 cup "half and half" or heavy cream
- 8 slices thick cut white or sourdough bread
- 2 tablespoons sugar
- 1 tablespoon cinnamon
- 1 teaspoon salt - butter
- powdered sugar
- maple syrup

Directions:

1. Heat your griddle to medium heat.
2. In a large bowl, combine the eggs, cream, sugar, cinnamon, and salt. Mix well until smooth.
3. Lightly grease the griddle with butter or vegetable oil.
4. Dip each slice of bread in the mixture until well saturated with egg then place onto the griddle.
5. When the French toast has begun to brown, flip and cook until the other side has browned as well. About four minutes. Remove the French toast from the griddle, dust with powdered sugar, and serve with warm maple syrup.

Nutrition: Calories: 332, Sodium: 593 mg, Dietary Fiber: 2.4g, Fat: 10.5.g, Carbs: 44.2g Protein: 16g

Simple French Crepes

Servings: 4 Preparation time: 1 hour
Cooking Time: 15 minutes
Ingredients:

- 1 1/4 cups flour
- 3/4 cup whole milk
- 1/2 cup water
- 2 eggs
- 3 tablespoons unsalted butter, melted
- 1 teaspoon vanilla
- 2 tablespoon sugar

Directions:

1. In a large bowl, add all the ingredients and mix with a whisk. Make sure the batter is smooth. Rest for 1 hour.
2. Heat your Blackstone Griddle to medium heat and add a thin layer of butter. Add about ¼ cup of the batter. Using a crepe spreading tool, form your crepe and cook for 1-2 minutes. Use your Crepe Spatula and flip. Cook for another minute.
3. Top with Nutella and strawberries for a sweet crepe, or top with scrambled eggs and black forest ham for a savory crepe

Nutrition: Calories: 303, Sodium: 112mg, Dietary Fiber: 1.1g, Fat: 12.7g, Carbs: 38.2g Protein: 8.4g

Classic Denver Omelet

Servings: 2 Preparation time: 5 minutes
Cooking Time: 10 minutes
Ingredients:

- 6 large eggs
- 1/4 cup country ham, diced
- 1/4 cup yellow onion, finely chopped
- 1/4 cup green bell pepper, chopped
- 2/3 cup cheddar cheese, shredded
- 1/4 teaspoon cayenne pepper
- salt and black pepper
- 2 tablespoons butter

Directions:

1. Heat your griddle to medium heat and place the butter onto the griddle.
2. Add the ham, onion, and pepper to the butter and cook until the vegetables have just softened.
3. Beat the eggs in a large bowl and add a pinch of salt and the cayenne pepper.
4. Split the vegetables into to portions on the griddle and add half of the eggs to each portion. Cook until the eggs have begun to firm up, and then add the cheese to each omelet.
5. Fold the omelets over and remove from the griddle. Serve immediately.

Nutrition: Calories: 507, Sodium: 747 mg, Dietary Fiber: 0.8g, Fat: 40.5g, Carbs: 4.9g Protein: 31.5g

Bacon Egg and Cheese Sandwich

Servings 4
Preparation time: 5 minutes
Cooking Time: 10 minutes
Ingredients:

- 4 large eggs
- 8 strips of bacon
- 4 slices cheddar or American cheese
- 8 slices sourdough bread
- 2 tablespoons butter
- 2 tablespoons vegetable oil

Directions:

1. Heat your griddle to medium heat and place the strips of bacon on one side. Cook until just slightly crispy.
2. When the bacon is nearly finished, place the oil on the other side of the griddle and crack with eggs onto the griddle. Cook them either sunny side up or over medium.
3. Butter one side of each slice of bread and place them butter side down on the griddle. Place a slice of cheese on 4 of the slices of bread and when the cheese has just started to melt and the eggs are finished, stack the eggs on the bread.
4. Add the bacon to the sandwiches and place the other slice of bread on top. Serve immediately.

Nutrition: Calories: 699, Sodium: 1148 mg, Dietary Fiber: 1.5g, Fat: 47.7g, Carbs: 37.8g Protein: 29.3g

Sausage and Vegetable Scramble

Servings: 4
Preparation time: 10 minutes
Cooking Time: 20 minutes
Ingredients:

- 8 eggs, beaten
- 1/2 lb sausage, sliced into thin rounds or chopped
- 1 green bell pepper, sliced
- 1 yellow onion, sliced
- 1 cup white mushrooms, sliced
- 1 teaspoon salt
- 1/2 teaspoon black pepper
- vegetable oil

Directions:

1. Preheat the griddle to medium-high heat.
2. Brush the griddle with vegetable oil and add the peppers and mushrooms.

3. Cook until lightly browned and then add the onions. Season with salt and pepper and cook until the onions are soft.
4. Add the sausage to the griddle and mix with the vegetables. Cook until lightly browned.
5. Add the eggs and mix with the vegetables and cook until eggs reach desired doneness. Use a large spatula to remove the scramble from the griddle and serve immediately.

Nutrition: Calories: 342, Sodium: 1131 mg, Dietary Fiber: 1.2g, Fat: 24.9.g, Carbs: 6.3g, Protein: 23.2g

Classic Steak and Eggs

Servings: 4
Preparation time: 10 minutes
Cooking Time: 10 minutes
Ingredients:

- 1 pound Sirloin, cut into 4 1/2-inch thick pieces
- 8 large eggs
- 3 tablespoons vegetable oil
- salt and black pepper

Directions:

1. Preheat griddle to medium-high heat on one side and medium heat on the other.
2. Season the steaks with a generous amount of salt and pepper.
3. Place steaks on the medium high side and cook for 3 minutes and add the oil to the medium heat side.
4. Flip the steaks and crack the eggs onto the medium heat side of the griddle.
5. After 3 minutes remove the steaks from the griddle and allow to rest 5 minutes. Finish cooking the eggs and place two eggs and one piece of steak on each plate to serve. Season the eggs with a pinch of salt and pepper.

Nutrition: Calories: 444, Sodium: 215 mg, Dietary Fiber: 0g, Fat: 27.2g, Carbs: 0.8g Protein: 47g

Toad in a Hole

Servings: 4
Preparation time: 10 minutes
Cooking Time: 5 minutes
Ingredients:

- 4 slices white, wheat, or sourdough bread
- 4 eggs
- 2 tablespoons butter
- salt and black pepper

Directions:

1. Preheat griddle to medium heat add the butter, spreading it around.
2. Cut a hole in the center of each slice of bread.
3. Place the slices of bread on the griddle and crack an egg into the holes in each slice of bread.
4. Cook until the bread begins to brown, then flip and cook until the egg whites are firm.
5. Remove from the griddle and season with salt and black pepper before serving.

Nutrition: Calories: 206, Sodium: 311 mg, Dietary Fiber: 0.8g, Fat: 10.7g, Carbs: 18.4g Protein: 9.4g

Ultimate Breakfast Burrito

Servings: 2
Preparation time: 5 minutes
Cooking Time: 20 minutes
Ingredients:

- 4 eggs
- 4 strips bacon
- 1 large russet potato, peeled and cut into small cubes
- 1 red bell pepper
- 1/2 yellow onion
- 1 ripe avocado, sliced
- 2 tablespoon hot sauce
- 2 large flour tortillas
- vegetable oil

Directions:

2. Preheat the griddle to medium-high heat on one side and medium heat on the other side. Brush with vegetable oil and add the bacon to the medium heat side and peppers and onions to the medium-high side. When the bacon finishes cooking, place on paper towels and chop into small pieces. Add the potatoes to the bacon fat on the griddle. Cook the potatoes until softened.
3. Add the eggs to the vegetable side and cook until firm. Place the ingredients onto the tortillas and top with slices of avocado and a tablespoon of hot sauce.

4. Fold the tortillas and enjoy.

Nutrition: Calories: 793, Sodium: 1800 mg, Dietary Fiber: 10.7g, Fat: 41.3.g, Carbs: 73.4g Protein: 35.8g

Mexican Scramble

Servings: 4 Preparation time: 5 minutes
Cooking Time: 10 minutes
Ingredients:

- 8 eggs, beaten - 1 lb Chorizo
- 1/2 yellow onion
- 1 cup cooked black beans
- 1/2 cup green chilies
- 1/2 cup jack cheese
- 1/4 cup green onion, chopped
- 1/2 teaspoon black pepper
- vegetable oil

Directions:

2. Preheat a griddle to medium heat. Brush the griddle with vegetable oil and add the chorizo to one side and the onions to the other side. When the onion has softened, combine it with the chorizo and add the beans and chilies. Add the eggs, cheese, and green onion and cook until eggs have reached desired firmness.
3. Remove the scramble from the griddle and season with black pepper before serving.

Nutrition: Calories: 843, Sodium: 1554 mg, Dietary Fiber: 9.2g, Fat: 54.1.g, Carbs: 38.2g Protein: 50.7g

Hash Brown Scramble

Servings: 4 Preparation time: 10 minutes
Cooking Time: 10 minutes
Ingredients:

- 2 russet potatoes, shredded, rinsed, and drained
- 8 eggs, beaten
- 1 cup cheddar cheese
- 6 slices bacon, cut into small pieces

- 1/3 cup green onion, chopped
- vegetable oil

Directions:

1. Preheat griddle to medium heat and brush with vegetable oil.
2. On one side, place the potatoes on the griddle and spread in a 1/2 inch thick layer. Cook the potatoes until golden brown and then flip. Add the bacon to the other side of the griddle and cook until the fat has rendered.
3. Add the eggs and cheese to the top of the hash browns and stir in the bacon and green onion. Cook until the cheese has melted and divide equally among 4 plates.

Nutrition: Calories: 470, Sodium: 965 mg, Dietary Fiber: 2.8g, Fat: 30.2g,Carbs: 18.8g Protein: 30.6g

Golden Hash Browns

Servings: 4
Preparation time: 10 minutes
Cooking Time: 15 minutes
Ingredients:

- 3 russet potatoes, peeled
- 1 tablespoon onion powder
- 1 tablespoon salt
- 1 teaspoon black pepper
- vegetable oil

Directions:

1. Using the largest holes on a box grater, grate the potatoes and place in a large bowl. When all of the potatoes have been grated, rinse with water.
2. Squeeze as much water out of the potatoes as possible and return to the bowl.
3. Add the onion powder, salt, and pepper to the bowl and stir to combine.
4. Preheat your griddle to medium heat and add a think layer of oil. Spread the potato mixture onto the grill creating a layer about 1/2 inch thick. Cook for approximately 8 minutes.
5. Working in sections using a large spatula, turn the potatoes and cook an additional 5 to 8 minutes or until both sides are golden brown.
6. Remove the potatoes from the griddle in sections and add to plates. Sprinkle with a pinch of salt and serve immediately.

Nutrition: Calories: 118. Sodium: 1755 mg, Dietary Fiber: 4.1g, Fat: 0.2.g, Carbs: 26.8g Protein: 2.9g

Potato Bacon Hash

Servings: 6 – 8
Preparation time: 30 minutes
Cooking Time: 3 hours
Ingredients:

- 6 slices thick cut bacon
- 2 russet potatoes, cut into 1/2 inch chunks
- 1 yellow onion, chopped
- 1 red bell pepper, chopped
- 1 clove garlic, finely chopped
- 1 teaspoon salt
- 1/2 teaspoon black pepper
- 1 tablespoon Tabasco sauce

Directions:

1. Set your griddle to medium heat and cook the bacon until just crispy.

2. Add the potato, onion, and bell pepper to the griddle and cook until the potato has softened. Use the large surface of the griddle to spread out the ingredients.
3. When the potato has softened, add the garlic, salt, and pepper.
4. Chop the bacon into small pieces and add it to the griddle. Stir the mixture well and add the hot sauce right before removing the hash from the griddle. Serve immediately.

Nutrition: Calories: 154, Sodium: 475 mg, Dietary Fiber: 1.8g, Fat: 10.2g, Carbs:11.3g Protein: 4.5g

CHAPTER 5
Burger Recipes

Big Burger

Preparation Time: 5 Minutes
Cooking Time: 9 Minutes
Servings: 4

- **Ingredients:**
  1¼ pounds lean ground beef
- ½ teaspoon salt
- ½ teaspoon freshly ground black pepper
- Seasoning of your choice (such as a dash of Worcestershire or hot sauce, or 1 teaspoon Spicy Spanish Rub
- 4 slices cheese such as American, cheddar, or Swiss (about 4 ounces), or ¼ cup
- crumbled blue or goat cheese
- 4 toasted buns
- 4 beefsteak tomato slices
- 4 leaves romaine lettuce

Directions:

1. Bring the griddle to medium-high heat. Put the beef in a medium bowl and add the salt, pepper, and your preferred seasonings.
2. Using a fork, mix the seasonings into the meat and then, with your hands, form the mixture into 4 patties, each about 1 inch thick. When the griddle is hot, place the burgers on the Griddle and cook for 4 minutes without flipping.
3. Cooking is complete when the internal temperature of the beef reaches at least 145°F on a food thermometer. If needed, cook for up to 5 more minutes.
4. Lay the cheese over the burgers and lower the griddle. Griddle for 30 seconds, just until the cheese melts.
5. Set the burgers onto the bottom halves of the buns, add a slice of tomato and a leaf of lettuce to each burger, and cover with the tops of the buns. Serve immediately.

Nutrition: Calories: 510; Fat: 30g; Protein: 36g

Pineapple Teriyaki Turkey Burgers

Preparation Time: 5 Minutes
Cooking Time: 9 Minutes **Servings:** 4
Ingredients:

- 1 tsp. BBQ rub
- 1 can sliced pineapple
- 4 slices Swiss cheese
- 1 cup fresh raw spinach, stems removed
- 4 sets of hamburger buns
- PATTY
- 1 lb. ground turkey
- ½ cup bread crumbs
- ¼ cup teriyaki sauce
- 1 small yellow onion, diced
- 2 Tbsp. finely chopped parsley
- 2 cloves garlic, minced
- 1 egg, beaten

Directions:

1. In a large mixing bowl, combine all patty ingredients and mix thoroughly by hand.
2. Divide mixture into four equal parts. Form the four portions into patties and lay on parchment paper. Sprinkle each patty evenly with BBQ rub. Place in refrigerator for 30 minutes.
3. Bring the griddle to high heat. When the griddle is hot, place the burgers and pineapple slices. Cook for 4 minutes without flipping. Remove the burgers and cover to keep warm.

4. After burgers are flipped over, add a slice of Swiss cheese to each patty and allow to melt as patty finishes cooking. Remove from griddle.
5. Layer burgers on buns with spinach and pineapple.

Nutrition: Calories: 554; Fat: 11g; Protein:26g; Fiber:2g

Tex-Mex Turkey Burgers

Preparation Time: 10 Minutes
Cooking Time: 15 Minutes
Servings: 4
Ingredients:

- ⅓ cup finely crushed corn tortilla chips
- 1 egg, beaten
- ¼ cup salsa
- ⅓ cup shredded pepper Jack cheese
- Pinch salt
- Freshly ground black pepper
- 1 pound ground turkey
- 1 tablespoon olive oil
- 1 teaspoon paprika

Directions:

1. In a medium bowl, combine the tortilla chips, egg, salsa, cheese, salt, and pepper, and mix well.
2. Add the turkey and mix gently but thoroughly with clean hands.
3. Form the meat mixture into patties about ½ inch thick. Make an indentation in the center of each patty with your thumb so the burgers don't puff up while cooking.
4. Brush the patties on both sides with the olive oil and sprinkle with paprika.
5. Griddle. Turn control knob to the high position. When the griddle is hot, griddle for 14 to 16 minutes or until the meat registers at least 165°F.

Nutrition: Calories: 354; Fat: 21g; Protein:36g; Fiber:2g

Beef Burgers

Preparation Time: 5 Minutes
Cooking Time: 4 Minutes **Servings:** 4
Ingredients:

- 1¼ pounds lean ground beef
- 1 small onion, minced
- ¼ cup teriyaki sauce
- 3 tablespoons I talian-flavored bread
- crumbs
- 2 tablespoons grated Parmesan cheese
- 1 teaspoon salt
- 1 teaspoon freshly ground black pepper
- 3 tablespoons sweet pickle relish
- 4 Kaiser rolls, toasted

Directions:

1. Put the beef in a medium bowl and add the onion, teriyaki sauce, bread crumbs, Parmesan cheese, salt, and pepper. Using a fork, mix the seasonings into the meat and then form the mixture into 4 patties, each about 1 inch thick. Bring the griddle to high heat. When the griddle is hot place the burgers and cook for 4 minutes without flipping.
2. Remove the burgers and cover to keep warm. Top each burger with a spoonful of sweet pickle relish before sandwiching between a bun. Serve immediately.

Nutrition: Calories: 519; Fat: 23g; Protein: 33g

Tzatziki Lamb Burgers

Preparation Time: 5 Minutes
Cooking Time:12 Minutes **Servings:** 5
Ingredients:

- 1½ pounds boneless lamb shoulder or leg or good-quality ground lamb
- 1 tablespoon chopped fresh oregano
- 1 teaspoon salt
- 1 teaspoon black pepper
- 1 tablespoon minced garlic
- ½ cup Greek yogurt
- 1 tablespoon olive oil, plus more for brushing
- 1 tablespoon red wine vinegar
- 2 tablespoons crumbled feta cheese
- 4 or 5 ciabatta rolls, split, or 8–10 slider buns (like potato or dinner rolls)
- Thinly sliced cucumbers for serving

Directions:

1 Put the lamb, oregano, salt, pepper, and garlic in a food processor and pulse until coarsely ground—finer than chopped, but not much. (If you're using preground meat, put it in a bowl with the seasonings and work them together gently with your hands.)
2 Take a bit of the mixture and fry it up to taste for seasoning; adjust if necessary.
3 Handling the meat as little as possible to avoid compressing it, shape the mixture lightly into 4 or 5 burgers or 8 to 10 sliders.
4 Refrigerate the burgers until you're ready to griddle; if you make them several hours in advance, cover with plastic wrap.
5 Whisk the yogurt, oil, and vinegar together in a small bowl until smooth. Stir in the feta. Taste and adjust the seasoning with salt and pepper.
6 Bring the griddle to high heat. When the griddle is hot, place the burgers and cook for 11 minutes.
7 Transfer the burgers to a plate. Brush the cut sides of the rolls lightly with oil and toast directly over the griddle, 1 to 2 minutes. Top with a burger, then several slices of cucumber, a dollop of the sauce, and the other half of the roll. Serve with the remaining sauce on the side.

Nutrition: Calories: 134; Fat: 21g; Protein:36g; Fiber:2g

New Mexican Salsa Verde

Preparation Time: 5 Minutes
Cooking Time: 15 Minutes
Servings: 1 Cup
Ingredients:

- cloves garlic (leave the skins on),
- skewered on a wooden toothpick or small bamboo skewer
- 1 cup roasted New Mexican green chiles or Anaheim chiles cut into ¼-inch strips (8 to 10 chiles
- 2 tablespoons chopped fresh cilantro
- 2 teaspoons fresh lime juice, or more to
- taste
- ½ teaspoon ground cumin
- ½ teaspoon dried oregano
- Coarse salt (kosher or sea) and freshly
- ground black pepper

Directions:

1. Preheat the griddle to high. When ready to cook, lightly oil the griddle surface. Place the burgers on the hot griddle. The burgers will be done after cooking 4 to 6 minutes. Put the garlic cloves until they are lightly browned and tender, 2 to 3 minutes per side (4 to 6 minutes in all). Scrape any really burnt skin off the garlic. Place the garlic, chile strips, cilantro, lime juice, cumin, oregano, and 4 tablespoons of water in a blender and purée until smooth, scraping down the sides of the blender with a spatula.
2. Transfer the salsa to a saucepan and bring to a gentle simmer over medium heat. Let simmer until thick and flavorful, 5 to 8 minutes, stirring with a wooden spoon. The salsa should be thick (roughly the consistency of heavy cream) but pourable; add more water as needed. Taste for seasoning, adding more lime juice as necessary and salt and pepper to taste; the salsa should be highly seasoned.

Nutrition: Calories: 214; Fat: 16g; Protein:36g; Fiber:2g

Chipotle Burgers With Avocado

Preparation Time: 5 Minutes
Cooking Time: 5 Minutes
Servings: 4
Ingredients:

- 1¼ pounds lean ground beef
- 2 tablespoons chipotle puree
- ½ teaspoon salt
- ¼ teaspoon freshly ground black pepper
- slices cheddar cheese (about 4 ounces)
- 1 avocado, halved, pitted, and sliced
- ¼ head iceberg lettuce, shredded
- 4 hamburger buns, toasted

Directions:

1. Put the beef in a medium bowl and add the chipotle puree, salt, and pepper. Using a fork, mix the seasonings into the meat and then, with your hands, form the mixture into 4 patties, each about 1 inch thick.
2. Turn control knob to the high position, when the griddle is hot, place the burgers and cook for 4 minutes without flippin. Topping each burger with a slice of cheese and cook for 1 minute more, until the cheese melts. Remove the burgers and cover to keep warm.
3. Top each burger with a few slices of avocado and some shredded lettuce before sandwiching between a bun.
4. Chipotle Puree: Put canned chipotles and their liquid in a blender or food processor and process until smooth.
5. The puree can be covered with plastic wrap and refrigerated for up to 2 weeks. This stuff is hot-hot-hot, so a little goes a long way. I use it in meat marinades and dips. The puree is sold in some grocery stores, in ethnic mark.

Nutrition: Calories: 590; Fat: 38g; Protein: 37g

Salmon Burgers

Preparation Time: 5 Minutes
Cooking Time: 11 Minutes **Servings:** 4
Ingredients:

- 1½ pounds salmon fillet, skin and any remaining pin bones removed, cut into chunks
- 2 teaspoons Dijon mustard
- 3 scallions, trimmed and chopped
- ¼ cup bread crumbs (preferably fresh)
- Salt and pepper
- Good-quality olive oil for brushing
- sesame hamburger buns or 8–10 slider buns (like potato or dinner rolls)
- 1 large tomato, cut into 4 thick slices

Directions:

1. Put about one quarter of the salmon and the mustard in a food processor and purée into a paste. Add the rest of the salmon and pulse until chopped. Transfer to a bowl, add the scallions, bread crumbs, and a sprinkle of salt and pepper. Mix gently just enough to combine. Form into 4 burgers ¾ to 1 inch thick. Transfer to a plate, cover with plastic wrap, and chill until firm, at least 2 or up to 8 hours.
2. Turn control knob to the high position, when the griddle is hot, brush the burgers with oil on both sides, then put them on the griddle. Cook for 11 minutes.
3. After 11 minutes, check the burgers for doneness. Cooking is complete when the internal temperature reaches at least 165°F on a food thermometer.
4. If necessary, close the hood and continue cooking for up to 2 minutes more.
5. Remove the burgers from the griddle. Put the buns on the griddle, cut side down, and toast for 1 to 2 minutes. Serve the burgers on the buns, topped with the tomato if using.

Nutrition: Calories: 123; Fat: 21g; Protein:16g; Fiber:12g

Bruch Burgers

Preparation Time: 5 Minutes
Cooking Time: 5 Minutes**Servings:** 4
Ingredients:

- ¼ cup light sour cream
- 5 tablespoons white horseradish
- ¼ teaspoon salt
- 1¼ pounds lean ground beef
- ¼ cup tomato sauce
- 2 tablespoons Worcestershire sauce
- A dash or 2 of hot sauce
- 1 teaspoon celery salt
- 4 beefsteak tomato slices
- 4 brioche buns or hamburger buns,
- toasted
- 2 celery stalks, with leafy greens, each cut into 4 pieces

Directions:

1. In a small bowl, combine the sour cream, 2 tablespoons of the horseradish, and the salt.
2. Put the beef in a medium bowl and add the remaining 3 tablespoons horseradish, the tomato sauce, the Worcestershire sauce, hot sauce, and celery salt.

3. Using a fork, mix the seasonings into the meat and then, with your hands, form the mixture into 4 patties, each about 1 inch thick.
4. Turn control knob to the high position, when the griddle is hot, place the burgers and cook for 4 minutes without flipping. Remove the burgers and cover to keep warm. Top with a tablespoon of the horseradish sour cream and a tomato slice before sandwiching between a toasted bun. Serve immediately with the celery sticks.

Nutrition: Calories: 447; Fat: 27g; Protein: 35g

Caesar Salad Poultry Burgers

Preparation Time: 5 Minutes
Cooking Time: 15 Minutes**Servings:** 4
Ingredients:

- ¼ cup mayonnaise
- 2 cloves garlic, 1 minced, 1 peeled and left whole
- 2 oil-packed anchovy fillets, drained and mashed
- 2 tablespoons freshly grated Parmesan cheese
- 1 tablespoon fresh lemon juice
- ½ teaspoon Worcestershire sauce
- 1½ pounds ground chicken or turkey
- Good-quality vegetable oil for oiling the grates
- ciabatta rolls, split, or 8–10 slider buns
- Good-quality olive oil for brushing the rolls
- leaves heart of romaine, trimmed
-

Directions:

1. Line a baking sheet with wax paper. Whisk the mayonnaise, minced garlic, anchovies, Parmesan, lemon juice, and Worcestershire together in a small bowl until smooth. Put the chicken in a medium bowl and add 2 tablespoons of the dressing. Cover and refrigerate the remaining dressing. Work the dressing into the chicken with your hands gently but completely. Form the mixture into 4 burgers ¾ to 1 inch thick. Put them on the **Prepa**red pan, cover, and refrigerate until firm, at least 1 hour.
2. Turn control knob to the high position, when the griddle is hot, brush the cut sides of the rolls with olive oil. Brush the burgers with oil on both sides, put them on the griddle. Carefully turning once with two spatulas, until browned on the outside and no longer pink in the center, 5 to 7 minutes per side.
3. 2 For the last couple of minutes, toast the rolls on the griddle, cut side down. To serve, rub the cut side of the top of each roll with the whole garlic clove.
4. Put a burger on the bottom half, add a dollop of the remaining dressing, a leaf of romaine, and the top of the roll.

Nutrition: Calories: 200; Fat: 11g; Protein: 12g; Fiber:2g

Turkey Burger

Preparation Time: 5 Minutes
Cooking Time: 4 Minutes**Servings:** 4
Ingredients:

- 1pound ground turkey

- cup pine nuts or walnut pieces
- tablespoons grated Parmesan cheese
- tablespoons store-bought pesto
- ¼ teaspoon salt
- ¼ teaspoon freshly ground black pepper
- whole wheat pitas
- romaine lettuce leaves or 1 small handful arugula
- Lemon

Directions:

1. Preheat the griddle to high.
2. Put the turkey in a medium bowl and add the pine nuts, Parmesan, pesto, salt, and pepper. Using a fork, mix the seasonings into the meat and then, with your hands, form the mixture into 4 patties, each about 1 inch thick.
3. Griddle the patties for about 4 minutes, until they have taken on griddle marks and are cooked through. Put each burger into a pita with some lettuce and a squeeze of lemon juice. Serve immediately.

Nutrition: Calories: 369; Fat: 21g; Protein: 28g

Nut Burgers

Preparation Time: 5 Minutes
Cooking Time: 10 Minutes
Servings: 4
Ingredients:

- cup raw rolled oats or cooked short-grain white or brown rice
    - cup walnuts, pecans, almonds, cashews, or other nuts
- 1 medium onion, cut into pieces
- 1 teaspoon chili powder
- 1 egg
- tablespoons ketchup, miso, tomato
- paste, nut butter, or tahini
- Salt and pepper
- Broth, soy sauce, wine, or other liquid if necessary

Directions:

1. Put the onion in a food processor and pulse to a paste. Add the nuts and oats and pulse to chop, but not too finely. Add the ketchup, chili powder, some salt and pepper, and the egg. Process briefly; don't grind the mixture too finely.
2. Add a little liquid—water, broth, soy sauce, wine, whatever is handy—if necessary; the mixture should be moist enough to hold together without being wet. With damp hands, shape the mixture into 8 burgers; put on a platter without touching and refrigerate for at least 1 hour.
3. Turn control knob to the high position, when the griddle is hot, put them and cook, carefully turning once with two spatulas, until browned on the outside and no longer pink in the center, 5 to 7 minutes per side.

Nutrition: Calories: 134; Fat: 31g; Protein:15g; Fiber:9g

Basil-Ginger Shrimp Burgers

Preparation Time: 5 Minutes
Cooking Time: 10 Minutes
Servings: 4
Ingredients:

    - large clove garlic, peeled
- 1 1-inch piece fresh ginger, peeled and
- sliced

- 1½ pounds shrimp, peeled (and deveined if you like)
- ½ cup lightly packed fresh basil leaves
- ¼ cup roughly chopped shallots, scallions, or red onion
- Salt and pepper
- Sesame oil for brushing the burgers
- sesame hamburger buns or 8–10 slider buns
- Lime wedges for serving
- Lettuce, sliced tomato, and other
- condiments for serving (optional)

Directions:

1. Put the garlic, ginger, and one-third of the shrimp in a food processor; purée until smooth, stopping the machine to scrape down the sides as necessary. Add the remaining shrimp, the basil, and shallots, season with salt and pepper, and pulse to chop. Form into 4 burgers about ¾ inch thick (or 8 to 10 sliders). Transfer to a plate, cover with plastic wrap, and chill until firm, at least 1 or up to 8 hours.
2. Turn control knob to the high position, when the griddle is hot, brush the burgers on both sides with oil then put them on the griddle-and cook until the bottoms brown and they release easily, 5 to 7 minutes. Carefully turn and cook until opaque all the way through, 3 to 5 minutes.
3. Put the buns, cut side down, on the griddle to toast. Serve the burgers on the toasted buns with lime wedges, as is or dressed however you like.

Nutrition: Calories: 194; Fat: 21g; Protein:6g; Fiber:2g

Spiced Lamb Burger

Preparation Time: 5 Minutes
Cooking Time: 5 Minutes **Servings:** 4
Ingredients:

- 1¼ pounds lean ground lamb
- tablespoon ground cumin
- ¼ teaspoon ground cinnamon
- ½ teaspoon salt
- ½ teaspoon freshly ground black pepper
- whole wheat pitas
- ½ medium cucumber, peeled and sliced
- ½ cup Simple Garlic Yogurt Sauce

Directions:

1. Put the lamb in a medium bowl with the cumin, cinnamon, salt, and pepper. Using a fork, mix the seasonings into the meat and then, with your hands, form the mixture into 4 patties, each about 1 inch thick.
2. Turn control knob to the high position, when the griddle is hot place the burgers and cook for 5 minutes without flipping. Remove the burgers and cover to keep warm. Put a burger into each pita, stuff a few cucumber slices in there too, and spoon some of the yogurt sauce over the top. Serve immediately.

Nutrition: Calories: 354; Fat: 21g; Protein:36g; Fiber:2g

Garlicky Pork Burgers

Preparation Time: 5 Minutes
Cooking Time: 10 Minutes **Servings:** 4
Ingredients:

- 1 teaspoon salt
- 1 teaspoon black pepper

- 4 cloves garlic, chopped
- 4 hard rolls, split, or 8–10 slider buns

Directions:

1 Put the meat, salt, pepper, and garlic in a food processor and pulse until coarsely ground—finer than chopped, but not much. (If using preground meat, put it in a bowl with the salt, pepper, and garlic and work them together gently with your hands.)

2 Handling the meat as little as possible to avoid compressing it, shape it lightly into 4 burgers, 1 to 1½ inches thick. (You can do this several hours in advance; cover with plastic wrap and refrigerate until you're ready to griddle.)

3 Turn control knob to the high position, when the griddle is hot, place the burgers on and cook for 10 minutes without flipping; the internal temperature should be 160°F (check with an instant-read thermometer, or nick with a small knife and peek inside).

4 Transfer to a platter.

5 Toast the rolls. Serve the burgers on the rolls.

Nutrition: Calories: 144; Fat: 22g; Protein:11g; Fiber:0g

Beet Burgers with Dates and Ginger

Preparation Time: 5 Minutes
Cooking Time: 10 Minutes **Servings:** 6
Ingredients:

- pound beets, peeled and grated (about
- cups)
- ½ cup packed pitted dates, broken into
- pieces
- ½ cup almonds
- 1 1-inch piece peeled fresh ginger, cut into coins
- ½ cup bulgur
- Salt and pepper
- ¾ cup boiling red wine or water
- 1 tablespoon Dijon or other mustard
- Cayenne or red chile flakes (optional)

Directions:

1. Put the beets in a food processor with the dates, almonds, and ginger; pulse until everything is well chopped but not quite a paste. Transfer the mixture to a large bowl and add the bulgur and a sprinkle of salt and pepper. Stir in the boiling wine, mustard, and cayenne to taste if you're using it and cover the bowl with a plate. Let sit for 20 minutes for the bulgur to soften. Taste and adjust the seasonings. Shape into 12 burgers, put on a platter without touching, and refrigerate for at least 1 hour.
2. Turn control knob to the high position, when the griddle is hot, place the burgers and cook for 10 minutes without flipping. Serve with your preferred fixings or toppings.

Nutrition: Calories: 465; Fat: 9g; Protein:13g; Fiber:2g

Preparation time: time: 15 minutes
Cooking Time: 35 minutes
Servings: 6
Ingredients:

- 2 lbs. ground beef, at least 20% fat
- kosher salt

- black pepper
- 1 tomato, sliced
- 1 yellow or red onion, sliced
- 1 head iceberg lettuce, cut into flats
- thick pieces of American or medium cheddar cheese
- seeded buns or potato buns, toasted

Directions:

1. Divide the ground beef into 6 equal loosely formed balls. Press the balls on a flat surface to make patties. Do not over work them.
2. Generously season the patties with salt and black pepper.
3. Heat your griddle to medium-high heat.
4. Place the patties on the griddle and press down to ensure that the surface makes contact. Cook for three to four minutes.
5. Flip the patties and top with cheese. Cook an additional three to four minutes. The cheese should melt by then.
6. Remove the burgers from the griddle and place them on the buns. Top with lettuce, tomato, and onion, as well as your favorite condiments.

Nutrition: Calories: 410, Sodium: 305 mg, Dietary Fiber: 0.9g, Fat: 18.8g, Carbs: 4.1g Protein: 53.4g

Layered Beef & Corn Burger

Preparation time: time: 20 minutes
Cooking Time: 30 minutes
Servings: 6
Ingredients:

  - large egg, lightly beaten
- 1 cup whole kernel corn, cooked
- 1/2 cup bread crumbs
  - tablespoons shallots, minced
- 1 teaspoon Worcestershire sauce
  - pounds ground beef
- 1 teaspoon salt
- 1/2 teaspoon pepper
- 1/2 teaspoon ground sage

Directions:

1. Combine the egg, corn, bread crumbs, shallots, and Worcestershire sauce in a mixing bowl and set aside.
2. Combine ground beef and seasonings in a separate bowl.
3. Line a flat surface with waxed paper.
4. Roll beef mixture into 12 thin burger patties.
5. Spoon corn mixture into the center of 6 patties and spread evenly across within an inch of the edge.
6. Top each with a second circle of meat and press edges to seal corn mixture in the middle of each burger.
7. Griddle over medium heat, for 12-15 minutes on each side or until thermometer reads 160°F and juices run clear.

Nutrition: Calories: 354, Sodium: 578 mg, Dietary Fiber: 1.2g Fat: 11.1g, Carbs: 12.3g Protein: 49.1g

Pork Tenderloin Sandwiches

Preparation time: time: 10 minutes
Cooking Time: 25 minutes **Servings:** 6
Ingredients:

- 2 (3/4-lb.) pork tenderloins
  - teaspoon garlic powder
- 1 teaspoon sea salt

- 1 teaspoon dry mustard
- 1/2 teaspoon coarsely ground pepper
- Olive oil, for brushing
- whole wheat hamburger buns
- tablespoons barbecue sauce

Directions:

1. Stir the garlic, salt, pepper, and mustard together in a small mixing bowl.
2. Rub pork tenderloins evenly with olive oil, then seasoning mix.
3. Preheat griddle to medium-high heat, and cook 10 to 12 minutes on each side or until a meat thermometer inserted into thickest portion registers 155°F.
4. Remove from griddle and let stand 10 minutes.
5. Slice thinly, and evenly distribute onto hamburger buns.
6. Drizzle each sandwich with barbecue sauce and serve.

Nutrition: Calories: 372, Sodium: 694 mg, Dietary Fiber: 2.9g, Fat: 13.4g, Carbs: 24.7g Protein: 37.2g

Cheesy Ham and Pineapple Sandwich

Preparation time: time: 10 minutes
Cooking Time: 20 minutes **Servings:** 4
Ingredients:

- (10 ounce) package deli sliced ham
- pineapple rings
- slices swiss cheese
- 8 slices of thick bread
- Butter, softened, for brushing

Directions:

1. Butter one side of all the slices of bread and heat your griddle to medium heat.
2. On top of each piece of bread, stack 1/4 of the ham, a pineapple ring, and 1 slice of cheese.
3. Place the sandwiches on the griddle and top with another slice of bread.
4. Cook until the bottom bread is golden brown, then flip and cook until the other side of the bread is browned and the cheese is melted.

Nutrition: Calories: 594, Sodium: 3184 mg, Dietary Fiber: 0.3g, Fat: 40.3g, Carbs: 4.7g Protein: 47.7g

Croque Madame

Preparation time: time: 10 minutes
Cooking Time: 10 minutes **Servings:** 2
Ingredients:

- tablespoons butter
- tablespoon flour
- 2/3 cup milk
- slices thick cut bread
- slices black forest ham
- slices gruyere cheese
- Salt and black pepper
- eggs

Directions:

1. In a small saucepan over medium heat, melt one tablespoon of butter and add the flour. Whisk until just browned and add the milk.
2. Stir until the sauce has thickened. Remove from heat and season with salt and pepper.

2. Heat your griddle to medium heat. Butter one side of each slice of bread and add a generous amount of the bechamel sauce to the other side.
3. Place two slices of ham on top of each sandwich and top with the other slice of bread. Place on the griddle and cook until golden brown. Flip the sandwiches and top with the gruyere cheese. On the other side of the griddle, crack the eggs and cook until the whites are firm.
4. Cook until the other side of the sandwich is golden brown and the gruyere has melted on top. Top each sandwich with a fried egg before serving.

Nutrition: Calories: 538, Sodium: 1019 mg, Dietary Fiber: 2.4g Fat: 35.2g, Carbs: 17.8g Protein: 36.9g

Ultimate Griddle Cheese

Preparation time: time: 10 minutes
Cooking Time: 10 minutes
Servings: 4
Ingredients:

- 8 slices sourdough bread
- slices provolone cheese
- slices yellow American cheese
- 4 slices sharp cheddar cheese
- 4 slices tomato
- 3 tablespoons mayonnaise
- 3 tablespoons butter

Directions:

1. Heat your griddle to medium heat.
2. Butter one side of each piece of bread and spread mayo on the other side.
3. Place the buttered side down on the griddle and stack the cheeses on top.
4. Place the other pieces of bread, butter side up on top of the cheese and cook until golden brown. Flip and cook until the other piece of bread is golden brown as well and the cheese is melted.
5. Remove from the griddle, slice in half and enjoy.

Nutrition: Calories: 521, Sodium: 1044 mg, Dietary Fiber: 1.7g Fat: 30.1g, Carbs: 41.4g Protein: 22g

Garlic Parmesan Griddle Cheese Sandwiches

Preparation time: time: 2 minutes
Cooking Time: 7 minutes
Servings: 1
Ingredients:

- 2 slices Italian bread, sliced thin
- 2 slices provolone cheese
- 2 tablespoons butter, softened
- Garlic powder, for dusting
- Dried parsley, for dusting
- Parmesan Cheese, shredded, for dusting

Directions:

1. Spread butter evenly across 2 slices of bread and sprinkle each buttered side with garlic and parsley.
2. Sprinkle a few tablespoons of Parmesan cheese over each buttered side of bread and gently press the cheese into the bread.

3. Preheat the griddle to medium heat and place one slice of bread, buttered side down, into the griddle.
4. Top with provolone slices and second slice of bread with the butter side up.
5. Cook 3 minutes, and flip to cook 3 minutes on the other side; cook until bread is golden and parmesan cheese is crispy.
6. Serve warm with your favorite sides!

Nutrition: Calories: 575, Sodium: 1065 mg, Dietary Fiber: 2.8g, Fat: 45.1g, Carbs: 18.1g Protein: 27.6g

Griddle Pizza Cheese

Preparation time: Time: 10 minutes
Cooking Time: 20 minutes
Servings: 4
Ingredients:

- 8 slices French bread
- 3 tablespoons butter, softened
- 1/2 cup pizza sauce
- 1/4 cup mozzarella cheese
- 1/2 cup pepperoni diced
- Garlic powder, for dusting
- Oregano, for dusting

Directions:

1. Spread butter on one side of each French bread slice.
2. Place butter side down on a piece of aluminum foil and dust with garlic powder and oregano.
3. Spread pizza sauce on opposite side of all French bread slices.
4. Top 4 slices of bread with mozzarella cheese, a few slices of pepperoni, and additional mozzarella.
5. Place remaining French bread slices on top of pizza topped bread, butter side up, to create 4 sandwiches.
6. Preheat the griddle to medium heat and place one slice of bread, buttered side down into the griddle.
7. Cook, 3 minutes and flip to cook 3 minutes on the other side; cook until bread is golden and cheese is melted.
8. Serve warm and enjoy!

Nutrition: Calories:305, Sodium: 664 mg, Dietary Fiber: 2.3g, Fat: 12g, Carbs: 40.4g Protein: 9.4g

Mini Portobello Burgers

Preparation time: time: 15 minutes
Cooking Time: 15 minutes
Servings: 4
Ingredients:

- portobello mushroom caps
- slices mozzarella cheese
- 4 buns, like brioche
- For the marinade:
- 1/4 cup balsamic vinegar
- 2 tablespoons olive oil
    - teaspoon dried basil
- 1 teaspoon dried oregano
- 1 teaspoon garlic powder
- ¼ teaspoon sea salt
- ¼ teaspoon black pepper

Directions:

1. Whisk together marinade ingredients in a large mixing bowl. Add mushroom caps and toss to coat.
2. Let stand at room temperature for 15 minutes, turning twice.

3. Preheat griddle for medium-high heat.
4. Place mushrooms on the griddle; reserve marinade for basting.
5. Cook for 5 to 8 minutes on each side, or until tender.
6. Brush with marinade frequently.
7. Top with mozzarella cheese during the last 2 minutes of cooking.
8. Remove from griddle and serve on brioche buns.

Nutrition: Calories: 248, Sodium: 429 mg, Dietary Fiber: 2.1g Fat: 13.5g, Carbs: 20.3g Protein: 13g

Veggie Pesto Flatbread

Preparation time: time: 40 minutes
Cooking Time: 10 minutes **Servings:** 4
Ingredients:

- 2 flatbreads
- jar pesto
    - cup shredded mozzarella cheese
- For the topping:
- 1/2 cup cherry tomatoes, halved
- 1 small red onion, sliced thin
- 1 red bell pepper, sliced
- 1 yellow bell pepper, sliced
- 1/2 cup mixed black and green olives, halved
- 1 small yellow squash or zucchini, sliced
- teaspoon olive oil
- ¼ teaspoon sea salt
- ¼ teaspoon black pepper

Directions:

1. Preheat the griddle to low heat.
2. Spread an even amount of pesto onto each flatbread.
3. Top with ½ cup mozzarella cheese each.
4. Mix all the topping ingredients together in a large mixing bowl with a rubber spatula.
5. Lay flatbreads on griddle, and top with an even amount of topping mixture; spreading to the edges of each.
6. Tent the flatbreads with foil for 5 minutes each, or until cheese is just melted.
7. Place flatbreads on a flat surface or cutting board, and cut each with a pizza cutter or kitchen scissors.
8. Serve warm!

Nutrition: Calories: 177 Sodium: 482 mg, Dietary Fiber: 1.7g Fat: 11.9g, Carbs: 12.6g Protein: 5.5g

Griddle Vegetable Pizza

Preparation time: time: 30 minutes
Cooking Time: 10 minutes
Servings: 6
Ingredients:

- 8 small fresh mushrooms, halved
- small zucchini, cut into 1/4-inch slices
    - small yellow pepper, sliced
- 1 small red pepper, sliced
- 1 small red onion, sliced
- 1 tablespoon white wine vinegar
- 1 tablespoon water
- teaspoons olive oil, divided
- 1/2 teaspoon dried basil
- 1/4 teaspoon sea salt
- 1/4 teaspoon pepper
- 1 prebaked, 12-inch thin whole wheat pizza crust

- 1 can (8 ounces) pizza sauce
- small tomatoes, chopped
- cups shredded part-skim mozzarella cheese

Directions:

1. Preheat your griddle to medium-high heat.
2. Combine mushrooms, zucchini, peppers, onion, vinegar, water, 3 teaspoons oil and seasonings in a large mixing bowl.
3. Transfer to griddle and cook over medium heat for 10 minutes or until tender, stirring often.
4. Brush crust with remaining oil and spread with pizza sauce.
5. Top evenly with Griddle vegetables, tomatoes and cheese.
6. Tent with aluminum foil and griddle over medium heat for 5 to 7 minutes or until edges are lightly browned and cheese is melted.
7. Serve warm!

Nutrition: Calories: 111, Sodium: 257 mg, Dietary Fiber: 1.7g Fat: 5.4g, Carbs: 12.2g Protein: 5g

Bacon Jalapeno Wraps

Preparation time: time: 5 minutes
Cooking Time: 10 minutes
Servings: 4
Ingredients:

- package bacon, uncured and nitrate free
- fresh jalapeno peppers, halved lengthwise and seeded
- 1 (8 ounce) package cream cheese
- 1 dozen toothpicks, soaked

Directions:

1. Preheat your griddle to high heat.
2. Fill jalapeno halves with cream cheese.
3. Wrap each with bacon. Secure with a toothpick.
4. Place on the griddle, and cook until bacon is crispy, about 5 to 7 minutes per side.
5. Remove to a platter to cool and serve warm.

Nutrition: Calories: 379, Sodium: 1453 mg, Dietary Fiber: 0.9g Fat: 33.4g, Carbs: 3.5g Protein: 16.3g

CHAPTER 6
Vegetable & Side Dishes

Lemon-Garlic Artichokes

Preparation Time: 10 minutes
Cooking Time: 15 minutes Servings: 4 slices
Ingredients:

- Juice of 1/2 lemon
- 1/2 cup canola oil
- 3 garlic cloves, chopped - Sea salt
- Freshly ground black pepper
- 2 large artichokes, trimmed and halved

Directions:

1. Preheat the griddle to medium high.
2. While the unit is preheating, in a medium bowl, combine the lemon juice, oil, and garlic. Season with salt and pepper, then brush the artichoke halves with the lemon-garlic mixture.
3. Place the artichokes on the Grill, cut side down. Gently press them down to maximize grill marks. Grill for 8 to 10 minutes, occasionally basting generously with the lemon-garlic mixture throughout cooking, until blistered on all sides.

Nutrition: Calories: 285kcal; Fat: 28g; Carbs: 10g; Protein: 3g

Blistered Green Beans

Preparation Time: 5 minutes
Cooking Time: 10 minutes Servings: 4 slices
Ingredients:

- 1 pound haricots verts or green beans, trimmed
- 2 tablespoons vegetable oil
- Juice of 1 lemon
- Pinch red pepper flakes
- Flaky sea salt
- Freshly ground black pepper

Directions:

1. Preheat the griddle to medium high. While the unit is preheating, in a medium bowl, toss the green beans in oil until evenly coated.
2. Place the green beans on the Grill and grill for 8 to 10 minutes, tossing frequently until blistered on all sides. When cooking is complete, place the green beans on a large serving platter. Squeeze lemon juice over the green beans, top with red pepper flakes, and season with sea salt and black pepper.

Nutrition:Calories: 100kcal; Fat: 7g; Carbs: 10g; Protein: 2g

Stir Fry Mushrooms

Preparation Time: 10 minutes
Cooking Time: 10 minutes **Servings:** 2
Ingredients:

- 10 oz mushrooms, sliced
- 1/4 cup olive oil
- 1 tbsp garlic, minced
- 1/4 tsp dried thyme
- Pepper - Salt

Directions:

1. Preheat the griddle to high heat.
2. Add 2 tablespoons of oil to the hot griddle top.
3. Add mushrooms, garlic, thyme, pepper, and salt and sauté mushrooms until tender.
4. Drizzle remaining oil and serve.

Nutrition:

- Calories 253 Fat 25.6 g
- Carbohydrates 6.2 g Sugar 2.5 g
- Protein 4.7 g Cholesterol 0 mg

Grilled Asian-Style Broccoli

Preparation Time: 10 minutes
Cooking Time: 10 minutes
Servings: 4 slices
Ingredients:

- 4 tablespoons soy sauce
- 4 tablespoons balsamic vinegar
- 2 tablespoons canola oil
- 2 teaspoons maple syrup
- 2 heads broccoli, trimmed into florets
- Red pepper flakes, for garnish
- Sesame seeds, for garnish

Directions:

1. Preheat the griddle to medium high.
2. While the unit is preheating, in a large bowl, whisk together the soy sauce, balsamic vinegar, oil, and maple syrup. Add the broccoli and toss to coat evenly.
3. Place the broccoli on the Grill and grill for 8 to 10 minutes, until charred on all sides.
4. When cooking is complete, place the broccoli on a large serving platter. Garnish with red pepper flakes and sesame seeds. Serve immediately.

Nutrition:
Calories: 133kcal; Fat: 8g; Carbs: 13g; Protein: 5g

Stir Fry Vegetables

Preparation Time: 10 minutes
Cooking Time: 20 minutes **Servings:** 4
Ingredients:

- 2 medium potatoes, cut into small pieces
- 3 medium carrots, peeled and cut into small pieces
- 1/4 cup olive oil
- 1 small rutabaga, peeled and cut into small pieces
- 2 medium parsnips, peeled and cut into small pieces
- Pepper
- Salt

Directions:

1. Preheat the griddle to high heat.
2. In a large bowl, toss vegetables with olive oil. Transfer vegetables onto the hot griddle top and stir fry until vegetables are tender.
3. Serve and enjoy.

Nutrition:

- Calories 218 Fat 12.8 g
- Carbohydrates 25.2 g Sugar 6.2 g
- Protein 2.8 g
- Cholesterol 0 mg

Easy Fried Rice

Preparation Time: 10 minutes
Cooking Time: 10 minutes
Servings: 2
Ingredients:

- 4 cups rice, cooked
- 2 large eggs
- 2 tbsp green onion, sliced
- 2 tbsp olive oil
- 1 tsp salt

Directions:

1. In a bowl, whisk eggs and set aside.
2. Preheat the griddle to high heat.
3. Spray griddle top with cooking spray.
4. Add cooked rice on hot griddle top and fry until rice separate from each other.

5. Push rice to one side of the griddle top. Add oil to the griddle and pour beaten egg.
6. Add salt and mix egg quickly with rice and cook until rice grains are covered by egg.
7. Add green onion and stir fry for 2 minutes. Serve and enjoy.

Nutrition:

- Calories 557 Fat 19.8 g
- Carbohydrates 79.6 g
- Sugar 0.7 g Protein 14 g
- Cholesterol 186 mg

Healthy Zucchini Noodles

Preparation Time: 10 minutes
Cooking Time: 10 minutes **Servings:** 4
Ingredients:

- 4 small zucchini, spiralized
- 1 tbsp soy sauce
- 2 onions, spiralized
- 2 tbsp olive oil
- 1 tbsp sesame seeds
- 2 tbsp teriyaki sauce

Directions:

1. Preheat the griddle to high heat.
2. Add oil to the hot griddle top.
3. Add onion and sauté for 4-5 minutes.
4. Add zucchini noodles and cook for 2 minutes.
5. Add sesame seeds, teriyaki sauce, and soy sauce and cook for 4-5 minutes. Serve and enjoy.

Nutrition:

- Calories 124 Fat 8.4 g
- Carbohydrates 11.3 g
- Sugar 5.7 g Protein 3.2 g
- Cholesterol 0 mg

Easy Seared Green Beans

Preparation Time: 10 minutes
Cooking Time: 10 minutes
Servings: 6
Ingredients:

- 1 1/2 lbs green beans, trimmed
- 1 1/2 tbsp rice vinegar
- 3 tbsp soy sauce
- 1 1/2 tbsp sesame oil
- 2 tbsp sesame seeds, toasted
- 1 1/2 tbsp brown sugar
- 1/4 tsp black pepper

Directions:

1. Cook green beans in boiling water for 3 minutes and drain well.
2. Transfer green beans to chilled ice water and drain again. Pat dry green beans.
3. Preheat the griddle to high heat.
4. Add oil to the hot griddle top.
5. Add green beans and stir fry for 2 minutes.
6. Add soy sauce, brown sugar, vinegar, and pepper and stir fry for 2 minutes more.
7. Add sesame seeds and toss well to coat. Serve and enjoy.

Nutrition:

- Calories 100 Fat 5 g
- Carbohydrates 11.7 g
- Sugar 3.9 g Protein 3.1 g
- Cholesterol 0 mg

Stir Fry Bok Choy

Preparation Time: 10 minutes
Cooking Time: 5 minutes **Servings:** 4
Ingredients:

- 2 heads bok choy, trimmed and cut crosswise

- 1 tsp sesame oil
- 2 tsp soy sauce
- 2 tbsp water
- 1 tbsp butter
- 1 tbsp peanut oil
- 1 tbsp oyster sauce
- 1/2 tsp salt

Directions:

1. In a small bowl, mix together soy sauce, oyster sauce, sesame oil, and water and set aside.
2. Preheat the griddle to high heat.
3. Add oil to the hot griddle top.
4. Add bok choy and salt and stir fry for 2 minutes.
5. Add butter and soy sauce mixture and stir fry for 1-2 minutes.
6. Serve and enjoy.

Nutrition:

- Calories 122
- Fat 8.2 g
- Carbohydrates 9.5 g
- Sugar 5 g
- Protein 6.5 g
- Cholesterol 8 mg

Sautéed Vegetables

Preparation Time: 10 minutes
Cooking Time: 5 minutes
Servings: 4
Ingredients:

- 2 medium zucchini, cut into matchsticks
- 2 tbsp coconut oil
- 2 tsp garlic, minced
- 1 tbsp honey
- 3 tbsp soy sauce
- 1 tsp sesame seeds
- 2 cups carrots, cut into matchsticks
- 2 cups snow peas

Directions:

1. In a small bowl, mix together soy sauce, garlic, and honey and set aside.
2. Preheat the griddle to high heat.
3. Add oil to the hot griddle top.
4. Add carrots, snow peas, and zucchini, and sauté for 1-2 minutes.
5. Add soy sauce mixture and stir fry for 1 minute.
6. Garnish with sesame seeds and serve.

Nutrition:

- Calories 160 Fat 7.5 g
- Carbohydrates 20.2 g
- Sugar 12.1 g
- Protein 5.3 g
- Cholesterol 0 mg

Stir Fry Cabbage

Preparation Time: 10 minutes
Cooking Time: 5 minutes **Servings:** 4
Ingredients:

- 1 cabbage head, tear cabbage leaves, washed and drained
- 2 green onion, sliced
- 1 tbsp ginger, minced
- 2 garlic cloves, minced
- 1 tbsp soy sauce
- 1/2 tbsp vinegar
- 4 dried chilies
- 2 tbsp olive oil
- 1/2 tsp salt

Directions:

1. Preheat the griddle to high heat.
2. Add oil to the hot griddle top.

3. Add ginger, garlic, and green onion and sauté for 2-3 minutes.
4. Add dried chilies and sauté for 30 seconds.
5. Add cabbage, vinegar, soy sauce, and salt and stir fry for 1-2 minutes over high heat until cabbage wilted.
6. Serve and enjoy.

Nutrition:

- Calories 115 Fat 7.3 g
- Carbohydrates 12.7 g Sugar 6 g
- Protein 2.9 g
- Cholesterol 0 mg

Pineapple Fried Rice

Preparation Time: 10 minutes
Cooking Time: 10 minutes
Servings: 4
Ingredients:

- 3 cups cooked brown rice
- 1/2 cup frozen corn
- 2 carrots, peeled and grated
- 1 onion, diced
- 2 garlic cloves, minced
- 2 tbsp olive oil
- 1/2 tsp ginger powder
- 1 tbsp sesame oil
- 3 tbsp soy sauce
- 1/4 cup green onion, sliced
- 1/2 cup ham, diced
- 2 cups pineapple, diced
- 1/2 cup frozen peas

Directions:

1. In a small bowl, whisk soy sauce, ginger powder, and sesame oil and set aside.
2. Preheat the griddle to high heat.
3. Add oil to the hot griddle top.
4. Add onion and garlic and sauté for 3-4 minutes.
5. Add corn, carrots, and peas and stir constantly for 3-4 minutes.
6. Stir in cooked rice, green onions, ham, pineapple, and soy sauce mixture and stir continuously for 2-3 minutes.
7. Serve and enjoy.

Nutrition:

- Calories 375
- Fat 13.3 g
- Carbohydrates 57.6 g
- Sugar 12.7 g
- Protein 9.4 g
- Cholesterol 10 mg

Italian Zucchini Slices

Preparation Time: 10 minutes
Cooking Time: 5 minutes
Servings: 4
Ingredients:

- 2 zucchini, cut into 1/2-inch thick slices
- 1 tsp Italian seasoning
- 2 garlic cloves, minced
- 1/4 cup butter, melted
- 1 1/2 tbsp fresh parsley, chopped
- 1 tbsp fresh lemon juice
- Pepper
- Salt

Directions:

1. In a small bowl, mix melted butter, lemon juice, Italian seasoning, garlic, pepper, and salt.
2. Brush zucchini slices with melted butter mixture.
3. Preheat the griddle to high heat.

4. Place zucchini slices on the griddle top and cook for 2 minutes per side.
5. Transfer zucchini slices on serving plate and garnish with parsley. Serve and enjoy.

Nutrition:

- Calories 125 Fat 12 g
- Carbohydrates 4.1 g
- Sugar 1.9 g Protein 1.5 g
- Cholesterol 31 mg

Green Beans with Bacon

Preparation Time: 10 minutes
Cooking Time: 20 minutes **Servings:** 6
Ingredients:

- 4 strips of bacon, chopped
- 1 1/2 pound green beans, ends trimmed
- 1 teaspoon minced garlic
- 1 teaspoon salt
- 4 tablespoons olive oil

Directions:

1. Switch on the griddle, set the temperature to 450 degrees F and let it preheat for a minimum of 15 minutes.
2. Meanwhile, take a sheet tray, place all the ingredients in it and toss until mixed.
3. When the griddle has preheated, open the lid, place **Prepar**ed sheet tray on the griddle grate, shut the griddle and smoke for 20 minutes until lightly browned and cooked. When done, transfer green beans to a dish and then serve.

Nutrition:

Calories: 93 Cal Fat: 4.6 g Carbs: 8.2 g Protein: 5.9 g Fiber: 2.9 g

Griddle Potato Salad

Preparation Time: 15 minutes
Cooking Time: 10 minutes
Servings: 8
Ingredients:

- 1 ½ pound fingerling potatoes, halved lengthwise
- 1 small jalapeno, sliced
- 10 scallions
- 2 teaspoons salt
- 2 tablespoons rice vinegar
- 2 teaspoons lemon juice
- 2/3 cup olive oil, divided

Directions:

1. Switch on the griddle, set the temperature to 450 degrees F and let it preheat for a minimum of 5 minutes.
2. Meanwhile, **Prepar**e scallions, and for this, brush them with some oil.
3. When the griddle has preheated, open the lid, place scallions on the griddle grate, shut the griddle and smoke for 3 minutes until lightly charred.
4. Then transfer scallions to a cutting board, let them cool for 5 minutes, then cut into slices and set aside until required.
5. Brush potatoes with some oil, season with some salt and black pepper, place potatoes on the griddle grate, shut the griddle and smoke for 5 minutes until thoroughly cooked.
6. Then take a large bowl, pour in remaining oil, add salt, lemon juice, and vinegar and stir until combined.

7. Add Griddle scallion and potatoes, toss until well mixed, taste to adjust seasoning and then serve.

Nutrition:

Calories: 223.7 Cal Fat: 12 g
Carbs: 27 g Protein: 1.9 g Fiber: 3.3 g

Vegetable Sandwich

Preparation Time: 30 minutes
Cooking Time: 45 minutes
Servings: 4
Ingredients:

For the Smoked Hummus:

- 1 1/2 cups cooked chickpeas
- 1 tablespoon minced garlic
- 1 teaspoon salt
- 4 tablespoons lemon juice
- 2 tablespoon olive oil
- 1/3 cup tahini

For the Vegetables:

- 2 large portobello mushrooms
- 1 small eggplant, destemmed, sliced into strips
- 1 teaspoon salt
- 1 small zucchini, trimmed, sliced into strips
- ½ teaspoon ground black pepper
- 1 small yellow squash, peeled, sliced into strips
- ¼ cup olive oil

For the Cheese:

- 1 lemon, juiced
- ½ teaspoon minced garlic
- ¼ teaspoon ground black pepper
- ¼ teaspoon salt
- 1/2 cup ricotta cheese

To Assemble:

- 1 bunch basil, leaves chopped
- 2 heirloom tomatoes, sliced
- 4 ciabatta buns, halved

Directions:

1. Switch on the griddle, set the temperature to 180 degrees F and let it preheat for a minimum of 15 minutes.
2. Meanwhile, **Prepa**re the hummus, and for this, take a sheet tray and spread chickpeas on it.
3. When the griddle has preheated, open the lid, place sheet tray on the griddle grate, shut the griddle and smoke for 20 minutes.
4. When done, transfer chickpeas to a food processor, add remaining ingredients for the hummus in it, and pulse for 2 minutes until smooth, set aside until required.
5. Change the smoking temperature to 500 degrees F, shut with lid, and let it preheat for 10 minutes.
6. Meanwhile, **Prepa**re vegetables and for this, take a large bowl, place all the vegetables in it, add salt and black pepper, drizzle with oil and lemon juice and toss until coated.
7. Place vegetables on the griddle grate, shut with lid and then smoke for eggplant, zucchini, and squash for 15 minutes and mushrooms for 25 minutes.
8. Meanwhile, **Prepa**re the cheese and for this, take a small bowl, place all of its ingredients in it and stir until well combined.

9. Assemble the sandwich for this, cut buns in half lengthwise, spread **Prepa**red hummus on one side, spread cheese on the other side, then stuff with Griddle vegetables and top with tomatoes and basil.
10. Serve straight away.

Nutrition:
Calories: 560 Cal Fat: 40 g
Carbs: 45 g Protein: 8.3 g Fiber: 6.8 g

Griddled Zucchini

Preparation Time: 5 minutes
Cooking Time: 10 minutes
Servings: 6
Ingredients:

- 4 medium zucchini
- 2 tablespoons olive oil
- 1 tablespoon sherry vinegar
- 2 sprigs of thyme, leaves chopped
- ½ teaspoon salt
- 1/3 teaspoon ground black pepper

Directions:

1. Switch on the griddle, set the temperature to 350 degrees F and let it preheat for a minimum of 5 minutes. Meanwhile, cut the ends of each zucchini, cut each in half and then into thirds and place in a plastic bag.
2. Add remaining ingredients, seal the bag, and shake well to coat zucchini pieces.
3. When the griddle has preheated, open the lid, place zucchini on the griddle grate, shut the griddle and smoke for 4 minutes per side.
4. When done, transfer zucchini to a dish, garnish with more thyme and then serve.

Nutrition:
Calories: 74 Cal
Fat: 5.4 g Carbs: 6.1 g Protein: 2.6 g
Fiber: 2.3 g

Griddle Sugar Snap Peas

Preparation Time: 15 minutes
Cooking Time: 10 minutes
Servings: 4
Ingredients:

- 2-pound sugar snap peas, ends trimmed
- ½ teaspoon garlic powder
- 1 teaspoon salt
- 2/3 teaspoon ground black pepper
- 2 tablespoons olive oil

Directions:

1. Switch on the griddle, or set the temperature to 450 degrees F and let it preheat for a minimum of 15 minutes.
2. Meanwhile, take a medium bowl, place peas in it, add garlic powder and oil, season with salt and black pepper, toss until mixed and then spread on the sheet pan.
3. When the griddle has preheated, open the lid, place the **Prepa**red sheet pan on the griddle grate, shut the griddle and smoke for 10 minutes until slightly charred.
4. Serve straight away.

Nutrition:
Calories: 91 Cal Fat: 5 g
Carbs: 9 g Protein: 4 g
Fiber: 3 g

Cauliflower with Parmesan and Butter

Preparation Time: 15 minutes
Cooking Time: 45 minutes
Servings: 4
Ingredients:

- 1 medium head of cauliflower
- 1 teaspoon minced garlic
- 1 teaspoon salt
- ½ teaspoon ground black pepper
- 1/4 cup olive oil
- 1/2 cup melted butter, unsalted
- 1/2 tablespoon chopped parsley
- 1/4 cup shredded parmesan cheese

Directions:

1. Switch on the griddle, set the temperature to 450 degrees F and let it preheat for a minimum of 15 minutes.
2. Meanwhile, brush the cauliflower head with oil, season with salt and black pepper and then place in a griddle pan.
3. When the griddle has preheated, open the lid, place **Prepa**red griddle pan on the griddle grate, shut the griddle and smoke for 45 minutes until golden brown and the center has turned tender.
4. Meanwhile, take a small bowl, place melted butter in it, and then stir in garlic, parsley, and cheese until combined.
5. Baste cheese mixture frequently in the last 20 minutes of cooking and, when done, remove the pan from heat and garnish cauliflower with parsley.
6. Cut it into slices and then serve.

Nutrition:
Calories: 128 Cal Fat: 7.6 g
Carbs: 10.8 g Protein: 7.4 g Fiber: 5 g

Griddle Carrots and Asparagus

Preparation Time: 10 minutes
Cooking Time: 30 minutes **Servings:** 6
Ingredients:

- 1 pound whole carrots, with tops
- 1 bunch of asparagus, ends trimmed
- Sea salt as needed
- 1 teaspoon lemon zest
- 2 tablespoons honey
- 2 tablespoons olive oil

Directions:

1. Switch on the griddle, or set the temperature to 450 degrees F and let it preheat for a minimum of 15 minutes.
2. Meanwhile, take a medium dish, place asparagus in it, season with sea salt, drizzle with oil and toss until mixed.
3. Take a medium bowl, place carrots in it, drizzle with honey, sprinkle with sea salt and toss until combined.
4. When the griddle has preheated, open the lid, place asparagus and carrots on the griddle grate, shut the griddle and smoke for 30 minutes.
5. When done, transfer vegetables to a dish, sprinkle with lemon zest, and then serve.

Nutrition:
Calories: 79.8 Cal Fat: 4.8 g Carbs: 8.6 g
Protein: 2.6 g Fiber: 3.5 g

Kale Chips

Preparation Time: 10 minutes
Cooking Time: 20 minutes
Servings: 6
Ingredients:

- 2 bunches of kale, stems removed
- ½ teaspoon of sea salt
- 4 tablespoons olive oil

Directions:

1. Switch on the griddle, set the temperature to 250 degrees F and let it preheat for a minimum of 15 minutes.
2. Meanwhile, rinse the kale leaves, pat dry, spread the kale on a sheet tray, drizzle with oil, season with salt and toss until well coated.
3. When the griddle has preheated, open the lid, place sheet tray on the griddle grate, shut the griddle and smoke for 20 minutes until crisp.
4. Serve straight away.

Nutrition:
Calories: 110 Cal
Fat: 5 g
Carbs: 15.8 g
Protein: 5.3 g
Fiber: 5.6 g

Roasted Root Vegetables

Preparation Time: 15 minutes
Cooking Time: 45 minutes
Servings: 6
Ingredients:

- 1 large red onion, peeled
- 1 bunch of red beets, trimmed, peeled
- 1 large yam, peeled
- 1 bunch of golden beets, trimmed, peeled
- 1 large parsnips, peeled
- 1 butternut squash, peeled
- 1 large carrot, peeled
- 6 garlic cloves, peeled
- 3 tablespoons thyme leaves
- Salt as needed
- 1 cinnamon stick
- Ground black pepper as needed
- 3 tablespoons olive oil
- 2 tablespoons honey

Directions:

1. Switch on the griddle, set the temperature to 450 degrees F and let it preheat for a minimum of 15 minutes.
2. Meanwhile, cut all the vegetables into ½-inch pieces, place them in a large bowl, add garlic, thyme, and cinnamon, drizzle with oil and toss until mixed.
3. Take a large cookie sheet, line it with foil, spread with vegetables, and then season with salt and black pepper.
4. When the griddle has preheated, open the lid, place **Prepar**ed cookie sheet on the griddle grate, shut the griddle and smoke for 45 minutes until tender.
5. When done, transfer vegetables to a dish, drizzle with honey, and then serve.

Nutrition:
Calories: 164 Cal
Fat: 4 g
Carbs: 31.7 g
Protein: 2.7 g
Fiber: 6.4 g

Vegetable Skewers

Preparation Time: 10 minutes
Cooking Time: 20 minutes
Servings: 4
Ingredients:

- 2 cups whole white mushrooms
- 2 large yellow squash, peeled, chopped
- 1 cup chopped pineapple
- 1 cup chopped red pepper
- 1 cup halved strawberries
- 2 large zucchini, chopped

For the Dressing:

- 2 lemons, juiced
- ½ teaspoon ground black pepper
- 1/2 teaspoon sea salt
- 1 teaspoon red chili powder
- 1 tablespoon maple syrup
- 1 tablespoon orange zest
- 2 tablespoons apple cider vinegar
- 1/4 cup olive oil

Directions:

1. Switch on the griddle, set the temperature to 450 degrees F and let it preheat for a minimum of 5 minutes.
2. Meanwhile, **Prepa**red thread vegetables and fruits on skewers alternately and then brush skewers with oil.
3. When the griddle has preheated, open the lid, place vegetable skewers on the griddle grate, shut the griddle, and smoke for 20 minutes until tender and lightly charred.
4. Meanwhile, **Prepa**re the dressing and for this, take a small bowl, place all of its ingredients in it and then whisk until combined.
5. When done, transfer skewers to a dish, top with **Prepa**red dressing and then serve.

Nutrition:
Calories: 130 Cal
Fat: 2 g
Carbs: 20 g
Protein: 2 g
Fiber: 0.3 g

Baked Green Bean Casserole

Preparation Time:10 mins
Cooking Time:50 mins **Servings:**10-12
Ingredients:

- 3 lbs. trimmed green beans
- Kosher salt
- 2 tbsp olive oil
- 2 tbsp unsalted butter
- 1/2 lb. shitake or king trumpet mushrooms, sliced
- 1/4 cup minced shallot
- 1/4 cup rice flour
- 2 cups chicken stock
- 1/2 cup sherry cooking wine
- 1 cup heavy cream
- 1 cup grated parmigiana Reggiano
- 1 cup slivered almonds, for topping
- 4 cups canola or vegetable oil
- 8 whole, peeled shallots
- 1/2 cup rice flour
- 1 tsp kosher salt

Directions:

1. When ready to cook, set the temperature to High and preheat, lid closed for 15 minutes.

2. Fill a large stockpot 2/3 full of water and bring to a boil over high heat. **Prepa**re a large ice bath. When the water is boiling, add 1 Tbsp of salt.
3. After the water has returned to a rolling boil, add half of the green beans. Cook until al dente, about 2 minutes. Remove with a strainer and place the beans in the ice bath to cool.
4. Remove the green beans from the water and place on paper towels to dry. Repeat with the remaining green beans. Alternatively, place the green beans on a clean dish cloth and roll up to remove the water.
5. To make the Sauce: Melt the butter and olive oil in a small saucepan over medium heat. Add the shallots and mushrooms and a generous pinch of salt and cook, stirring, until the mushrooms are soft, about 5 minutes.
6. Sprinkle the rice flour over the top and stir to coat the mushrooms and cook off the raw flour taste, about 2 minutes. Add the sherry, stir and reduce, then slowly stir in the stock, allowing to thicken and ensuring there are no lumps, about 3 minutes.
7. Stir in the cream and Parmigiano-Reggiano. Taste, adding salt and pepper as needed.
8. Combine the green beans with the sauce.
9. While the green beans are on the griddle, fry the shallots. Place the oil in a deep saucepan or Dutch oven and heat oil to 350°F.
10. Combine the rice flour and salt in a shallow bowl and mix with a fork
11. When the casserole is ready, garnish with the fried shallots. Enjoy!

Nutrition:
Calories: 130
Carbs: 14g
Fat: 6g Protein: 2g

Mashed Potatoes

Preparation Time:5 mins
Cooking Timc:40 mins
Servings:8-12
Ingredients:

- 5 lbs. Yukon gold potatoes, large dice
- 1 1/2 sticks butter, softened
- 1 1/2 cup cream, room temperature
- kosher salt, to taste
- white pepper, to taste

Directions:

1. When ready to cook, set temperature to 300 degree F and preheat, lid closed for 15 minutes
2. Peel and dice potatoes into 1/2" cubes.
3. Place the potatoes in a foil tin and cover. Roast on the griddle until tender (about 40 minutes).
4. In a medium saucepan, combine cream and butter. Cook over medium heat until butter is melted.

5. Mash potatoes using a potato masher. Gradually add in cream and butter mixture, and mix using the masher. Be careful not to overwork, or the potatoes will become gluey.
6. Season with salt and pepper to taste. Enjoy!

Nutrition:
Calories: 122 Carbs: 12g
Fat: 2g Protein: 2g

Corn & Cheese Chile Rellenos

Preparation Time:30 mins
Cooking Time:65 mins
Servings:8-12
Ingredients:

- 2 lbs. Ripe tomatoes, chopped
- 4 cloves garlic, chopped
- 1/2 cup sweet onion, chopped
- 1 jalapeno, stemmed, seeded, and chopped
- 8 large green new Mexican or poblano chiles
- 3 ears sweet corn, husked
- 1/2 tsp. Dry oregano, Mexican, crumbled
- 1 tsp. Ground cumin
- 1 tsp. Mild chile powder
- 1/8 tsp. Ground cinnamon
- Salt and freshly ground pepper
- 3 cups grated Monterey jack
- 1/2 cup Mexican crema
- 1 cup queso fresco, crumbled
- Fresh cilantro leaves

Directions:

1. Put the tomatoes, garlic, onion, and jalapeno in a shallow baking dish and place on the griddle
2. Put the cooled tomato mixture in a blender and liquefy. Pour into a saucepan.
3. Stir in the cumin, oregano, chile powder, cinnamon, and salt and pepper to taste.
4. Carefully peel the blistered outer skin off the New Mexican chiles: Leave the stem ends intact and try not to tear the flesh.
5. Slice the corn off the cobs and put in a large mixing bowl.
6. Bake the rellenos for 25 to 30 minutes, or until the filling is bubbling and the cheese has melted.
7. Sprinkle with queso fresco and garnish with fresh cilantro leaves, if desired. Enjoy!

Nutrition:
Calories: 206 Carbs: 5g
Fat: 14g Protein: 9g

Roasted Tomatoes with Hot Pepper Sauce

Preparation Time:20 mins
Cooking Time:90 mins **Servings:**4-6
Ingredients:

- 2 lbs. roman fresh tomatoes
- 3 tbsp parsley, chopped
- 2 tbsp garlic, chopped
- Black pepper, to taste
- 1/2 cup olive oil
- Hot pepper, to taste
- 1 lb. spaghetti or other pasta

Directions:

1. When ready to cook, set the temperature to 400°F and preheat, lid closed for 15 minutes

2. Wash tomatoes and cut them in half, length width. Place them in a baking dish cut side up.
3. Sprinkle with chopped parsley, garlic, add salt and black pepper and pour 1/4 cup of olive oil over them.
4. Place on pre-heated griddle and bake for 1 1/2 hours. Tomatoes will shrink and the skins will be partly blackened.
5. Remove tomatoes from baking dish and place in a food processor leaving the cooked oil and puree them.
6. Drop pasta into boiling salted water and cook until tender. Drain and toss immediately with the pureed tomatoes.
7. Add the remaining 1/4 cup of raw olive oil and crumbled hot red pepper to taste. Toss and serve. Enjoy!

Nutrition:

Calories: 111 Carbs: 5g Fat: 11g Protein: 1g

Griddle Fingerling Potato Salad

Preparation Time:15 mins

Cooking Time:15 mins

Servings:6-8

Ingredients:

- 1-1/2 lbs. Fingerling potatoes cut in half lengthwise
- 10 scallions
- 2/3 cup Evo (extra virgin olive oil), divided use
- 2 tbsp rice vinegar
- 2 tsp lemon juice
- 1 small jalapeno, sliced
- 2 tsp kosher salt

Directions:

1. When ready to cook, set temperature to High and preheat, lid closed for 15 minutes. Brush the scallions with the oil and place on the griddle. Cook until lightly charred, about 2-3 minutes. Remove and let cool. Once the scallions have cooled, slice and set aside.
2. Brush the Fingerlings with oil (reserving 1/3 cup for later use), then salt and pepper. Place cut side down on the griddle until cooked through, about 4-5 minutes.
3. In a bowl, whisk the remaining 1/3 cup olive oil, rice vinegar, salt, and lemon juice, then mix in the scallions, potatoes, and sliced jalapeno. Season with salt and pepper and serve. Enjoy!

Nutrition:

Calories: 270 Carbs: 18g Fat: 18g Protein: 3g

Smoked Jalapeño Poppers

Preparation Time: 15 minutes

Cooking Time: 60 minutes

Servings: 4-6

Ingredients:

- 12 medium jalapeños
- 6 slices bacon, cut in half
- 8 oz cream cheese, softened
- 1 cup cheese, grated
- 2 tbsp pork & poultry rub

Directions:

1. When ready to cook, set temperature to 180 degree F and preheat, lid closed for 15 minutes.

2. Slice the jalapeños in half lengthwise. Scrape out any seeds and ribs with a small spoon or paring knife.
3. Mix softened cream cheese with Pork & Poultry rub and grated cheese.
4. Spoon mixture onto each jalapeño half. Wrap with bacon and secure with a toothpick.
5. Place the jalapeños on a rimmed baking sheet. Place on griddle and smoke for 30 minutes.
6. Increase the griddle temperature to 375 degree F and cook an additional 30 minutes or until bacon is cooked to desired doneness. Serve warm, enjoy!

Nutrition:
Calories: 280
Carbs: 24g
Fat: 19g
Protein: 4g

Griddle Veggie Sandwich

Preparation Time: 30 minutes
Cooking Time: 30 minutes
Servings: 4-6
Ingredients:

- Smoked hummus
- 1-1/2 cups chickpeas
- 1/3 cup tahini
- 1 tbsp minced garlic
- 2 tbsp olive oil
- 1 tsp kosher salt
- 4 tbsp lemon juice
- Griddle veggie sandwich
- 1 small eggplant, sliced into strips
- 1 small zucchini, sliced into strips
- 1 small yellow squash, sliced into strips
- 2 large portobello mushrooms
- Olive oil
- Salt and pepper to taste
- 2 heirloom tomatoes, sliced
- 1 bunch basil, leaves pulled
- 4 ciabatta buns
- 1/2 cup ricotta
- Juice of 1 lemon
- 1 garlic clove minced
- Salt and pepper to taste

Directions:

1. When ready to cook, set temperature to 180 degree F and preheat, lid closed for 15 minutes.
2. In the bowl of a food processor, combine smoked chickpeas, tahini, garlic, olive oil, salt and lemon juice and process until mixed well but not completely smooth. Transfer to a bowl and reserve.
3. Increase griddle temp to high (400-500 degree F).
4. While the veggies are cooking combine the ricotta, lemon juice, garlic, salt and pepper in a small bowl.
5. Cut the ciabatta buns in half and open them up. Spread hummus on one side and ricotta on the other. Stack the Griddle veggies and top with tomatoes and basil. Enjoy!

Nutrition:
Calories: 376
Carbs: 57g
Fat: 16g
Protein: 10g

Smoked Healthy Cabbage

Preparation Time: 10 minutes
Cooking Time: 2 hours
Servings: 5
Ingredients:

- 1 head cabbage, cored
- 4 tablespoons butter
- 2 tablespoons rendered bacon fat
- 1 chicken bouillon cube
- 1 teaspoon fresh ground black pepper
- 1 garlic clove, minced

Directions:

1. Pre-heat your griddle to 240 degrees Fahrenheit.
2. Fill the hole of your cored cabbage with butter, bouillon cube, bacon fat, pepper and garlic
3. Wrap the cabbage in foil about two-thirds of the way up
4. Make sure to leave the top open
5. Transfer to your griddle rack and smoke for 2 hours
6. Unwrap and enjoy!

Nutrition:
Calories: 231
Fats: 10g
Carbs: 26g
Fiber: 1g

Garlic and Rosemary Potato Wedges

Preparation Time: 15 minutes
Cooking Time: 1 hour 30 minutes
Servings:4
Ingredients:

- 4-6 large russet potatoes, cut into wedges
- ¼ cup olive oil
- 2 garlic cloves, minced
- 2 tablespoons rosemary leaves, chopped
- 2 teaspoon salt
- 1 teaspoon fresh ground black pepper
- 1 teaspoon sugar
- 1 teaspoon onion powder

Directions:

1. Pre-heat your griddle to 250 degrees Fahrenheit
2. Take a large bowl and add potatoes and olive oil
3. Toss well
4. Take another small bowl and stir garlic, salt, rosemary, pepper, sugar, onion powder
5. Sprinkle the mix on all sides of the potato wedge
6. Transfer the seasoned wedge to your griddle rack and smoke for 1 and a ½ hours
7. Serve and enjoy!

Nutrition:
Calories: 291 Fats: 10g Carbs: 46g
Fiber: 2g

Smoked Tomato and Mozzarella Dip

Preparation Time: 5 minutes
Cooking Time: 1 hour
Servings:4
Ingredients:

- 8 ounces smoked mozzarella cheese, shredded
- 8 ounces Colby cheese, shredded
- ½ cup parmesan cheese, grated
- 1 cup sour cream
- 1 cup sun-dried tomatoes
- 1 and ½ teaspoon salt
- 1 teaspoon fresh ground pepper

- 1 teaspoon dried basil
- 1 teaspoon dried oregano
- 1 teaspoon red pepper flakes
- 1 garlic clove, minced
- ½ teaspoon onion powder
- French toast, serving

Directions:

1. Pre-heat your griddle to 275 degrees Fahrenheit
2. Take a large bowl and stir in the cheeses, tomatoes, pepper, salt, basil, oregano, red pepper flakes, garlic, onion powder and mix well
3. Transfer the mix to a small metal pan and transfer to a griddle
4. Smoke for 1 hour
5. Serve with toasted French bread
6. Enjoy!

Nutrition:

Calories: 174

Fats: 11g

Carbs: 15g

Fiber: 2g

Feisty Roasted Cauliflower

Preparation Time: 15 minutes

Cooking Time:10 minutes **Servings:**4

Ingredients:

- 1 cauliflower head, cut into florets
- 1 tablespoon oil
- 1 cup parmesan, grated
- 2 garlic cloves, crushed
- ½ teaspoon pepper
- ½ teaspoon salt
- ¼ teaspoon paprika

Directions:

1. Pre-heat your Griddle to 180 degrees F
2. Transfer florets to griddle and smoke for 1 hour
3. Take a bowl and add all ingredients except cheese
4. Once smoking is done, remove florets
5. Increase temperature to 450 degrees F, brush florets with the brush and transfer to griddle
6. Smoke for 10 minutes more
7. Sprinkle cheese on top and let them sit (Lid closed) until cheese melts
8. Serve and enjoy!

Nutrition:

Calories: 45

Fats: 2g

Carbs: 7g

Fiber: 1g

Griddle Zucchini Squash Spears

Preparation Time: 5 minutes

Cooking Time: 10 minutes

Servings: 4-6

Ingredients:

- 4 medium zucchinis
- 2 tbsp olive oil
- 1 tbsp cherry vinegar
- 2 springs thyme, leaves pulled
- Salt and pepper, to taste

Directions:

1. Clean the zucchini and cut each end off. Cut each in half, then each half into thirds.
2. When ready to cook, set the temperature to 350 degree F and preheat, lid closed for 15 minutes.
3. Cooking Time for 3-4 minutes per side, until griddle marks appear, and zucchini is tender.

4. Remove from griddle and finish with more thyme leaves if desired. Enjoy!

Nutrition:
Calories: 76
Carbs: 17g
Fat: 1g
Protein: 4g

Smoked Pickled Green Beans

Preparation Time:15 mins
Cooking Time:45 mins **Servings:**4-6
Ingredients:

- 1 lb. green beans, blanched
- 1/2 cup salt
- 1/2 cup sugar
- 1 tbsp red pepper flake
- 2 cups white wine vinegar
- 2 cups ice water

Directions:

1. When ready to cook, set temperature to 180°F and preheat, lid closed for 15 minutes.
2. Place the blanched green beans on a mesh griddle mat and place mat directly on the griddle grate. Smoke the green beans for 30-45 minutes until they've picked up the desired amount of smoke. Remove from griddle and set aside until the brine is ready.
3. In a medium sized saucepan, bring all remaining ingredients, except ice water, to a boil over medium high heat on the stove. Simmer for 5-10 minutes then remove from heat and steep 20 minutes more. Pour brine over ice water to cool.
4. Once brine has cooled, pour over the green beans and weigh them down with a few plates to ensure they are entirely submerged. Let sit 24 hours before use.
5. Enjoy!

Nutrition:
Calories: 20
Carbs: 3g
Fat: 0g
Protein: 1g

Sweet Maple Smoked Brussels Sprouts

Preparation Time: 10 minutes
Cooking Time: 40 minutes
Servings: 10
Ingredients:

- Brussels sprouts (2-lbs., 0.9-kg.)
- Maple syrup – 3 tablespoons
- Olive oil – 2 tablespoons
- Salt – ¼ teaspoon
- Pepper – ¼ teaspoon
- Smoked paprika – ¼ teaspoon

Directions:

1. Combine maple syrup with olive oil, salt, pepper, and smoked paprika then stir until incorporated.
2. Drizzle the mixture over the Brussels sprouts then shake to coat. Spread the seasoned Brussels sprouts over a disposable aluminum pan.
3. Set the griddle for indirect heat then adjust the temperature to 400°F (204°C).
4. Place the glazed Brussels sprouts on the griddle and smoke for 30 minutes, until brown and tender.

5. Once the smoked Brussels sprouts are done, remove from the griddle and transfer to a serving dish.
6. Serve and enjoy.

Nutrition:
Calories: 380
Carbs: 30g
Fat: 26g
Protein: 8g

Brown Sugar Glazed Smoked Acorn Squash

Preparation Time: 20 minutes
Cooking Time: 2 hours
Servings: 10
Ingredients:

- Acorn squash (2-lbs., 0.9-kg.)
- Butter – 3 tablespoons
- Brown sugar – ¼ cup
- Salt – ¼ teaspoon
- Ground cinnamon – ¼ teaspoon
- Ground ginger – ¼ teaspoon
- Ground nutmeg – ¼ teaspoon

Directions:

1. Combine brown sugar, salt, ground cinnamon, ground ginger, and ground nutmeg in a bowl then mix well. Set aside.
2. Cut the acorn squash into halves then place in a disposable aluminum pan with the cut sides on top.
3. Brush butter onto the halved acorn squash then sprinkle the brown sugar mixture over the squash. Set aside.
4. Set the griddle for indirect heat then adjust the temperature to 225°F (107°C).
5. Place the acorn squash in the griddle and smoke for 2 hours or until tender.
6. Once it is done, remove the smoked acorn squash from the griddle and place on a serving dish.
7. Serve and enjoy.

Nutrition:
Calories: 125
Carbs: 25g
Fat: 4g
Protein: 2g

Sticky Caramel Smoked Onion

Preparation Time: 30 minutes
Cooking Time: 1 hour
Servings: 10
Ingredients:

- Onions (2.5-lb., 1.1-kg.)
- Salted butter – ½ cup
- Brown sugar – 3 tablespoons
- Molasses – 1 tablespoon
- Apple cider vinegar – 2 tablespoons
- Worcestershire sauce – 1 tablespoon
- Dry mustard – 2 teaspoons
- Smoked paprika – 1 teaspoon
- Onion powder – 1 teaspoon

Directions:

1. Peel the onions then cut into slices. Place in a disposable aluminum pan.
2. Mix brown sugar, molasses, apple cider vinegar, Worcestershire sauce, dry mustard, smoked paprika, and onion powder then sprinkle over the sliced onions. Shake to coat.
3. Drop butter on top of the sliced onion then set aside.

4. Set the griddle for indirect heat then adjust the temperature to 225°F (107°C).
5. Place the disposable aluminum pan in the griddle and smoke for an hour and a half, until the spice mixture is caramelized.
6. Once it is done, take the smoked onion out of the griddle and transfer to a serving dish. Stir a little.
7. Serve and enjoy.

Nutrition:
Calories: 170
Carbs: 0g
Fat: 9g
Protein: 2g

Beer Smoked Cabbage with Garlic Rub

Preparation Time: 40 minutes
Cooking Time: 3 hours
Servings: 10
Ingredients:

- Whole cabbages (3-lb., 1.4-kg.)
- Olive oil – 3 tablespoons
- Garlic powder – 2 teaspoons
- Salt – ¼ teaspoon
- Chili powder – ¼ teaspoon
- Ground cinnamon – ½ teaspoon
- Beer – 1 can

Directions:

1. Combine garlic powder, salt, chili powder, and ground cinnamon in a bowl.
2. Drizzle olive oil over the spices then mix well.
3. Rub the spice mixture over the cabbage and in between the cabbage leaves.
4. Set the griddle for indirect heat then adjust the temperature to 275°F (135°C).
5. Place the seasoned cabbage on a sheet of aluminum foil then wrap the cabbage. Let the top of the cabbage open.
6. Pour beer over the cabbage then place it on the griddle. Smoke the cabbage for 3 hours, until tender.
7. Once it is done, remove the smoked cabbage from the griddle and unwrap it.
8. Cut the smoked cabbage into wedges then serve.
9. Enjoy!

Nutrition:
Calories: 300 Carbs: 70g
Fat: 2g
Protein: 18g

Smoked Asparagus with Sesame Aroma

Preparation Time: 20 minutes
Cooking Time: 1 hour **Servings:** 10
Ingredients:

- Asparagus (2-lbs., 0.9-kg.)
- Sesame oil – 2 tablespoons
- Lemon juice – 2 tablespoons
- Grated lemon zest – ¼ teaspoon
- Garlic powder – 1 teaspoon
- Salt – ½ teaspoon
- Pepper – ¼ teaspoon

Directions:

1. Combine grated lemon zest, garlic powder, salt, and pepper in a bowl then drizzle lemon juice and sesame oil over the spices. Mix well.

2. Cut and trim the asparagus then rub with the spice mixture.
3. Next, wrap the seasoned asparagus with aluminum foil then set aside.
4. Set the griddle for indirect heat then adjust the temperature to 225°F (107°C).
5. Place the wrapped asparagus in the griddle and smoke for an hour, until tender.
6. Once it is done, remove the smoked asparagus from the griddle then transfer to a serving dish.
7. Serve and enjoy.

Nutrition:
Calories: 250
Carbs: 26g
Fat: 9g
Protein: 19g

CHAPTER 7
Poultry Recipes

Classic BBQ Chicken

Preparation time: time: 5 minutes
Cooking Time: 1 hour 45 minutes
Servings: 4-6
Ingredients:

- pounds of your favorite chicken, including legs, thighs, wings, and breasts, skin-on
- Salt
- Olive oil
- cup barbecue sauce, like Hickory Mesquite or homemade

Directions:

1. Rub the chicken with olive oil and salt.
2. Preheat the griddle to high heat.
3. Sear chicken skin side down on the griddle for 5-10 minutes.
4. Turn the griddle down to medium low heat, tent with foil and cook for 30 minutes.
5. Turn chicken and baste with barbecue sauce.
6. Cover the chicken again and allow to cook for another 20 minutes.
7. Baste, cover and cook again for 30 minutes; repeat basting and turning during this time.
8. The chicken is done when the internal temperature of the chicken pieces are 165°F and juices run clear.
9. Baste with more barbecue sauce to serve!

Nutrition: Calories: 539, Sodium: 684 mg, Dietary Fiber: 0.3 g, Fat: 11.6 g, Carbs: 15.1 g, Protein: 87.6 g.

California Seared Chicken

Preparation time: time: 35 minutes
Cooking Time: 20 minutes **Servings:** 4
Ingredients:

- boneless, skinless chicken breasts
- 3/4 cup balsamic vinegar
- tablespoons extra virgin olive oil
    - tablespoon honey
- 1 teaspoon oregano
- 1 teaspoon basil
- 1 teaspoon garlic powder
- For garnish:
- Sea salt
- Black pepper, fresh ground
- slices fresh mozzarella cheese
- 4 slices avocado
- 4 slices beefsteak tomato
- Balsamic glaze, for drizzling

Directions:

1. Whisk together balsamic vinegar, honey, olive oil, oregano, basil and garlic powder in a large mixing bowl.
2. Add chicken to coat and marinate for 30 minutes in the refrigerator.
3. Preheat griddle to medium-high. Sear chicken for 7 minutes per side, or until a meat thermometer reaches 165°F.
4. Top each chicken breast with mozzarella, avocado, and tomato and tent with foil on the griddle to melt for 2 minutes.
5. Garnish with a drizzle of balsamic glaze, and a pinch of sea salt and black pepper.

Nutrition: Calories: 883, Sodium: 449 mg, Dietary Fiber: 15.2 g, Fat: 62.1 g, Carbs: 29.8 g, Protein: 55.3 g.

Sweet Chili Lime Chicken

Preparation time: time: 35 minutes
Cooking Time: 15 minutes **Servings:** 4
Ingredients:

- ½ cup sweet chili sauce
- ¼ cup soy sauce - teaspoon mirin
- teaspoon orange juice, fresh squeezed
- 1 teaspoon orange marmalade
- tablespoons lime juice
- 1 tablespoon brown sugar
- 1 clove garlic, minced
- boneless, skinless chicken breasts
- Sesame seeds, for garnish

Directions:

1. Whisk sweet chili sauce, soy sauce, mirin, orange marmalade, lime and orange juice, brown sugar, and minced garlic together in a small mixing bowl.
2. Set aside ¼ cup of the sauce.
3. Toss chicken in sauce to coat and marinate 30 minutes.
4. Preheat your griddle to medium heat.Put the chicken on the griddle and cook each side for 7 minutes. Baste the cooked chicken with remaining marinade and garnish with sesame seeds to serve with your favorite sides.

Nutrition: Calories: 380, Sodium: 1274 mg, Dietary Fiber: 0.5 g, Fat: 12 g, Carbs:19.7g, Protein: 43.8 g.

Seared Spicy Citrus Chicken

Preparation time: time: 8 - 24 hours
Cooking Time: 20 minutes **Servings:** 4
Ingredients:

- 2 lbs. boneless, skinless chicken thighs
- For the marinade:
- 1/4 cup fresh lime juice
- 2 teaspoon lime zest
- 1/4 cup honey
- 2 tablespoons olive oil
- tablespoon balsamic vinegar
- 1/2 teaspoon sea salt
- 1/2 teaspoon black pepper
- garlic cloves, minced
- 1/4 teaspoon onion powder

Directions:

1. Whisk together marinade ingredients in a large mixing bowl; reserve 2 tablespoons of the marinade for basting.
2. Add chicken and marinade to a sealable plastic bag and marinate 8 hours or overnight in the refrigerator.
3. Preheat griddle to medium high heat and brush lightly with olive oil.
4. Place chicken on griddle and cook 8 minutes per side.
5. Baste each side of chicken with reserved marinade during the last few minutes of cooking; chicken is done when the internal temperature reaches 165°F.
6. Plate chicken, tent with foil, and allow to rest for 5 minutes.
7. Serve and enjoy!

Nutrition: Calories: 381, Sodium: 337mg, Dietary Fiber: 1.1 g, Fat: 20.2 g, Carbs: 4.7 g, Protein: 44.7 g.

Honey Balsamic Marinated Chicken

Preparation time: time: 30 minutes - 4 hours
Cooking Time: 20 minutes
Servings: 4
Ingredients:

- 2 lbs. boneless, skinless chicken thighs
- teaspoon olive oil
- 1/2 teaspoon sea salt
- 1/4 teaspoon black pepper
- 1/2 teaspoon paprika
- 3/4 teaspoon onion powder
- For the Marinade:
- tablespoons honey
- tablespoons balsamic vinegar
- 2 tablespoons tomato paste
    - teaspoon garlic, minced

Directions:

1. Add chicken, olive oil, salt, black pepper, paprika, and onion powder to a sealable plastic bag. Seal and toss to coat, covering chicken with spices and oil; set aside.
2. Whisk together balsamic vinegar, tomato paste, garlic, and honey.
3. Divide the marinade in half. Add one half to the bag of chicken and store the other half in a sealed container in the refrigerator.
4. Seal the bag and toss chicken to coat. Refrigerate for 30 minutes to 4 hours.
5. Preheat a griddle to medium-high.
6. Discard bag and marinade. Add chicken to the griddle and cook 7 minutes per side or until juices run clear and a meat thermometer reads 165°F.
7. During last minute of cooking, brush remaining marinade on top of the chicken thighs.
8. Serve immediately.

Nutrition: Calories: 485, Sodium: 438 mg, Dietary Fiber: 0.5 g, Fat: 18.1 g, Carbs: 11 g, Protein: 66.1 g.

Salsa Verde Marinated Chicken

Preparation time: time: 4 hours 35 minutes
Cooking Time: 4 hours 50 minutes
Servings: 6
Ingredients:

- boneless, skinless chicken breasts
    - tablespoon olive oil
- 1 teaspoon sea salt
- 1 teaspoon chili powder
- 1 teaspoon ground cumin
- 1 teaspoon garlic powder
- For the salsa verde marinade:
    - teaspoons garlic, minced
- 1 small onion, chopped
- tomatillos, husked, rinsed and chopped
- 1 medium jalapeño pepper, cut in half, seeded
- ¼ cup fresh cilantro, chopped
- ½ teaspoon sugar or sugar substitute

Directions:

1. Add salsa verde marinade ingredients to a food processor and pulse until smooth.
2. Mix sea salt, chili powder, cumin, and garlic powder together in a small mixing bowl.

3. Season chicken breasts with olive oil and seasoning mix, and lay in glass baking dish.
4. Spread a tablespoon of salsa verde marinade over each chicken breast to cover; reserve remaining salsa for serving.
5. Cover dish with plastic wrap and refrigerate for 4 hours.
6. Preheat griddle to medium-high and brush with olive oil.
7. Add chicken to griddle and cook 7 minutes per side or until juices run clear and a meat thermometer reads 165°F.
8. Serve each with additional salsa verde and enjoy!

Nutrition: Calories: 321, Sodium: 444 mg, Dietary Fiber: 1.3 g, Fat: 13.7 g, Carbs: 4.8 g, Protein: 43 g.

Hasselback Stuffed Chicken

Preparation time: time: 15 minutes
Cooking Time: 30 minutes
Servings: 4
Ingredients:

- boneless, skinless chicken breasts
- 2 tablespoons olive oil
- 2 tablespoons taco seasoning
- 1/2 red, yellow and green pepper, very thinly sliced
- small red onion, very thinly sliced
- 1/2 cup Mexican shredded cheese
- Guacamole, for serving
- Sour cream, for serving
- Salsa, for serving

Directions:

1. Preheat griddle to med-high.
2. Cut thin horizontal cuts across each chicken breast; like you would hasselback potatoes.
3. Rub chicken evenly with olive oil and taco seasoning.
4. Add a mixture of bell peppers and red onions to each cut, and place the breasts on the griddle.
5. Cook chicken for 15 minutes.
6. Remove and top with cheese.
7. Tent loosely with foil and cook another 5 minutes, until cheese is melted. Remove from griddle and top with guacamole, sour cream and salsa. Serve alongside your favorite side dishes!

Nutrition: Calories:643 , Sodium:1549 mg, Dietary Fiber: 3.8 g, Fat: 18.6g, Carbs: 26.3g, Protein: 93.3g.

Creole Chicken Stuffed With Cheese & Peppers

Preparation time: time: 10 minutes
Cooking Time: 20 minutes **Servings:** 4
Ingredients:

- boneless, skinless chicken breasts
- 8 mini sweet peppers, sliced thin and seeded
- 2 slices pepper jack cheese, cut in half
- 2 slices colby jack cheese, cut in half
- tablespoon creole seasoning, like Emeril's
- 1 teaspoon black pepper
- 1 teaspoon garlic powder
- 1 teaspoon onion powder
- teaspoons olive oil, separated
- Toothpicks

Directions:

1. Rinse chicken and pat dry.
2. Mix creole seasoning, pepper, garlic powder, and onion powder together in a small mixing bowl and set aside.

3. Cut a slit on the side of each chicken breast; be careful not to cut all the way through the chicken.
4. Rub each breast with 1 teaspoon each of olive oil.
5. Rub each chicken breast with seasoning mix and coat evenly.
6. Stuff each breast of chicken with 1 half pepper jack cheese slice, 1 half colby cheese slice, and a handful of pepper slices.
7. Secure chicken shut with 4 or 5 toothpicks.
8. Preheat the griddle to medium-high and cook chicken for 8 minutes per side; or until chicken reaches an internal temperature of 165°F. Allow chicken to rest for 5 minutes, remove toothpicks, and serve.

Nutrition: Calories: 509, Sodium:1117 mg, Dietary Fiber: 3.4 g, Fat: 25.1g, Carbs: 19.8g, Protein: 51.4g.

Root Beer Can Chicken

Preparation time: time: 8 hours and 10 minutes

Cooking Time: 20 minutes **Servings:** 2 -4

Ingredients:

- lb. boneless chicken thighs
- (12 ounce) cans root beer, like A&W
- Olive oil
- For the rub:
    - tablespoon garlic powder
- 3/4 tablespoon sea salt
- 1/2 tablespoon white pepper
- teaspoons smoked paprika
    - teaspoons garlic powder
- 1 teaspoon dried thyme
- 1/8 teaspoon cayenne pepper

Directions:

2. Combine rub ingredients in a bowl; reserve half in a separate air tight container until ready to cook. Rub chicken thighs evenly with olive oil and coat each with some rub.
3. Lay chicken in a 13 by 9 inch baking dish. Cover with 2 cans of root beer. Preheat griddle to medium-high heat.
4. Discard marinade and brush griddle with olive oil.
5. Gently fold remaining rub and a half of the third can of root beer in a small bowl.
6. Sear chicken for 7 minutes on each side, basting often with root beer rub mix. Serve when cooked through or chicken reaches 165°F and juices run clear.

Nutrition: Calories: 363, Sodium: 1185 mg, Dietary Fiber: 0.9g, Fat: 12.1g, Carbs: 29.9g, Protein: 33.4g.

Chipotle Adobe Chicken

Preparation time: Time: 1 - 24 hours

Cooking Time: 20 minutes **Servings:** 4 - 6

Ingredients:

- 2 lbs chicken thighs or breasts (boneless, skinless)
- For the marinade:
- ¼ cup olive oil
- 2 chipotle peppers, in adobo sauce, plus 1 teaspoon adobo sauce from the can
    - tablespoon garlic, minced
- 1 shallot, finely chopped
- 1 ½ tablespoons cumin

- 1 tablespoon cilantro, super-finely chopped or dried
    - o teaspoons chili powder
- 1 teaspoon dried oregano
- 1/2 teaspoon salt
- Fresh limes, garnish
- Cilantro, garnish

Directions:

1. Preheat griddle to medium-high.
2. Add marinade ingredients to a food processor or blender and pulse into a paste.
3. Add the chicken and marinade to a sealable plastic bag and massage to coat well.
4. Place in the refrigerator for 1 hour to 24 hours before cooking.
5. Sear chicken for 7 minutes, turn and cook and additional 7 minutes.
6. Turn heat to low and continue to cook until chicken has reached an internal temperature of 165°F. Remove chicken from griddle and allow to rest 5 to 10 minutes before serving. Garnish with a squeeze of fresh lime and a sprinkle of cilantro to serve.

Nutrition: Calories: 561, Sodium: 431 mg, Dietary Fiber: 0.3 g, Fat: 23.8 g, Carbs: 18.7 g, Protein: 65.9 g.

Chicken Tacos With Avocado Crema

Preparation time: Time: 1 hour 5 minutes
Cooking Time: 10 minutes
Servings: 4-5
Ingredients:

- 1/2 lbs. Boneless, skinless chicken breasts, sliced thin
- For the chicken marinade:
- 1 serrano pepper, minced
    - o teaspoons garlic, minced
- 1 lime, juiced
- 1 teaspoon ground cumin
- 1/3 cup olive oil
- Sea salt, to taste
- Black pepper, to taste
- For the avocado crema:
- 1 cup sour cream
    - o teaspoons lime juice
- 1 teaspoon lime zest
- 1 serrano pepper, diced and seeded
- 1 clove garlic, minced
- 1 large hass avocado
- For the garnish:
- 1/2 cup queso fresco, crumbled
- 2 teaspoons cilantro, chopped
- 1 lime sliced into wedges
- 10 corn tortillas

Directions:

1. Mix chicken marinade together in a sealable plastic bag. Add chicken and toss to coat well.
2. Marinate for 1 hour in the refrigerator.
3. Combine avocado crema ingredients in a food processor or blender and pulse until smooth.
4. Cover and refrigerate until you are ready to assemble tacos.
5. Preheat griddle to medium heat and griddle chicken for 5 minutes per side; rotating and turning as needed.
6. Remove from griddle and tent loosely with aluminum foil. Allow chicken to rest 5 minutes.

7. Serve with warm tortillas, a dollop of avocado crema, queso fresco, cilantro and lime wedges.
8. To meal Preparation time: simply divide chicken into individual portion containers with a serving of the garnish, and take with tortillas wrapped in parchment paper to warm in a microwave to serve.

Nutrition: Calories: 703, Sodium: 357 mg, Dietary Fiber: 6.3 g, Fat: 44.5 g, Carbs:30.5g, Protein: 47.9g.

Sizzling Chicken Fajitas

Preparation time: time: 5 minutes
Cooking Time: 25 minutes
Servings: 4
Ingredients:

- boneless chicken breast halves, thinly sliced
- yellow onion, sliced
  - large green bell pepper, sliced
- 1 large red bell pepper, sliced
- 1 teaspoon ground cumin
- 1 teaspoon garlic powder
- 1 teaspoon onion powder
- tablespoons lime juice
- 1 tablespoon olive oil
- 1/2 teaspoon black pepper
- 1 teaspoon salt
- tablespoons vegetable oil
- 10 flour tortillas

Directions:

1. In a zipperlock bag, combine the chicken, cumin, garlic, onion, lime juice, salt, pepper, and olive oil. Allow to marinate for 30 minutes.
2. Preheat griddle to medium heat.
3. On one side of the griddle add the olive oil and heat until shimmering. Add the onion and pepper and cook until slightly softened.
4. On the other side of the griddle add the marinated chicken and cook until lightly browned.
5. Once chicken is lightly browned, toss together with the onion and pepper and cook until chicken registers 165°F.
6. Remove chicken and vegetables from the griddle and serve with warm tortillas.

Nutrition: Calories: 408, Sodium:664 mg, Dietary Fiber: 5.5 g, Fat: 18.3g, Carbs:37.1g, Protein: 25.9g.

Hawaiian Chicken Skewers

Preparation time: Time: 1 hour 10 minutes
Cooking Time: 15 minutes
Servings: 4 - 5
Ingredients:

  - lb. boneless, skinless chicken breast, cut into 1 ½ inch cubes
  - cups pineapple, cut into 1 ½ inch cubes
  - large green peppers, cut into 1 ½ inch pieces
- 1 large red onion, cut into 1 ½ inch pieces
- 2 tablespoons olive oil, to coat veggies
- For the marinade:
- 1/3 cup tomato paste
- 1/3 cup brown sugar, packed
- 1/3 cup soy sauce
- 1/4 cup pineapple juice
- 2 tablespoons olive oil

- 1 1/2 tablespoon mirin or rice wine vinegar
    - o teaspoons garlic cloves, minced
- 1 tablespoon ginger, minced
- 1/2 teaspoon sesame oil
- Pinch of sea salt
- Pinch of ground black pepper
- 10 wooden skewers, for assembly

Directions:

1. Combine marinade ingredients in a mixing bowl until smooth. Reserve a 1/2 cup of the marinade in the refrigerator.
2. Add chicken and remaining marinade to a sealable plastic bag and refrigerate for 1 hour.
3. Soak 10 wooden skewer sticks in water for 1 hour.
4. Preheat the griddle to medium heat.
5. Add red onion, bell pepper and pineapple to a mixing bowl with 2 tablespoons olive oil and toss to coat. Thread red onion, bell pepper, pineapple and chicken onto the skewers until all of the chicken has been used. Place skewers on griddle and grab your reserved marinade from the refrigerator; cook for 5 minutes then brush with remaining marinade and rotate.
6. Brush again with marinade and sear about 5 additional minutes or until chicken reads 165°F on a meat thermometer. Serve warm.

Nutrition: Calories: 311, Sodium: 1116 mg, Dietary Fiber: 4.2 g, Fat: 8.8 g, Carbs: 38.1 g, Protein: 22.8g.

Fiery Italian Chicken Skewers

Preparation time: 1 hour 20 minutes
Cooking Time: 20 minutes
Servings: 2 -4
Ingredients:

- 10 boneless, skinless chicken thighs, cut into chunks
    - o large red onion, cut into wedges
- 1 large red pepper, stemmed, seeded, and cut into chunks
- For the marinade:
- 1/3 cup toasted pine nuts
- 1 1/2 cups sliced roasted red peppers
- hot cherry peppers, stemmed and seeded, or to taste
- 1 cup packed fresh basil leaves, plus more to serve
- cloves garlic, peeled
- 1/4 cup grated Parmesan cheese
- 1 tablespoon paprika
- extra virgin olive oil, as needed

Directions:

1. Combine the toasted pine nuts, roasted red peppers, hot cherry peppers, basil, garlic, Parmesan, and paprika in a food processor or blender and process until well-combined.
2. Add in olive oil until the pesto reaches a thin consistency in order to coat the chicken as a marinade.
3. Transfer half of the pesto to a large sealable plastic bag, and reserve the other half for serving.
4. Add the chicken thigh chunks to the bag of pesto, seal, and massage the bag to coat the chicken.

5. Refrigerate for 1 hour.
6. Preheat griddle to medium-high heat and brush with olive oil.
7. Thread the chicken cubes, red onion, and red pepper onto metal skewers.
8. Brush the chicken with the reserved pesto.
9. Cook until the chicken reaches an internal temperature of 165°F; about 5 minutes per side. Serve warm with your favorite salad or vegetables!

Nutrition: Calories: 945, Sodium: 798 mg, Dietary Fiber: 3.2 g, Fat: 46.7 g, Carbs: 14.7g, Protein: 112.2g.

Chicken Thighs With Ginger-Sesame Glaze

Preparation time: time: 10 minutes
Cooking Time: 20 minutes
Servings: 4 - 8
Ingredients:

- 8 boneless, skinless chicken thighs
- For the glaze:
- 3 tablespoons dark brown sugar
- 2 1/2 tablespoons soy sauce
    - tablespoon fresh garlic, minced
    - teaspoons sesame seeds
- 1 teaspoon fresh ginger, minced
- 1 teaspoon sambal oelek
- 1/3 cup scallions, thinly sliced
- Non-stick cooking spray

Directions:

1. Combine glaze ingredients in a large mixing bowl; separate and reserve half for serving.
2. Add chicken to bowl and toss to coat well.
3. Preheat the griddle to medium-high heat.
4. Coat with cooking spray.
5. Cook chicken for 6 minutes on each side or until done.
6. Transfer chicken to plates and drizzle with remaining glaze to serve.

Nutrition: Calories: 301, Sodium: 413 mg, Dietary Fiber: 0.3 g, Fat: 11.2g, Carbs: 4.7g, Protein: 42.9g.

Honey Sriracha Griddle Chicken Thighs

Preparation time: 5 minutes
Cooking Time: 35 minutes
Servings: 6
Ingredients:

- lbs. boneless chicken thighs
- 3 tablespoons butter, unsalted
- tablespoon fresh ginger, minced
- garlic cloves, minced
- 1/4 teaspoon smoked paprika
- 1/4 teaspoon chili powder
- tablespoons honey
- tablespoons Sriracha
- tablespoon lime juice

Directions:

1. Preheat griddle to medium high.
2. Melt butter in a small saucepan on medium low heat; when melted add ginger and garlic. Stir until fragrant, about 2 minutes.
3. Fold in smoked paprika, ground cloves, honey, Sriracha and lime juice. Stir to combine, turn heat to medium and simmer for 5 minutes.
4. Rinse and pat chicken thighs dry.

5. Season with salt and pepper on both sides.
6. Spray griddle with non-stick cooking spray.
7. Place chicken thighs on griddle, skin side down first. Griddle for 5 minutes. Flip the chicken over and griddle on the other side for 5 minutes.
8. Continue to cook chicken, flipping every 3 minutes, so it doesn't burn, until the internal temperature reads 165°F on a meat thermometer.
9. During the last 5 minutes of griddling brush the glaze on both sides of the chicken.
10. Remove from griddle and serve warm.

Nutrition: Calories: 375, Sodium: 221 mg, Dietary Fiber: 0.3g, Fat: 22.5g, Carbs: 14.7g Protein: 32g

Buffalo Chicken Wings

Preparation time: time: 10 minutes
Cooking Time: 20 minutes
Servings: 6 - 8
Ingredients:

- tablespoon sea salt
- teaspoon ground black pepper
    - teaspoon garlic powder
- lbs. chicken wings
- tablespoons unsalted butter
- 1/3 cup buffalo sauce, like Moore's
- 1 tablespoon apple cider vinegar
- 1 tablespoon honey

Directions:

1. Combine salt, pepper and garlic powder in a large mixing bowl.
2. Toss the wings with the seasoning mixture to coat.
3. Preheat griddle to medium heat.
4. Place the wings on the griddle; make sure they are touching so the meat stays moist on the bone while griddling.
5. Flip wings every 5 minutes, for a total of 20 minutes of cooking.
6. Heat the butter, buffalo sauce, vinegar and honey in a saucepan over low heat; whisk to combine well.
7. Add wings to a large mixing bowl, toss the wings with the sauce to coat.
8. Turn griddle up to medium high and place wings back on the griddle until the skins crisp; about 1 to 2 minutes per side.
9. Add wings back into the bowl with the sauce and toss to serve.

Nutrition: Calories:410, Sodium: 950 mg, Dietary Fiber: 0.2 g, Fat: 21.3g, Carbs: 2.7g, Protein: 49.4g.

Chicken Wings With Sweet Red Chili And Peach Glaze

Preparation time: time: 15 minutes
Cooking Time: 30 minutes **Servings:** 4
Ingredients:

- (12 oz.) jar peach preserves
- cup sweet red chili sauce
- 1 teaspoon lime juice
- 1 tablespoon fresh cilantro, minced
- 1 (2-1/2 lb.) bag chicken wing sections
- Non-stick cooking spray

Directions:

1. Mix preserves, red chili sauce, lime juice and cilantro in mixing bowl. Divide in half, and place one half aside for serving.

2. Preheat griddle to medium heat and spray with non-stick cooking spray.
3. Cook wings for 25 minutes turning several times until juices run clear.
4. Remove wings from griddle, toss in a bowl to coat wings with remaining glaze.
5. Return wings to griddle and cook for an additional 3 to 5 minutes turning once.
6. Serve warm with your favorite dips and side dishes!

Nutrition: Calories: 790, Sodium: 643 mg, Dietary Fiber: 1 g, Fat: 16.9 g, Carbs:87.5g, Protein: 66g.

Yellow Curry Chicken Wings

Preparation time: time: 35 minutes
Cooking Time: 30 minutes to 1 hour
Servings: 6
Ingredients:

- 2 lbs. chicken wings
- For the marinade:
- 1/2 cup Greek yogurt, plain
- tablespoon mild yellow curry powder
    - tablespoon olive oil
- ½ teaspoon sea salt
- ½ teaspoon black pepper
- 1 teaspoon red chili flakes

Directions:

1. Rinse and pat wings dry with paper towels.
2. Whisk marinade ingredients together in a large mixing bowl until well-combined.
3. Add wings to bowl and toss to coat.
4. Cover bowl with plastic wrap and chill in the refrigerator for 30 minutes.
5. Preparation time are one side of the griddle for medium heat and the other side on medium-high.
6. Working in batches, griddle wings over medium heat, turning occasionally, until skin starts to brown; about 12 minutes.
7. Move wings to medium-high area of griddle for 5 minutes on each side to char until cooked through; meat thermometer should register 165°F when touching the bone.
8. Transfer wings to a platter and serve warm.

Nutrition: Calories: 324, Sodium:292 mg, Dietary Fiber: 0.4 g, Fat: 14g, Carbs:1.4g, Protein: 45.6g.

Korean Griddle Chicken Wings With Scallion

Preparation time: time: 30 minutes
Cooking Time: 30 minutes to 1 hour
Servings: 6
Ingredients:

- 2 pounds chicken wings (flats and drumettes attached or separated)
- For the marinade:
- tablespoon olive oil
- teaspoon sea salt, plus more
- 1/2 teaspoon black pepper
- 1/2 cup gochujang, Korean hot pepper paste
- 1 scallion, thinly sliced, for garnish

Directions:

1. Rinse and pat wings dry with paper towels.

2. Whisk marinade ingredients together in a large mixing bowl until well-combined.
3. Add wings to bowl and toss to coat.
4. Cover bowl with plastic wrap and chill in the refrigerator for 30 minutes.
5. Preparation time are one side of the griddle for medium heat and the other side on medium-high.
6. Working in batches, cook wings over medium heat, turning occasionally, until skin starts to brown; about 12 minutes.
7. Move wings to medium-high area of griddle for 5 minutes on each side to sear until cooked through; meat thermometer should register 165°F when touching the bone. Transfer wings to a platter, garnish with scallions, and serve warm with your favorite dipping sauces.

Nutrition: Calories: 312, Sodium:476 mg, Dietary Fiber: 0.4 g, Fat: 13.5g, Carbs:1.1g, Protein: 43.9g.

Kale Caesar Salad With Seared Chicken

Preparation time: time: 10 minutes
Cooking Time: 8 minutes **Servings:** 1
Ingredients:

- chicken breast
- 1 teaspoon garlic powder
- ½ teaspoon black pepper
- ½ teaspoon sea salt
    - kale leaves, chopped
- shaved parmesan, for serving
- For the dressing:
- 1 tablespoon mayonnaise
- 1/2 tablespoon dijon mustard
- ½ teaspoon garlic powder
- 1/2 teaspoon worcestershire sauce
- 1/4 lemon, juice of (or 1/2 a small lime)
- ¼ teaspoon anchovy paste
- Pinch of sea salt
- Pinch of black pepper

Directions:

1. Mix garlic powder, black pepper, and sea salt in a small mixing bowl. Coat chicken with seasoning mix.
2. Preheat griddle to medium-high heat.
3. Sear chicken on each side for 7 minutes or until a meat thermometer reads 165°F when inserted in the thickest part of the breast.
4. Whisk all of the dressing ingredients together.
5. Plate your kale and pour the dressing over, and toss to combine.
6. Cut the chicken on a diagonal and place on top of the salad. Garnish with shaved parmesan, and serve.

Nutrition: Calories:643, Sodium:1549 mg, Dietary Fiber: 3.8 g, Fat: 18.6g, Carbs: 26.3g, Protein: 93.3g.

Seared Chicken With Fruit Salsa

Preparation time: time: 1 hour
Cooking Time: 20 minutes
Servings: 4
Ingredients:

- boneless, skinless chicken breasts
- For the marinade:
- 1/2 cup fresh lemon juice

- 1/2 cup soy sauce
- tablespoon fresh ginger, minced
- 1 tablespoon lemon pepper seasoning
- garlic cloves, minced
- For the salsa:
- 1 1/2 cups pineapple, chopped
- 3/4 cup kiwi fruit, chopped
- 1/2 cup mango, chopped
- 1/2 cup red onion, finely chopped
- tablespoons fresh cilantro, chopped
- 1 small jalapeño pepper, seeded and chopped
- 1 1/2 teaspoons ground cumin
- 1/4 teaspoon sea salt
- 1/8 teaspoon black pepper
- ½ teaspoon olive oil, more for brushing griddle

Directions:

1. Combine marinade ingredients in a large sealable plastic bag.
2. Add chicken to bag, seal, and toss to coat. Marinate in refrigerator for 1 hour.
3. Combine salsa ingredients in a mixing bowl and toss gently to combine. Set aside until ready to serve. Preheat the griddle to medium heat.
4. Remove chicken from bag and discard marinade. Brush griddle with olive oil and cook chicken for 7 minutes on each side or until chicken is cooked through. Serve chicken topped with salsa alongside your favorite side dishes.

Nutrition: Calories: 391, Sodium:2051 mg, Dietary Fiber: 3.7 g, Fat: 12.3g, Carbs:23.6g, Protein: 46.1g.

Teriyaki Chicken And Veggie Rice Bowls

Preparation time: time: 8 hours 10 minutes **Cooking Time:** 20 minutes **Servings:** 4

Ingredients:

- bag brown rice
- For the skewers:
- boneless skinless chicken breasts, cubed
- 1 red onion, quartered
- 1 red pepper, cut into cube slices
- 1 green pepper, cut into cube slices
- 1/2 pineapple, cut into cubes
- For the marinade:
- 1/4 cup light soy sauce
- 1/4 cup sesame oil
- 1 tablespoon ginger, fresh grated
- 1 garlic clove, crushed
- 1/2 lime, juiced

Directions:

1. Whisk the marinade ingredients together in a small mixing bowl.
2. Add chicken and marinade to a resealable plastic bag, seal and toss well to coat.
3. Refrigerate for one hour or overnight.
4. Preheat the griddle to medium-high heat.
5. Thread the chicken and the cubed veggies onto 8 metal skewers and cook for 8 minutes on each side until seared and cooked through.
6. Portion rice out into bowls and top with two skewers each, and enjoy!

Nutrition: Calories: 477, Sodium:362 mg, Dietary Fiber: 3.8 g, Fat: 20.6g, Carbs:48.1g, Protein: 26.1g.

Chicken Satay with Almond Butter Sauce

Preparation time: 2 hours 20 minutes
Cooking Time: 8 minutes
Servings: 4
Ingredients:

  - lb. boneless, skinless chicken thighs, cut into thin strips
- Olive oil, for brushing
- For the marinade:
- 1/2 cup canned light coconut milk
- 1/2 lime, juiced
- 1 tablespoon honey
  - teaspoons soy sauce
- 1 1/2 teaspoons fish sauce
- 1/2 teaspoon red chili flakes
  - teaspoons ginger, grated
- 1 clove of garlic, grated
- 1/2 teaspoon curry powder
- 1/4 teaspoon ground coriander
- For the almond butter sauce:
- 1/4 cup almond butter
- 1/4 cup water
- 2 tablespoons canned, light coconut milk
- 1 tablespoon honey
- 1/2 lime, juiced
- 1 teaspoon fish sauce
- 1 teaspoon fresh grated ginger
- 1/2 teaspoon low sodium soy sauce
- 1/2 teaspoon Sriracha

Directions:

1. Whisk together all of the ingredients for the marinade in a medium mixing bowl.
2. Add chicken to mixing bowl and toss to coat.
3. Cover and refrigerate 2 hours or overnight.
4. Preheat griddle to medium high heat and brush with olive oil.
5. Thread the chicken strips onto metal skewers.
6. Place the chicken skewers on the **Prepa**red griddle and cook 3 minutes, rotate, and cook another 4 minutes or until the chicken is cooked through.
7. Whisk together all of the ingredients for the almond butter sauce in a small saucepan.
8. Bring the sauce to a boil on medium heat, then lower to medium low and simmer for 1 to 2 minutes or until the sauce thickens.
9. Serve chicken satay warm with the almond butter sauce and enjoy.

Nutrition: Calories: 347, Sodium: 743 mg, Dietary Fiber: 1.2g, Fat: 19.7g, Carbs: 8.6g, Protein: 34.3g.

Chicken Fried Rice

Preparation time: time: 10 minutes
Cooking Time: 20 minutes **Servings:** 4
Ingredients:

- 2 boneless, skinless chicken breasts, cut into small pieces
- cups long grain rice, cooked and allowed to air dry
- 1/3 cup soy sauce
- yellow onion, finely chopped
- cloves garlic, finely chopped
  - cups petite peas
- carrots sliced into thin rounds
- 1/2 cup corn kernels
- 1/4 cup vegetable oil
- tablespoons butter

Directions:

1. Preheat griddle to medium-high.
2. Add the vegetable oil to the griddle.
3. When the oil is shimmering, add the onion, carrot, peas, and corn.
4. Cook for several minutes, until lightly charred.
5. Add the chicken and cook until just browned.
6. Add the rice, soy sauce, garlic, and butter.
7. Toss until the rice is tender and the vegetables are just softened.
8. Serve immediately.

Nutrition: Calories: 485, Sodium: 1527 mg, Dietary Fiber: 4.7g, Fat: 20.8g, Carbs: 60.9g Protein: 13.4g

Smoked Chicken in Maple Flavor

Preparation Time: 30 minutes
Cooking Time: 6 Hours **Servings:** 1
Ingredients:

- Boneless chicken breast (5-lbs., 2.3-kgs)
- The Spice
- Chipotle powder – 1 tablespoon
- Salt – 1 ½ teaspoons
- Garlic powder – 2 teaspoons
- Onion powder – 2 teaspoons
- Pepper – 1 teaspoon
- The Glaze
- Maple syrup – ½ cup

Directions:

1. Preheat a griddle to 225°F.
2. Place chipotle, salt, garlic powder, onion powder, and pepper in a bowl then mix to combine.
3. Rub the chicken with the spice mixture then place on the griddle's rack.
4. Smoke the chicken for 4 hours and brush with maple syrup once every hour.
5. When the internal temperature has reached 160°F (71°C), remove the smoked chicken breast from the griddle and transfer to a serving dish.
6. Serve and enjoy right away.

Nutrition:
Carbohydrates: 27 g
Protein: 19 g
Sodium: 65 mg
Cholesterol: 49 mg

Hot and Spicy Smoked Chicken Wings

Preparation Time: 30 minutes
Cooking Time: 3 Hours
Servings: 1
Ingredients:

- Chicken wings (6-lbs., 2.7-kgs)
- The Rub
- Olive oil – 3 tablespoons
- Chili powder – 2 ½ tablespoons
- Smoked paprika – 3 tablespoons
- Cumin – ½ teaspoon
- Garlic powder – 2 teaspoons
- Salt – 1 ¾ teaspoons
- Pepper – 1 tablespoon
- Cayenne – 2 teaspoons
- Preheat the griddle an hour prior to smoking.

Directions:

1. Divide each chicken wing into two then place in a bowl. Set aside.

2. Combine olive oil with chili powder, smoked paprika, cumin, garlic powder, salt, pepper, and cayenne then mix well.
3. Rub the chicken wings with the spice mixture then let them sit for about an hour.
4. Meanwhile, preheat a griddle to 225°F
5. When the griddle is ready, arrange the spiced chicken wings on the griddle's rack.
6. Smoke the chicken wings for 2 hours or until the internal temperature of the chicken wings has reached 160°F (71°C).
7. Take the smoked chicken wings from the griddle and transfer to a serving dish.
8. Serve and enjoy immediately.

Nutrition:
Carbohydrates: 17 g
Protein: 29 g Sodium: 55 mg
Cholesterol: 48 mg

Sweet Smoked Chicken in Black Tea Aroma

Preparation Time: 30 minutes
Cooking Time: 10 Hours
Servings: 1
Ingredients:

- Chicken breast (6-lbs., 2.7-kgs)
- The Rub
- Salt – ¼ cup
- Chili powder – 2 tablespoons
- Chinese five-spice – 2 tablespoons
- Brown sugar – 1 ½ cups
- The Smoke
- Preheat the griddle an hour prior to smoking.
- Black tea – 2 cups

Directions:

1. Place salt, chili powder, Chinese five-spice, and brown sugar in a bowl then stir to combine.
2. Rub the chicken breast with the spice mixture then marinate overnight. Store in the refrigerator to keep it fresh.
3. In the morning, preheat a griddle to 225°F (107°C)
4. Pour black tea into a disposable aluminum pan then place in the griddle.
5. Remove the chicken from the refrigerator then thaw while waiting for the griddle.
6. Once the griddle has reached the desired temperature, place the chicken on the griddle's rack.
7. Smoke the chicken breast for 2 hours then check whether the internal temperature has reached 160°F (71°C).
8. Take the smoked chicken breast out from the griddle and transfer to a serving dish.
9. Serve and enjoy immediately.

Nutrition:
Carbohydrates: 27 g
Protein: 19 g
Sodium: 65 mg
Cholesterol: 49 mg

Sweet Smoked Gingery Lemon Chicken

Preparation Time: 30 minutes
Cooking Time: 6 Hours
Servings: 1
Ingredients:

- Whole chicken 2 (4-lbs., 1.8-kgs)
- Olive oil – ¼ cup

- The Rub
- Salt – ¼ cup
- Pepper – 2 tablespoons
- Garlic powder – ¼ cup
- The Filling
- Fresh Ginger – 8, 1-inch each
- Cinnamon sticks – 8
- Sliced lemon – ½ cup
- Cloves - 6
- The Smoke
- Preheat the griddle an hour prior to smoking.

Directions:

1. Preheat a griddle to 225°F (107°C).
2. Rub the chicken with salt, pepper, and garlic powder then set aside.
3. Fill the chicken cavities with ginger, cinnamon sticks, cloves, and sliced lemon then brush olive oil all over the chicken.
4. When the griddle is ready, place the whole chicken on the griddle's rack.
5. Smoke the whole chicken for 4 hours then check whether the internal temperature has reached 160°F (71°C).
6. When the chicken is done, remove the smoked chicken from the griddle then let it warm for a few minutes.
7. Serve and enjoy right away or cut into slices.

Nutrition:

Carbohydrates: 27 g
Protein: 19 g
Sodium: 65 mg
Cholesterol: 49 mg

Hellfire Chicken Wings

Preparation Time: 30 minutes
Cooking Time: 6 Hours
Servings: 1
Ingredients:

- For Hellfire chicken wings
- 3 lbs. of chicken wings
- 2 tablespoon of vegetable oil
- For the rub
- 1 teaspoon of onion powder
- 1 tablespoon of paprika
- 1 teaspoon of celery seed
- 1 teaspoon of salt
- 1 teaspoon of cayenne pepper
- 1 teaspoon of freshly ground black pepper
- 1 teaspoon of granulated garlic
- 2 teaspoons of brown sugar
- For the sauce
- 2 -4 thinly sliced crosswise jalapeno poppers
- 2 tablespoons of butter; unsalted
- ½ cup of hot sauce
- ½ cup of cilantro leaves

Directions:

1. Take the chicken wings and cut off the tips and discard them
2. Now cut each of the wings into two separate pieces through the joint
3. Move this in a large mixing bowl and pour oil right over it
4. For the rub: Take a small-sized bowl and add sugar, black pepper, paprika, onion powder, salt, celery seed, cayenne, and granulated garlic in it
5. Now sprinkle this mixture over the chicken and toss it gently to coat the wings thoroughly

6. Put the griddle to preheat by putting the temperature to 350 degrees F
7. Griddle the wings for approximately 40 minutes or till the time the skin turns golden brown and you feel that it has cooked through. Make sure to turn it once when you are halfway.
8. For the sauce: Take a small saucepan and melt the butter by keeping the flame on medium-low heat. Now add jalapenos to it and cook for 3 minutes, stir cilantro along with a hot sauce
9. Now, pour this freshly made sauce over the wings and toss it to coat well Serve and enjoy

Nutrition:
Carbohydrates: 27 g
Protein: 19 g Sodium: 65 mg
Cholesterol: 49 mg

Buffalo Chicken Thighs

Preparation Time: 30 minutes
Cooking Time: 6 Hours **Servings:** 1
Ingredients:

- 4-6 skinless, boneless chicken thighs
- Pork and poultry rub
- 4 tablespoons of butter
- 1 cup of sauce; buffalo wing
- Bleu cheese crumbles
- Ranch dressing

Directions:

1. Set the griddle to preheat by keeping the temperature to 450 degrees F and keeping the lid closed
2. Now season the chicken thighs with the poultry rub and then place it on the griddle grate
3. Cook it for 8 to 10 minutes while making sure to flip it once midway
4. Now take a small saucepan and cook the wing sauce along with butter by keeping the flame on medium heat. Make sure to stir in between to avoid lumps
5. Now take the cooked chicken and dip it into the wing sauce and the butter mix. Make sure to coat both the sides in an even manner
6. Take the chicken thighs that have been sauced to the griddle and then cook for further 15 minutes. Do so until the internal temperature reads 175 degrees
7. Sprinkle bleu cheese and drizzle the ranch dressing
8. Serve and enjoy

Nutrition:
Carbohydrates: 29 g Protein: 19 g Sodium: 25 mg Cholesterol: 19 mg

Sweet and Sour Chicken Drumsticks

Preparation Time: 30 minutes
Cooking Time: 2 Hours
Servings: 1
Ingredients:

- 8 pieces of chicken drumsticks
- 2 tablespoon of rice wine vinegar
- 3 tablespoon brown sugar
- 1 cup of ketchup
- ¼ cup of soy sauce
- Minced garlic
- 2 tablespoons of honey

- 1 tablespoon of sweet heat rub
- Minced ginger
- ½ lemon; juice
- 1/2 juiced lime

Directions:

1. Take a mixing bowl and add soy sauce along with brown sugar, ketchup, lemon, rice wine vinegar, sweet heat rub, honey, ginger, and garlic.
2. Now keep half of the mixture for dipping sauce and therefore set it aside
3. Take the leftover half and pour it in a plastic bag that can be re-sealed
4. Now add drumsticks to it and then seal the bag again
5. Refrigerate it for 4 to 12 hours
6. Take out the chicken from the bag and discard the marinade
7. Fire the griddle and set the temperature to 225 degrees F
8. Now smoke the chicken over indirect heat for 2 to 3 hours a make sure to turn it once or twice
9. Add more glaze if needed
10. Remove it from the griddle and let it stand aside for 10 minutes
11. Add more sauce or keep it as a dipping sauce
12. Serve and enjoy

Nutrition:

Carbohydrates: 29 g
Protein: 19 g
Sodium: 25 mg
Cholesterol: 19 mg

Smoked Whole Chicken with Honey Glaze

Preparation Time: 30 minutes
Cooking Time: 3 Hours
Servings: 1
Ingredients:

- 1 4 pounds of chicken with the giblets thoroughly removed and patted dry
- 1 ½ lemon
- 1 tablespoon of honey
- 4 tablespoons of unsalted butter
- 4 tablespoon of chicken seasoning

Directions:

1. Fire up your griddle and set the temperature to 225 degrees F
2. Take a small saucepan and melt the butter along with honey over a low flame
3. Now squeeze ½ lemon in this mixture and then move it from the heat source
4. Take the chicken and smoke by keeping the skin side down. Do so until the chicken turns light brown and the skin starts to release from the grate.
5. Turn the chicken over and apply the honey butter mixture to it
6. Continue to smoke it making sure to taste it every 45 minutes until the thickest core reaches a temperature of 160 degrees F
7. Now remove the chicken from the griddle and let it rest for 5 minutes Serve with the leftover sliced lemon and enjoy

Nutrition:

Carbohydrates: 29 g Protein: 19 g
Sodium: 25 mg
Cholesterol: 19 mg

Beer-Braised Chicken Tacos with Jalapenos Relish

Preparation Time: 30 minutes
Cooking Time: 3 Hours **Servings:** 1
Ingredients:

- For the braised chicken
- 2 lbs. of chicken thighs; boneless, skinless
- ½ small-sized diced onion
- 1 de-seeded and chopped jalapeno
- 1 (12 oz) can of Modelo beer
- 1 tablespoon of olive oil
- 1 EA chipotle Chile in adobo
- 1 clove of minced garlic
- 4 tablespoon of adobo sauce
- 1 teaspoon of chili powder
- 1 teaspoon of garlic powder
- 1 teaspoon of salt
- 1 teaspoon of black pepper
- Juice of 2 limes
- For the tacos
- 8-12 tortillas; small flour
- Hot sauce
- Cilantro
- Cotija cheese
- For the jalapeno relish
- ¼ cup of finely diced red onion
- 3 seeded and diced jalapenos
- 1 clove of minced garlic
- 1/3cup of water
- 1 tablespoon of sugar
- 2/3 cup of white wine vinegar
- 1 tablespoon of salt
- For pickled cabbage
- 2 cups of red cabbage; shredded
- ½ cup of white wine vinegar
- 1 tablespoon of sugar
- 1 tablespoon of salt

Directions:

1. For the jalapeño relish: take all the ingredients and mix then in a non-reactive dish and then keep it aside to be used.
2. For the pickled cabbage: take another non-reactive dish and mix all its respective ingredients and keep it aside
3. Now, transfer both the relish along with the pickled cabbage to your refrigerator and allow it to see for a couple of hours or even overnight if you so desire
4. Take the chicken thighs and season it with an adequate amount of salt and pepper
5. Take a Dutch oven and keep the flame over medium-high heat. Heat 1 tablespoon of olive oil in it
6. Now place the chicken thighs skin side down and brown
7. Remove them from the heat and then set it aside
8. Now, add 1 tablespoon of butter and keep the flame to medium-high
9. When the butter has melted, add jalapeno along with onion and sauté it for 3 to 5 minutes until they turn translucent
10. Add minced garlic to it and sauté it for 30 more seconds
11. Now add adobo sauce along with lime juice, chili powder, and chipotle chile.
12. Add the chicken thighs in the oven and pour in the beer
13. Now set the griddle to pre-heat by keeping the temperature to 350 degrees F

14. Place the oven on the griddle and let it braise for 30 minutes
15. Remove the chicken from the braising liquid and slowly shred it
16. For the tacos: place the shredded part of chicken on the tortillas. Top it with jalapeno relish along with cotija, cabbage, and cilantro and pour the hot sauce
17. Serve and enjoy

Nutrition:

Carbohydrates: 29 g
Protein: 19 g
Sodium: 25 mg
Cholesterol: 19 mg

Smoked Teriyaki Chicken Wings with Sesame Dressing

Preparation Time: 30 minutes
Cooking Time: 4 Hours
Servings: 1
Ingredients:

- Chicken wings
- For the homemade Teriyaki Glaze:
- 2/3 cup mirin
- 2 tablespoons of minced ginger
- 3 tablespoons of cornstarch
- 2 tablespoon of rice vinegar
- 1 cup of soy sauce
- 1/3 cup of brown sugar
- 8 minced garlic cloves
- 2 teaspoon of sesame oil
- 3 tablespoons of water
- For creamy sesame dressing:
- 1 green onion, chopped
- 1/2 cup of mayonnaise
- 1/4 cup rice wine vinegar
- 1 teaspoon of ground garlic
- 1 tablespoon of soy sauce
- 2 tablespoon of sesame oil
- 1/2 teaspoon of ground ginger
- 1 teaspoon siracha
- 2 tablespoon of maple syrup
- Salt and pepper to taste

Directions:

1. Set the griddle to smoke mode by keeping the temperature to 225 degrees F
2. Now trim the wings and make them into drumettes and season with sea salt and black pepper
3. Smoke them for nearly 45 minutes
4. For the teriyaki glaze
5. Mince both garlic and ginger by using a teaspoon of sesame oil
6. Then mix all the ingredients except for cornstarch and water
7. Take a pan and boil cornstarch and water on low heat
8. Simmer for 15 minutes and then when done, mix it with an immersion blender
9. Now add cornstarch and water and stir it until it has mixed well
10. Add this mix to the teriyaki glaze and mix it well until it thickens. Set it aside
11. For the creamy dressing
12. Take a blender and blend all the ingredients thoroughly until you get a smooth mixture
13. Now set the griddle for direct flame griddling and put the temperature to medium
14. Griddle the wings for approx. 10 minutes

15. The internal temperature should reach 165 degrees F when you remove the wings from the griddle
16. Toss them in the glaze when done
17. Sprinkle some sesame seeds along with green onion
18. Serve hot and spicy

Nutrition:
Carbohydrates: 39 g
Protein: 29 g Sodium: 15 mg
Cholesterol: 19 mg

Smoked Turkey Legs

Preparation Time: 30 minutes
Cooking Time: 6 Hours **Servings:** 1
Ingredients:

- 4 turkey legs
- 2 bay leaves
- 1 cup of BBQ rubs
- 1 tablespoon of crushed allspice berries
- 2 teaspoons of liquid smoke
- ½ gal of cold water
- 4 cups of ice
- 1 gal of warm water
- ½ cup of brown sugar
- ½ cup of curing salt
- 1 tablespoon of peppercorns; whole black

Directions:

1. Take a large stockpot and mix a gallon of warm water to curing salt, rub, peppercorns, brown sugar, liquid smoke, allspice and bay leaves
2. Bring this mix to boil by keeping the flame on high heat and let all salt granules dissolve thoroughly
3. Now let it cool to room temperature
4. Now add ice and cold water and let the whole thing chill in the refrigerator
5. Add turkey legs and make sure they are submerged in the brine
6. Let it stay for a day
7. Now drain the turkey legs and get rid of the brine
8. Wash off the brine from the legs with the help of cold water and then pat it dry
9. Set the griddle to preheat by keeping the temperature to 250 degrees F
10. Lay the legs directly on the grate of the griddle
11. Smoke it for 4 to 5 hours till the internal temperature reaches 165 degrees F
12. Serve and enjoy

Nutrition:
Carbohydrates: 39 g
Protein: 29 g
Sodium: 15 mg
Cholesterol: 19 mg

Spiced Lemon Chicken

Preparation Time: 30 minutes
Cooking Time:5 Hours
Servings: 1
Ingredients:

- 1 whole chicken
- 4 cloves of minced garlic
- Zest of 2 fresh lemons
- 1 tablespoon of olive oil
- 1 tablespoon of smoked paprika
- 1 ½ teaspoon of salt
- ½ teaspoon of black pepper
- ½ teaspoon of dried oregano

- 1 tablespoon of ground cumin

Directions:

1. Preheat the griddle by pushing the temperature to 375 degrees F
2. Now take the chicken and spatchcock it by cutting it on both the sides right from the backbone to the tail via the neck
3. Lay it flat and push it down on the breastbone. This would break the ribs
4. Take all the leftover ingredients in a bowl except ½ teaspoon of salt and crush them to make a smooth rub
5. Spread this rub evenly over the chicken making sure that it seeps right under the skin
6. Now place the chicken on the griddle grates and let it cook for an hour until the internal temperature reads 165 degrees F
7. Let it rest for 10 minutes
8. Serve and enjoy

Nutrition:

Carbohydrates: 39 g Protein: 29 g
Sodium: 15 mg Cholesterol: 19 mg

Slow Roasted Shawarma

Preparation Time: 30 minutes
Cooking Time: 4 Hours
Servings: 1
Ingredients:

- 5 ½ lbs. of chicken thighs; boneless, skinless
- 4 ½ lbs. of lamb fat
- Pita bread
- 5 ½ lbs. of top sirloin
- 2 yellow onions; large
- 4 tablespoons of rub
- Desired toppings like pickles, tomatoes, fries, salad and more

Directions:

1. Slice the meat and fat into ½" slices and place then in 3 separate bowls
2. Season each of the bowls with the rub and massage the rub into the meat to make sure it seeps well
3. Now place half of the onion at the base of each half skewer. This will make for a firm base
4. Add 2 layers from each of the bowls at a time
5. Make the track as symmetrical as you can
6. Now, put the other 2 half onions at the top of this
7. Wrap it in a plastic wrap and let it refrigerate overnight
8. Set the griddle to preheat keeping the temperature to 275 degrees F
9. Lay the shawarma on the griddle grate and let it cook for approx. 4 hours. Make sure to turn it at least once
10. Remove from the griddle and shoot the temperature to 445 degrees F
11. Now place a cast iron griddle on the griddle grate and pour it with olive oil
12. When the griddle has turned hot, place the whole shawarma on the cast iron and smoke it for 5 to 10 minutes per side
13. Remove from the griddle and slice off the edges
14. Repeat the same with the leftover shawarma
15. Serve in pita bread and add the chosen toppings Enjoy

Nutrition:

Carbohydrates: 39 g
Protein: 29 g Sodium: 15 mg
Cholesterol: 19 mg

Duck Poppers

Preparation Time: 30 minutes
Cooking Time: 4 Hours
Servings: 1
Ingredients:

- 8 – 10 pieces of bacon, cut event into same-sized pieces measuring 4 inches each
- 3 duck breasts; boneless and with skin removed and sliced into strips measuring ½ inches
- Sriracha sauce
- 6 de-seeded jalapenos, with the top cut off and sliced into strips

Directions:

1. Wrap the bacon around one trip of pepper and one slice of duck
2. Secure it firmly with the help of a toothpick
3. Fire the griddle on low flame and keep this wrap and griddle it for half an hour until the bacon turns crisp
4. Rotate often to ensure even cooking
5. Serve with sriracha sauce

Nutrition:
Carbohydrates: 39 g
Protein: 29 g
Sodium: 15 mg
Cholesterol: 19 mg

BBQ Pulled Turkey Sandwiches

Preparation Time: 30 minutes
Cooking Time: 4 Hours
Servings: 1
Ingredients:

- 6 skin-on turkey thighs
- 6 split and buttered buns
- 1 ½ cups of chicken broth
- 1 cup of BBQ sauce
- Poultry rub

Directions:

1. Season the turkey thighs on both the sides with poultry rub
2. Set the griddle to preheat by pushing the temperature to 180 degrees F
3. Arrange the turkey thighs on the grate of the griddle and smoke it for 30 minutes
4. Now transfer the thighs to an aluminum foil which is disposable and then pour the brine right around the thighs
5. Cover it with a lid
6. Now increase the griddle, temperature to 325 degrees F and roast the thigh till the internal temperature reaches 180 degrees F
7. Remove the foil from the griddle but do not turn off the griddle
8. Let the turkey thighs cool down a little
9. Now pour the dripping and serve
10. Remove the skin and discard it
11. Pull the meat into shreds and return it to the foil
12. Add 1 more cup of BBQ sauce and some more dripping
13. Now cover the foil with lid and re-heat the turkey on the griddle for half an hour Serve and enjoy

Nutrition: Carbohydrates: 39 g Protein: 29 g Sodium: 15 mg Cholesterol: 19 mg

Chicken Breasts Griddle With Feta And Fresh Mint

Preparation Time: 5 Minutes
Cooking Time: 14 Minutes **Servings:** 4
Ingredients:

- 2 whole skinless, boneless chicken breasts
- 1piece (1½ ounces) feta cheese, thinly sliced

- 8 fresh mint leaves, rinsed, blotted dry,
- and cut into thin slivers
- Coarse salt (kosher or sea)
- Freshly ground black pepper
    - tablespoon fresh lemon juice
- 1 tablespoon extra-virgin olive oil
- Lemon wedges, for serving
- YOU'LL ALSO NEED:
- Wooden toothpicks

Directions:

1. If using whole chicken breasts, cut each in half. Trim any sinews or excess fat off the chicken breasts and discard. Remove the tenders from the chicken breasts and set them aside. Place a half breast at the edge of a cutting board.
2. Cut a deep horizontal pocket in the breast, taking care not to pierce the edges. Repeat with the remaining breast halves. Place 2 or 3 slices of feta and a few slivers of mint in the pocket of each chicken breast. Pin the pockets shut with lightly oiled toothpicks. Place the breasts in a baking dish just large enough to hold them. Season the breasts on both sides with salt and pepper and sprinkle any remaining mint over them. Drizzle the lemon juice and olive oil over both sides of the chicken breasts, patting them onto the meat with your fingers.
3. Let the chicken breasts marinate in the refrigerator, covered, for 20 minutes, turning once or twice.
4. Turn control knob to the high position, when the griddle is hot, place the chicken breasts on the griddle and cook for 10 to 14 minutes. Insert an instant-read meat thermometer into the thick part of a breast through one end: The internal temperature should be about 160°F.

Transfer the chicken breasts to a platter or plates and remove and discard the toothpicks. Serve the chicken at once with lemon wedges.

Nutrition: Calories: 321; Fat: 9g; Protein:13g; Fiber:2g

Salt-and-Pepper Boneless Chicken

Preparation Time: 5 Minutes
Cooking Time: 15 Minutes **Servings:** 4
Ingredients:

- 1½ pounds boneless, skinless, chicken breasts
- 2 tablespoons good-quality olive oil
- Salt and pepper

Directions:

1. Pat the chicken dry with paper towels, then pound to an even thickness if necessary. Brush with the oil and sprinkle with salt and pepper on both sides.
2. Turn control knob to the high position, when the griddle is hot, place the chicken breasts and cook for 10 to 14 minutes.
3. Transfer the chicken to a platter, let rest for 5 minutes, slice across the grain if you like, and serve.

Nutrition: Calories: 111; Fat: 19g; Protein: 22g; Fiber:2g

Chicken Satay With Thai Peanut Sauce

Preparation Time:: 5 Minutes
Cooking Time: 8 Minutes
Servings: 4
Ingredients:

- 3 large boneless skinless chicken breasts or 6 boneless skinless thighs
- satay sticks
- THAI PEANUT SAUCE
    - cup creamy peanut butter
- ¾ cup coconut milk
    - Tbsp. soy sauce
    - Tbsp. fresh lime juice
    - Tbsp. brown sugar
- 2 Tbsp. sesame oil
- 2 tsp. crushed red pepper flakes
- 1 Tbsp. fish sauce
- 1 Tbsp. sriracha sauce
- 1 (3-in.) piece of ginger, peeled and diced
- 2 cloves garlic, minced
- ¼ cup chopped cilantro

Directions:

1. Cut chicken into 1.5-inch squares and place onto satay sticks. Lightly season with salt. Combine all ingredients for sauce except the cilantro into a saucepan. Place saucepan over medium heat, mix ingredients together using a whisk, and let simmer for 5 minutes. Once ingredients have melded together, use either a blender or an immersion blender to blend until smooth. Pour into bowl and top with cilantro.
2. Turn control knob to the high position, when the griddle is hot, place the chicken breasts and cook for 8 minutes. Because the chicken is cut into small pieces, it will cook rather quick. But don't risk undercooked chicken. Ensure internal temperature meets minimum requirements of 165° Fahrenheit. Remove from griddle. Serve with sauce and cilantro.

Nutrition: Calories: 391; Fat: 8g; Protein:23g; Fiber:9g

Lemony Chicken Paillards with Asparagus and Feta

Preparation Time: 5 Minutes
Cooking Time: 6 Minutes **Servings:** 4
Ingredients:

- pound thin asparagus
- 1 tablespoon good-quality olive oil, plus more for brushing
- Salt and pepper
- 1½ pounds boneless, skinless chicken breasts, cut and pounded into paillards
- ½ cup crumbled feta cheese
- Lemon wedges for serving

Directions:

1. Cut off the bottoms of the asparagus, then toss the spears with 1 tablespoon oil and sprinkle with salt. Put them on the griddle and cook, turning once, until browned and crisp-tender, 3 to 5 minutes. Transfer to a plate.
2. Brush the paillards with oil and sprinkle with salt and pepper on both sides.

3. Put them on the griddle and cook, turning once, until the chicken is no longer pink in the center, 2 to 3 minutes per side. (Nick with a small knife and peek inside.) Transfer to individual plates, top with the asparagus, sprinkle with feta, and serve with the lemon wedges.

Nutrition: Calories: 145; Fat: 3g; Protein:12g; Fiber:11g

Chicken Salad with Mango and Fresh Herbs

Preparation Time:: 10 Minutes
Cooking Time: 8 Minutes
Servings: 4
Ingredients:

- 1½ pounds boneless, skinless chicken breasts
- ¼ cup olive oil, plus more for brushing
- Salt and pepper
- Grated zest of 1 lime
- 2 tablespoons fresh lime juice
- head Boston lettuce, torn into pieces
- ½ cup whole fresh mint leaves
- 1 ripe mango, peeled, pitted, and cut into 1-inch pieces

Directions:

1. Brush with oil and sprinkle with salt and pepper on both sides.
2. Turn control knob to the high position, when the griddle is hot, place the chicken on the griddle and cook for 8 minutes. Transfer the chicken to a plate and let rest while you put the rest of the salad together.
3. Make the dressing: Put the ¼ cup oil in a small bowl with the lime zest and juice and a pinch of salt.
4. Whisk until the dressing thickens; taste and adjust the seasoning. Put the lettuce and mint in a salad bowl and toss to mix. Cut the chicken across the grain into ½-inch slices and put over the greens. Top with the mango pieces, then drizzle with the dressing and serve (or toss before serving if you like).

Nutrition: Calories: 115; Fat: 8g; Protein: 28g; Fiber: 9g

Chicken and Vegetable Kebabs

Preparation Time: 5 Minutes
Cooking Time: 15 Minutes **Servings:** 4
Ingredients:

- 1½ to 2 pounds boneless, skinless chicken breasts or thighs
- 2 cups cherry or grape tomatoes
- 3 tablespoons good-quality olive oil
- Salt and pepper

Directions:

1. If you're using bamboo or wooden skewers, soak them in water for 30 minutes. Cut the chicken into 1-to 1½-inch pieces, depending on the size of the tomatoes. Toss the chicken and tomatoes with the oil in a medium bowl and sprinkle with some salt and pepper. Alternate the chicken and tomatoes on the skewers.
2. Put the skewers on the griddle and cook until the chicken is no longer pink in the center, 10 to 15 minutes total. Transfer to a platter and serve hot or at room temperature.

Nutrition: Calories: 467; Fat: 19g; Protein:19g; Fiber:12g

Chicken Breast

Preparation Time: 5 Minutes
Cooking Time: 8 Minutes **Servings:** 5
Ingredients:

- boneless, skinless chicken breasts, leveled out to a similar thickness
- olive oil - salt and pepper to taste

Directions:

1. Brush the chicken breasts with the olive oil until they are coated liberally.
2. Add salt and pepper to taste, and let the breasts relax at room temperature for about 10 minutes. Turn control knob to the medium position, when the griddle is hot, place the chicken breasts on the griddle and cook for 5 minutes. Remove the breasts from the griddle and let them relax for several minutes to allow the juices to redistribute.Turn the griddle to medium heat.
3. Return the breasts to the griddle, and cook them until the internal temperature is 160 degrees (they will continue to cook after you remove them from the heat until they are over 165 degrees).
4. Let the breasts relax for 5–10 minutes before cutting and serving.

Nutrition: Calories: 576; Fat: 6g; Protein:3g; Fiber:12g

Double-Stuffed Bone-In Chicken Breasts

Preparation Time: 5 Minutes
Cooking Time: 20 Minutes
Servings: 4
Ingredients:

- lemon
- tablespoons (3/4 stick) butter, softened
- 1–2 tablespoons any chopped fresh herb
- Salt and pepper
- bone-in, skin-on chicken breast halves (1 3/4 to 2 pounds total)

Directions:

1. Finely grate the zest of the lemon, then cut the lemon into thin slices. Mash the butter, zest, and herb together in a small bowl with some salt and pepper. Taste and adjust the seasoning.
2. Working with the skin side up, cut a slit into the thickest part of the breast with the tip of a small sharp knife. Keeping the opening slit just large enough for your finger (this will help the filling stay in the pocket), work the knife back and forth to create as big a pocket as possible inside the breast; be careful not to cut through to the other side.
3. Divide the compound butter evenly between the breasts, pushing it into the slit and massaging it to fill the pocket.
4. Still using your fingers, separate the skin from the meat on one edge so you can work 2 lemon slices underneath to cover as much of the breast as possible. Sprinkle the breasts with salt and pepper and refrigerate. (You can make these to this point up to several hours ahead.)
5. Bring the griddle to high heat, when the griddle is hot, put the chicken skin side up and cook until firm when pressed and browned on top, 15 to 20 minutes.

6. Turn to crisp the skin; cook for another 5 minutes. If the chicken is still pink at the bone at the thickest point, turn skin side up again to finish cooking. (Nick with a small knife and peek inside.) Transfer the chicken to a platter and let rest for 5 minutes.

Nutrition: Calories: 412; Fat: 12g; Protein: 16g; Fiber:14g

Bone-In Chicken Thighs with Caramelized Fish Sauce

Preparation Time: 10 Minutes
Cooking Time: 55 Minutes
Servings: 4
Ingredients:

- 3 pounds bone-in, skin-on chicken thighs
- Salt and pepper
- ¼ cup fish sauce
- 2 tablespoons turbinado sugar
- tablespoon minced garlic
- dried red chiles

Directions:

1. Trim excess fat and skin from the chicken without exposing the meat. Sprinkle with salt and pepper on both sides.
2. Turn control knob to the high position, when the griddle is hot, put the thighs on the griddle, skin side up, and cook for about 20 minutes, then turn the pieces and rotate them 180 degrees for even browning. Cook until the meat is no longer pink at the bone, 40 to 55 minutes total, depending on the size of the pieces.
3. While the thighs cook, put the fish sauce, sugar, garlic, and chiles in a small saucepan over low heat. Stir until the sugar dissolves completely. Let cool a few minutes before pouring into a large heatproof bowl; remove the chiles. When the thighs are done, transfer them to the bowl and toss to coat evenly with the glaze, using tongs. Turn the heat to medium. Remove the thighs from the glaze, let any excess glaze drip off, then arrange the thighs skin side up on the griddle. Cook, turning once, until crisp and brown, 1 to 3 minutes per side; move the thighs away from the flames if the glaze starts to burn. Transfer to a platter and serve.

Nutrition: Calories: 400; Fat: 10g; Protein:34g; Fiber:17 g

Jerk Chicken

Preparation Time: 5 Minutes
Cooking Time: 40 Minutes
Servings: 4
Ingredients:

- scallions, cut into chunks
- or 2 habanero or Scotch bonnet chiles, or to taste, stemmed (remove the seeds and pith if you want it a bit milder)
- cloves garlic, peeled
- small shallot, peeled
- 1 1-inch piece fresh ginger, peeled and sliced
- tablespoons good-quality vegetable oil
- tablespoons fresh lime juice

- 1 tablespoon brown sugar
- 1 tablespoon fresh thyme leaves
- 1 teaspoon ground allspice
- 1 teaspoon salt
- 1 teaspoon black pepper
- ½ teaspoon freshly grated nutmeg
- pounds bone-in, skin-on chicken thighs, drumsticks, or a mix

Directions:

1. Put the scallions, chiles, garlic, shallot, ginger, oil, lime juice, sugar, thyme, allspice, salt, pepper, and nutmeg in a blender or food processor and purée to a rough paste. Trim excess skin and fat from the chicken without exposing the meat. Pat the chicken dry with paper towels, then rub the jerk paste all over the pieces. Let the chicken sit at room temperature.
2. Turn control knob to the medium position, when the griddle is hot, put the chicken on the griddle, and cook until the meat is no longer pink at the bone, 40 minutes total, depending on the size of the pieces. (Nick with a small knife and peek inside.)
3. Transfer to a platter and serve.

Nutrition: Calories: 500; Fat: 6g; Protein:2g; Fiber: 3

Penne With Griddle Chicken, Portobellos, And Walnuts

Preparation Time: 5 Minutes
Cooking Time: 11 Minutes
Servings: 5
Ingredients:

- portobello mushrooms, stemmed
- cup olive oil
- ½ teaspoon salt
- ½ teaspoon freshly ground black pepper
- pound dried penne
- pounds boneless, skinless chicken
- breasts, pounded to ½-inch thickness
    - cup walnut pieces
- ½ cup grated Parmesan cheese, preferably freshly grated
- ¼ cup chopped fresh basil or parsley leaves
- garlic cloves, minced

Directions:

1. Bring a medium pot of salted water to a boil, then reduce to a simmer. Brush the portobellos lightly with a couple of tablespoons of the olive oil and season with ¼ teaspoon of the salt and ¼ teaspoon of the pepper.
2. Turn control knob to the high position, when the griddle is hot, place the mushrooms, gill-side down, on the griddle, and griddle for 8 minutes, until the mushrooms are tender.
3. Transfer to a cutting board; keep the griddle on high. Bring the water up to a full boil, add the penne, and cook.
3. Sprinkle the chicken with the remaining ¼ teaspoon salt and ¼ teaspoon pepper. Griddle for about 3 minutes. Transfer to the cutting board with the mushrooms.
4. Cut the cooked breasts in half lengthwise and then cut them into ½-inch strips. Slice the portobello caps into pieces approximately the same size.

5. Drain the penne and transfer to a serving bowl. Add the remaining olive oil (about ¼ cup), the mushrooms, chicken, walnuts, Parmesan, basil, and garlic. Toss gently to combine and serve immediately.

Nutrition: Calories: 510; Fat: 11g; Protein:41g

Tandoori Chicken

Preparation Time: 5 Minutes
Cooking Time: 45 Minutes **Servings:** 4
Ingredients:

- cup yogurt
- ¼ cup fresh lemon juice
    - o tablespoon minced garlic
- 1 tablespoon minced fresh ginger
- 1 tablespoon ground cumin
- 1 tablespoon ground coriander
- teaspoons smoked paprika (pimentón)
- teaspoons salt
- 1 whole chicken (3–4 pounds), cut into pieces, or 3 pounds bone-in, skin-on - chicken parts
- 1 medium onion, cut into wedges
- Good-quality olive oil for brushing
- 1 lemon, halved

Directions:

1. Whisk the yogurt, lemon juice, garlic, ginger, cumin, coriander, paprika, and salt together in a large bowl to combine. Trim excess fat and skin from the chicken without exposing the meat. Add the chicken pieces to the marinade, turning to coat them completely. Cover with plastic wrap and refrigerate for 2 to 4 hours.
2. If you're using bamboo or wooden skewers, soak them in water for 30 minutes. Thread the onion wedges onto 2 skewers, then brush with oil. Remove the chicken from the marinade, letting any excess drip off.
3. Turn control knob to the high position, when the griddle is hot, put the chicken on the griddle, skin side up, and cook, turning the pieces and rotating them 180 degrees for even browning after 15 to 20 minutes (breasts) and 20 to 25 minutes (dark meat). Cook the chicken until the meat is no longer pink at the bone; depending on the size of the pieces, this can take 25 to 40 minutes total for the breasts and 40 to 50 minutes for the dark meat. (Nick with a small knife and peek inside.)
4. Put the lemon halves cut side down on the griddle grate. As the chicken and onions char, transfer them to a platter, squeeze the lemon halves over all, and serve.

Nutrition: Calories: 278; Fat: 11g; Protein:13g; Fiber:6g

Chicken "steaks"

Preparation Time: 5 Minutes
Cooking Time: 8 Minutes
Servings: 4
Ingredients:

- 2 whole boneless chicken breasts (each 12 to 16 ounces), or 4 half chicken breasts (each half 6 to 8 ounces)

- Coarse salt (kosher or sea) and freshly ground black pepper
- ¼ cup white wine vinegar or red wine vinegar
- ½ sweet onion, finely diced (about ½ cup)
- 3 cloves garlic, coarsely chopped
- teaspoon dried oregano
- ½ teaspoon ground cumin
- ¾ cup extra-virgin olive oil
- ⅓ cup chopped fresh flat-leaf parsley

Directions:

1. If using whole breasts, cut each breast in half. Remove the tenders from the chicken breasts, place a breast half between 2 pieces of plastic wrap and gently pound it to a thickness of ½ inch using a meat pounder, the side of a heavy cleaver, a rolling pin, or the bottom of a heavy saucepan. Repeat with the remaining breast halves. Place the chicken breasts in a large baking dish and season them on both sides with salt and pepper.
2. Place the vinegar, onion, garlic, oregano, and cumin in a nonreactive mixing bowl. Add ½ teaspoon of salt and ¼ teaspoon of pepper and whisk until the salt dissolves. Whisk in the olive oil. Correct the seasoning, adding salt and pepper to taste. The mixture should be highly seasoned. Pour half of this mixture into another nonreactive serving bowl and set aside for use as a sauce. Whisk 2 tablespoons of the parsley into the mixture in the mixing bowl then pour it over the chicken, turning the breasts to coat on both sides. Let the chicken breasts marinate in the refrigerator, covered, for at least 2 hours or as long as overnight, turning them a few times so that they marinate evenly.
3. Drain the chicken breasts well and discard the marinade.
4. Turn control knob to the high position, when the griddle is hot, place the chicken breasts and cook for 5 minutes. Use the poke test to check for doneness; the chicken should feel firm when pressed. Or insert an instant-read meat thermometer into the breast through one end: The internal temperature should be about 160°F. You may need to cook the chicken breasts in more than one batch; cover the Griddle chicken with aluminum foil to keep warm until ready to serve.

Whisk the remaining parsley into the reserved bowl of vinegar mixture. Spoon half of it over the chicken breasts and serve the remainder on the side.

Nutrition: Calories: 211; Fat: 5g; Protein:32g; Fiber:23g

Salt-and-Pepper Duck Breasts

Preparation Time:: 5 Minutes
Cooking Time: 15 Minutes **Servings:** 6
Ingredients:

- skin-on duck breasts (about 8 ounces each)
- Salt and pepper

Directions:

1. Trim the excess fat and skin from the duck without exposing the meat; reserve the scraps. With a sharp knife, cut slashes into the skin without slicing all the way down to the flesh; this will help render the fat as the duck cooks. Pat the duck dry with paper towels, then sprinkle both sides with salt and pepper.
2. Put the breasts in a cold large, heavy griddle, skin side down, along with the trimmings, and turn the heat to low. Let the breasts cook, rendering their fat, until the skin is golden brown and dry, 13 to 15 minutes; the flesh side of the breast should still be cool or room temperature to the touch. Remove the breasts from the griddle. (At this point, you can let the breasts cool, cover them, and refrigerate for up to a day.)
3. Bring the griddle to high heat. When the griddle is hot, put the duck skin side up and cook until the breasts are one stage less done than you eventually want them, 3 to 10 minutes; nick the thickest places with a small knife and peek inside.
4. Turn the breasts over to let the skin crisp, just 1 to 2 minutes. Transfer the duck breasts to a platter, let rest for 5 minutes, slice, and serve with any accumulated juices.

Nutrition: Calories: 127; Fat: 7g; Protein: 23g; Fiber: 5g

Caesar Marinated Griddle Chicken

Preparation Time: 10 Minutes
Cooking Time: 24 Minutes **Servings:** 3
Ingredients:

- ¼ cup crouton
- teaspoon lemon zest. Form into ovals, skewer and griddle.
- 1/2 cup Parmesan
- 1/4 cup breadcrumbs
- 1-pound ground chicken
- tablespoons Caesar dressing and more for drizzling
- 2-4 romaine leaves

Directions:

1. In a shallow dish, mix well chicken, 2 tablespoons Caesar dressing, parmesan, and breadcrumbs. Mix well with hands. Form into 1-inch oval patties.
2. Thread chicken pieces in skewers. Bring the griddle to high heat. When the griddle is hot, put the skewers and cook for 12 minutes. Halfway through cooking time, turnover skewers. Serve and enjoy on a bed of lettuce and sprinkle with croutons and extra dressing.

Nutrition: Calories: 339; Fat: 18.9g; Protein:32.6g; Sugar:1g

Chicken Fajitas

Preparation Time: 10 Minutes
Cooking Time: 15 Minutes **Servings:** 4
Ingredients:

- boneless, skinless chicken breasts, sliced
- small red onion, sliced
- red bell peppers, sliced
- ½ cup spicy ranch salad dressing, divided

- ½ teaspoon dried oregano
- 8 corn tortillas
- cups torn butter lettuce
- avocados, peeled and chopped

Directions:

1. Place the chicken, onion, and pepper in a bowl. Drizzle with 1 tablespoon of the salad dressing and add the oregano. Toss to combine.
2. Bring the griddle to high heat. When the griddle is hot, put the chicken and cook for 10 to 14 minutes or until the chicken is 165°F on a food thermometer. Transfer the chicken and vegetables to a bowl and toss with the remaining salad dressing. Serve the chicken mixture with the tortillas, lettuce, and avocados and let everyone make their own creations.

Nutrition: Calories: 783; Fat: 38g; Protein:72; Fiber:12g

Five-Spice Squab

Preparation Time: 10 Minutes
Cooking Time: 20 Minutes **Servings:** 4
Ingredients:

- 3 tablespoons hoisin sauce
- 2 tablespoons rice wine or dry sherry
- tablespoon soy sauce
- tablespoon rice vinegar
- teaspoons sugar
- teaspoon five-spice powder
- squabs (10–18 ounces each, semiboneless or spatchcocked)

Directions:

1. Whisk the hoisin sauce, rice wine, soy sauce, vinegar, sugar, and five-spice powder together in a small bowl. Brush the mixture evenly over both sides of the squabs. (You can marinate the squabs for several hours in the refrigerator before griddleing.)
2. Bring the griddle to high heat. When the griddle is hot, let excess marinade drip off the squabs and put them on the griddle, skin side up and cook, turning once, until they are crisp on the outside and rosy pink inside, 5 to 10 minutes per side depending on their size. Carve into pieces if you like, transfer to a platter, and serve.

Nutrition: Calories: 456; Fat: 5g; Protein:54g; Fiber:8g

Balsamic-Rosemary Chicken Breasts

Preparation Time:: 5 Minutes
Cooking Time: 6 Minutes **Servings:** 4
Ingredients:

- ½ cup balsamic vinegar
- 2 tablespoons olive oil
- 2 rosemary sprigs, coarsely chopped
- 2 pounds boneless, skinless chicken breasts, pounded to ½-inch thickness

Directions:

1. Combine the balsamic vinegar, olive oil, and rosemary in a shallow baking dish.
2. Add the chicken breasts and turn to coat. Cover with plastic wrap and refrigerate for at least 30 minutes or overnight.
3. Bring the griddle to high heat. When the griddle is hot, place the s chicken breasts on the Griddle and cook for 6 minutes until they have taken on griddle marks and are cooked through.

Nutrition: Calories: 299; Fat: G; Protein:52g;

Italian-Style Sweet Pork Sausage with Fennel Seeds

Preparation Time: 5 Minutes
Cooking Time: 10 Minutes
Servings: 8
Ingredients:

- 2½ pounds fatty boneless pork shoulder, cut into 1-inch cubes
- 3 cloves garlic, minced
    - tablespoon fennel seeds
- 1 teaspoon salt
- 1 teaspoon black pepper
- Sausage casings (optional)

Directions:

1. Working in batches if necessary, put the meat in a food processor and pulse until coarsely ground—finer than chopped, but not much. Take your time and be careful not to pulverize the meat. As you finish each batch, transfer it to a bowl. Add the garlic, fennel seeds, salt, and pepper and work the mixture gently with your hands to incorporate them into the meat; add a little water if the mixture seems dry and crumbly. Cook up a spoonful in a small griddle to taste it; adjust the seasoning. Shape into 8 or more patties, or stuff into casings if you prefer. (You can freeze some or all of them, wrapped well, for up to several months.)
2. Bring the griddle to high heat. When the griddle is hot, put the sausages on the griddle, and cook until they release from the grates easily, 5 to 10 minutes, then turn and cook the other side until the sausages are no longer pink in the center; the internal temperature should be 160°F (check with an instant-read thermometer, or nick with a small knife and peek inside). Transfer to a platter and serve.

Nutrition: Calories: 221; Fat: 9g; Protein:13g; Fiber:2g

Griddle Chicken Fajitas

Preparation Time: 5 Minutes
Cooking Time: 6 Minutes
Servings: 6
Ingredients:

- CHICKEN
- ¼ cup olive oil, divided
- juice from 1 lime
- 3 large boneless skinless chicken breasts, butterflied
    - each red, yellow, and orange peppers
- 1 medium Vidalia onion
- a pinch of salt
- 12 small soft flour tortillas
- SEASONING
- 1½ Tbsp. chili powder
    - tsp. ground cumin
    - tsp. kosher salt
- 2 tsp. smoked paprika
- 1 tsp. ground cinnamon
- 1 tsp. onion powder
- 1 tsp. garlic powder
- 1 tsp. cayenne pepper
- ½ tsp. white sugar
- zest from 1 lime

Directions:

1. Combine all the seasoning ingredients into small bowl and whisk together.

2. Whisk 2 tablespoons olive oil and the lime juice together in medium mixing bowl. Add butterflied chicken breasts. Toss to coat evenly.
3. Evenly sprinkle seasoning on both sides of chicken, ensuring uniform coverage.
4. Thinly slice peppers and onion.
5. In a large mixing bowl, toss sliced vegetables with remaining 2 tablespoons of olive oil and a pinch of salt.
6. Bring the griddle to high heat. When the griddle is hot, place the vegetables and cook for 4 minutes.
7. As veggies near completion, place seasoned chicken on the griddle, and cook for 4 minutes.
8. Remove both meat and vegetables from the griddle, slice chicken into thin strips, and keep warm.
9. Toss flour tortillas on griddle for 15 to 30 seconds per side, just to warm them up and slightly toast them. Don't cook them to the point that they are no longer flexible.
10. Serve hot with toppings of your choice: cheese, fresh limes, sour cream, cilantro, and so on.

Nutrition: Calories: 457; Fat: 12g; Protein:16g; Fiber:2g

Honey-Mustard Chicken Tenders

Preparation Time: 5 Minutes
Cooking Time: 3 Minutes
Servings: 4
Ingredients:

- ½ cup Dijon mustard
- 2 tablespoons honey
- 2 tablespoons olive oil
- teaspoon freshly ground black pepper
- pounds chicken tenders
- ½ cup walnuts

Directions:

1. Whisk together the mustard, honey, olive oil, and pepper in a medium bowl. Add the chicken and toss to coat.
2. Finely grind the walnuts by pulsing them in a food processor or putting them in a heavy-duty plastic bag and pounding them with a rolling pin or heavy griddle.
3. Toss the chicken tenders in the ground walnuts to coat them lightly.
4. Bring the griddle to high heat. When the griddle is hot, griddle the chicken tenders for about 3 minutes, until they have taken on griddle marks and are cooked through. Serve hot, at room temperature, or refrigerate and serve cold.

Nutrition: Calories: 444; Fat: 20g; Protein:5g

Chicken Roast with Pineapple Salsa

Preparation Time: 10 Minutes
Cooking Time: 45 Minutes
Servings: 2
Ingredients:

- ¼ cup extra virgin olive oil
- ¼ cup freshly chopped cilantro
- avocado, diced
- 1-pound boneless chicken breasts
- cups canned pineapples
- teaspoons honey
- Juice from 1 lime
- Salt and pepper to taste

Directions:

1. Season the chicken breasts with lime juice, olive oil, honey, salt, and pepper. Bring the griddle to high heat. When the griddle is hot, place on the griddle and cook for 45 minutes. Flip the chicken every 10 minutes to griddle all sides evenly.
2. Once the chicken is cooked, serve with pineapples, cilantro, and avocado.

Nutrition: Calories: 744; Fat: 32.8g; Protein:4.7g; Sugar:5g

Tarragon Chicken Tenders

Preparation Time: 5 Minutes
Cooking Time: 5 Minutes **Servings:** 4
Ingredients:
FOR THE CHICKEN:

- 1½ pounds chicken tenders (12 to 16
- tenders)
- Coarse salt (kosher or sea) and freshly
- ground black pepper
- 3 tablespoons chopped fresh tarragon
- leaves, plus 4 whole sprigs for garnish
- teaspoon finely grated lemon zest
- tablespoons fresh lemon juice
- tablespoons extra-virgin olive oil

FOR THE SAUCE (OPTIONAL):

- 2 tablespoons fresh lemon juice
- 2 tablespoons salted butter
- ½ cup heavy (whipping) cream

Directions:

1. Make the chicken: Place the chicken tenders in a nonreactive baking dish just large enough to hold them in a single layer.
2. Season the tenders generously on both sides with salt and pepper. Sprinkle the chopped tarragon and lemon zest all over the tenders, patting them onto the chicken with your fingertips. Drizzle the lemon juice and the olive oil over the tenders and pat them onto the chicken. Let the tenders marinate in the refrigerator, covered, for 10 minutes. Drain the chicken tenders well by lifting one end with tongs and letting the marinade drip off. Discard the marinade.
3. Bring the griddle to high heat. When the griddle is hot, place the chicken tenders on the griddle. The chicken tenders will be done after cooking 3 to 5 minutes. Use the poke test to check for doneness; the chicken should feel firm when pressed.
4. Transfer the chicken tenders to a platter or plates. If making the sauce, place the lemon juice and the butter in a small saucepan or in the griddle pan over medium heat. Add the cream and bring to a boil (use a wooden spoon to scrape up the brown bits from between the ridges of the griddle pan). Let the sauce boil until thickened, 3 to 5 minutes. Pour the lemon cream sauce over the chicken tenders and serve at once.

Nutrition: Calories: 245; Fat: 8g; Protein:33g; Fiber: 12g

Griddle Chicken With Salsa Criolla

Preparation Time: 5 Minutes
Cooking Time: 6 Minutes **Servings:** 5
Ingredients:

- 8 chicken thighs, with skin and bones (about 2 pounds total)

- tablespoon extra-virgin olive oil
- Coarse salt (kosher or sea) and freshly ground or cracked black peppercorns
- About 1 tablespoon dried oregano
- SALSA CRIOLLA
    - luscious ripe red tomato, seeded (but not peeled) and cut into ¼-inch dice
- 1 small or ½ large red bell pepper, seeded and cut into ¼-inch dice
- 1 small or ½ medium-size onion, cut into ¼-inch dice
- 1 tablespoon finely chopped fresh flat-leaf parsley
- ¼ cup extra-virgin olive oil
- tablespoons red wine vinegar
- Coarse salt (kosher or sea) and freshly ground black pepper

Directions:

1. Rinse the thighs under cold running water, then drain and blot dry with paper towels. Place a thigh on a work surface skin side down. Using a sharp paring knife, cut along the length of the thigh bone. Cut the meat away from one end of the bone, then pull or scrape the meat from the bone. Cut the meat away from the other end of the bone. Repeat with the remaining thighs. Discard the bones or set them aside for making stock or another use.
2. Lightly brush the chicken thighs all over with olive oil, then season them generously with salt, pepper, and oregano.
3. Bring the griddle to high heat. When the griddle is hot, place the chicken thighs on the griddle, and cook for 6 minutes.
4. Use the poke test to check for doneness; the chicken should feel firm when pressed.
5. Place the tomato, bell pepper, onion, parsley, olive oil, and vinegar in an attractive nonreactive serving bowl and toss to mix. Season with salt and pepper to taste. The sauce can be made several hours ahead.
6. Transfer the chicken thighs to a platter or plates and serve at once with the Salsa Criolla on top or on the side.

Nutrition: Calories: 301; Fat: 7g; Protein:43g; Fiber:12g

Chicken BBQ with Sweet And Sour Sauce

Preparation Time: 5 Minutes
Cooking Time: 40 Minutes
Servings: 6
Ingredients:

- ¼ cup minced garlic
- ¼ cup tomato paste
- ¾ cup minced onion
- ¾ cup sugar
- cup soy sauce
    - cup water
- 1 cup white vinegar
- chicken drumsticks
- Salt and pepper to taste

Directions:

1. Place all Ingredients in a Ziploc bag
2. Allow to marinate for at least 2 hours in the fridge.
3. Bring the griddle to high heat. When the griddle is hot, griddle the chicken for 40 minutes.
4. Flip the chicken every 10 minutes for even griddling.

5. Meanwhile, pour the marinade in a saucepan and heat over medium flame until the sauce thickens.
6. Before serving the chicken, brush with the glaze.

Nutrition: Calories: 4607; Fat: 19.7g; Protein:27.8g; Sugar:3g

Sweet Thai Cilantro Chili Chicken Quarters

Preparation Time: 5 Minutes
Cooking Time: 5 Minutes
Servings: 5
Ingredients:

- chicken leg quarters, lightly coated with olive oil
    - cup and 1 tsp. water
- ¾ cup rice vinegar
- ½ cup white sugar
    - Tbsp. freshly chopped cilantro
    - Tbsp. freshly minced ginger root
- 2 tsp. freshly minced garlic
- 2 Tbsp. crushed red pepper flakes
- 2 Tbsp. ketchup
- 2 Tbsp. cornstarch
- 2 Tbsp. fresh basil chiffonade ("chiffonade" is fancy for "thinly sliced")

Directions:

1. In a medium-sized saucepan, bring 1 cup water and the vinegar to a boil over high heat.
2. Stir in sugar, cilantro, ginger, garlic, red pepper flakes, and ketchup; simmer for 5 minutes.
3. In small mixing bowl, mix together 1 teaspoon warm water and 2 tablespoons cornstarch.
4. Use a fork for mixing this, and what you'll end up with will resemble white school glue.
5. Slowly whisk the cornstarch mixture into the simmering sauce, and continue mixing until sauce thickens. Set aside.
6. Bring the griddle to high heat. When the griddle is hot, place the chicken quarters skin side down and cook for 8 minutes.
7. At 155°F internal temperature, glaze chicken with sauce and allow to finish cooking to an internal temperature of 165°F. Plate, garnish with basil, and serve.

Nutrition: Calories: 321; Fat: 14g; Protein:12g; Fiber:8g

Tangy Chicken Sandwiches

Preparation time: 30 minutes
Cooking Time: 20 Minutes
Servings: 4
Ingredients:

- 2 lbs. chicken breast, sliced into 4 cutlets
- potato buns, toasted
- For the marinade:
- 1/2 cup pickle juice
    - tablespoon dijon mustard
- 1 teaspoon paprika
- 1/2 teaspoon black pepper
- 1/2 teaspoon salt

Directions:

1. Mix marinade ingredients together in a mixing bowl.
2. Place chicken in marinade and marinate for 30 minutes in the refrigerator.

3. Preheat griddle to medium-high. Wipe off extra marinade and sear chicken for 7 minutes per side, or until a meat thermometer reaches 165°F.
4. Allow chicken to rest for 5 minutes after griddleing and serve on toasted buns.

Nutrition: Calories:265, Sodium:685 mg, Dietary Fiber: 0.6 g, Fat: 6g, Carbs:1.1g, Protein: 48.4g.

Savory Chicken Burgers

If you're looking for a great alternative to traditional beef burgers, these chicken burgers are lighter and packed with flavor.

Servings: 3

Preparation time: time: 10 minutes

COOKing TIME: 20 minutcs

Ingredients:

1 lb. ground chicken
1/2 red onion, finely chopped
1 teaspoon garlic powder
1/2 teaspoon onion powder
1/4 teaspoon black pepper
1/2 teaspoon salt
3 tablespoons vegetable oil
3 potato buns, toasted

Directions:

1. In a large bowl, combine the ground chicken, onion, garlic powder, onion powder, pepper, and salt. Mix well to combine. Form the chicken mixture into three equal patties. Don't work the mixture too much or the burgers will be too dense.
2. Heat your griddle to medium-high heat. Add the vegetable oil.
3. When the oil is shimmering, add the chicken patties and cook 5 minutes per side, or until the patties reach 165°F.
4. Remove the patties from the griddle and allow to rest for five minutes before serving on the toasted buns.

Nutrition: Calories: 420, Sodium: 519 mg, Dietary Fiber: 0.6 g, Fat: 24.8g, Carbs: 2.8g, Protein: 44.2g.

Sun-Dried Tomato and Chicken Flatbreads

Preparation time: time: 5 minutes

Cooking Time: 7 minutes

Servings: 4

Ingredients:

- flat breads or thin pita bread
- For the topping:
  - 1/2 cups of sliced Griddle chicken, pre-cooked or leftovers
- 1/2 cup sun-dried tomatoes, coarsely chopped
- leaves fresh basil, coarsely chopped
  - cups mozzarella cheese, shredded
- 1 teaspoon salt
- 1 teaspoon ground black pepper
- 1 teaspoon red pepper flakes
- Olive or chili oil, for serving

Directions:

1. Preheat the griddle to low heat.
2. Mix all the topping ingredients together in a large mixing bowl with a rubber spatula.
3. Lay flatbreads on griddle, and top with an even amount of topping mixture; spreading to the edges of each.

4. Tent the flatbreads with foil for 5 minutes each, or until cheese is just melted.
5. Place flatbreads on a flat surface or cutting board, and cut each with a pizza cutter or kitchen scissors.
6. Drizzle with olive or chili oil to serve!

Nutrition: Calories: 276, Sodium: 1061 mg, Dietary Fiber: 1.9g Fat: 5.7g, Carbs: 35.7g Protein: 19.8g

Turkey Pesto Panini

Preparation time: time: 5 minutes
Cooking Time: 6 minutes
Servings: 2
Ingredients:

- o tablespoon olive oil
- slices French bread
- 1/2 cup pesto sauce
- slices mozzarella cheese
- o cups chopped leftover turkey
- 1 Roma tomato, thinly sliced
- 1 avocado, halved, seeded, peeled and sliced

Directions:

1. Preheat griddle to medium-high heat.
2. Brush each slice of bread with olive oil on one side.
3. Place 2 slices olive oil side down on the griddle.
4. Spread 2 tablespoons pesto over 1 side of French bread.
5. Top with one slice mozzarella, turkey, tomatoes, avocado, a second slice of mozzarella, and top with second half of bread to make a sandwich; repeat with remaining slices of bread.
6. Cook until the bread is golden and the cheese is melted, about 2-3 minutes per side.
7. Serve warm with your favorite salad or soup.

Nutrition: Calories: 1129, Sodium: 1243 mg, Dietary Fiber: 10g, Fat: 70.9g, Carbs: 53.2g Protein: 73g

CHAPTER 8
Turkey Recipes

Herb Roasted Turkey

Preparation Time: 15 Minutes
Cooking Time: 3 Hours 30 Minutes
Servings: 12
Ingredients:

- 14 pounds turkey, cleaned
- 2 tablespoons chopped mixed herbs
- Pork and poultry rub as needed
- ¼ teaspoon ground black pepper
- 3 tablespoons butter, unsalted, melted
- 8 tablespoons butter, unsalted, softened
- 2 cups chicken broth

Directions:

1. Clean the turkey by removing the giblets, wash it inside out, pat dry with paper towels, then place it on a roasting pan and tuck the turkey wings by tiring with butcher's string.
2. Switch on the griddle, set the temperature to 325 degrees F and let it preheat for a minimum of 15 minutes.
3. Meanwhile, **Prepa**red herb butter and for this, take a small bowl, place the softened butter in it, add black pepper and mixed herbs and beat until fluffy.
4. Place some of the **Prepa**red herb butter underneath the skin of turkey by using a handle of a wooden spoon, and massage the skin to distribute butter evenly.
5. Then rub the exterior of the turkey with melted butter, season with pork and poultry rub, and pour the broth in the roasting pan. When the griddle has preheated, open the lid, place roasting pan containing turkey on the griddle grate, shut the griddle and smoke for 3 hours and 30 minutes until the internal temperature reaches 165 degrees F and the top has turned golden brown.
6. When done, transfer turkey to a cutting board, let it rest for 30 minutes, then carve it into slices and serve.

Nutrition: Calories: 154.6 Fat: 3.1 g Carbs: 8.4 g Protein: 28.8 g

Turkey Legs

Preparation Time: 10 Minutes
Cooking Time: 5 Hours Servings: 4
Ingredients:

- 4 turkey legs - For the Brine:
- ½ cup curing salt
- 1 tablespoon whole black peppercorns - 1 cup BBQ rub
- ½ cup brown sugar
- 2 bay leaves
- 2 teaspoons liquid smoke
- 16 cups of warm water
- 4 cups ice -8 cups of cold water

Directions:

1. **Prepa**re the brine and for this, take a large stockpot, place it over high heat, pour warm water in it, add peppercorn, bay leaves, and liquid smoke

2. Stir in salt, sugar, and BBQ rub and bring it to a boil.
3. Remove pot from heat, bring it to room temperature, then pour in cold water, add ice cubes and let the brine chill in the refrigerator. Then add turkey legs in it, submerge them completely, and let soak for 24 hours in the refrigerator.
4. After 24 hours, remove turkey legs from the brine, rinse well and pat dry with paper towels.
5. When ready to cook, switch on the griddle, set the temperature to 250 degrees F and let it preheat for a minimum of 15 minutes.
6. When the griddle has preheated, open the lid, place turkey legs on the griddle grate, shut the griddle, and smoke for 5 hours until nicely browned and the internal temperature reaches 165 degrees F. Serve immediately.

Nutrition: Calories: 416 Fat: 13.3 g Carbs: 0 g Protein: 69.8 g

Turkey Breast

Preparation Time: 12 Hours
Cooking Time: 8 Hours **Servings:** 6
Ingredients:

For the Brine:

- 2 pounds turkey breast, deboned
- 2 tablespoons ground black pepper
- ¼ cup salt
- 1 cup brown sugar
- 4 cups cold water

For the BBQ Rub:

- 2 tablespoons dried onions
- 2 tablespoons garlic powder
- ¼ cup paprika
- 2 tablespoons ground black pepper - 1 tablespoon salt
- 2 tablespoons brown sugar
- 2 tablespoons red chili powder
- 1 tablespoon cayenne pepper
- 2 tablespoons sugar
- 2 tablespoons ground cumin

Directions:

1. **Prepa**re the brine and for this, take a large bowl, add salt, black pepper, and sugar in it, pour in water, and stir until sugar has dissolved. Place turkey breast in it, submerge it completely and let it soak for a minimum of 12 hours in the refrigerator.
2. Meanwhile, **Prepa**re the BBQ rub and for this, take a small bowl, place all of its ingredients in it and then stir until combined, set aside until required.Then remove turkey breast from the brine and season well with the **Prepa**red BBQ rub. When ready to cook, switch on the griddle, set the temperature to 180 degrees F and let it preheat for a minimum of 15 minutes. When the griddle has preheated, open the lid, place turkey breast on the griddle grate, shut the griddle, change the smoking temperature to 225 degrees F, and smoke for 8 hours until the internal temperature reaches 160 degrees F.

3. When done, transfer turkey to a cutting board, let it rest for 10 minutes, then cut it into slices and serve.

Nutrition: Calories: 250 Fat: 5 g Carbs: 31 g Protein: 18 g

Smoked Whole Turkey

Preparation Time: 10 minutes
Cooking Time: 5 hours **Servings:** 6
Ingredients:

- 1 (10- to 12-pound) turkey, giblets removed
- Extra-virgin olive oil, for rubbing
- ¼ cup poultry seasoning
- 8 tablespoons (1 stick) unsalted butter, melted
- ½ cup apple juice
- 2 teaspoons dried sage
- 2 teaspoons dried thyme

Directions:

1. Supply your griddle follow the manufacturer's specific start-up procedure. Preheat, with the lid closed, to 250°F.
2. Rub the turkey with oil and season with the poultry seasoning inside and out, getting under the skin.
3. In a bowl, combine the melted butter, apple juice, sage, and thyme to use for basting.
4. Put the turkey in a roasting pan, place on the griddle, close the lid, and griddle for 5 to 6 hours, basting every hour, until the skin is brown and crispy, or until a meat thermometer inserted in the thickest part of the thigh reads 165°F.
5. Let the turkey meat rest for about 15 to 20 minutes before carving.

Nutrition: Calories: 180 Carbs: 3g Fat: 2g Protein: 39g

Savory-Sweet Turkey Legs

Preparation Time: 10 minutes
Cooking Time: 5 hours **Servings:** 4
Ingredients:

- 1 gallon hot water
- 1 cup curing salt (such as Morton Tender Quick)
- ¼ cup packed light brown sugar
- 1 teaspoon freshly ground black pepper
- 1 teaspoon ground cloves
- 1 bay leaf
- 2 teaspoons liquid smoke
- 4 turkey legs
- Mandarin Glaze, for serving

Directions:

1. In a huge container with a lid, stir together the water, curing salt, brown sugar, pepper, cloves, bay leaf, and liquid smoke until the salt and sugar are dissolved; let come to room temperature.
2. Submerge the turkey legs in the seasoned brine, cover, and refrigerate overnight.
3. When ready to smoke, remove the turkey legs from the brine and rinse them; discard the brine. Supply your griddle Preheat, with the lid closed, to 225°F.

4. Arrange the turkey legs on the griddle, close the lid, and smoke for 4 to 5 hours, or until dark brown and a meat thermometer inserted in the thickest part of the meat reads 165°F.
5. Serve with Mandarin Glaze on the side or drizzled over the turkey legs.

Nutrition: Calories: 190 Carbs: 1g Fat: 9g Protein: 24g

Marinated Smoked Turkey Breast

Preparation Time: 15 minutes
Cooking Time: 4 hours **Servings:** 6
Ingredients:

- 1 (5 pounds) boneless chicken breast
- 4 cups water
- 2 tablespoons kosher salt
- 1 teaspoon Italian seasoning
- 2 tablespoons honey
- 1 tablespoon cider vinegar
- Rub:
- ½ teaspoon onion powder
- 1 teaspoon paprika
- 1 teaspoon salt
- 1 teaspoon ground black pepper
- 1 tablespoons brown sugar
- ½ teaspoon garlic powder
- 1 teaspoon oregano

Directions:

1. In a huge container, combine the water, honey, cider vinegar, Italian seasoning and salt.
2. Add the chicken breast and toss to combine. Cover the bowl and place it in the refrigerator and chill for 4 hours.
3. Rinse the chicken breast with water and pat dry with paper towels.
4. In another mixing bowl, combine the brown sugar, salt, paprika, onion powder, pepper, oregano and garlic.
5. Generously season the chicken breasts with the rub mix.
6. Preheat the griddle to 225°F with lid closed for 15 minutes.
7. Arrange the turkey breast into a griddle rack. Place the griddle rack on the griddle.
8. Smoke for about 3 to 4 hours or until the internal temperature of the turkey breast reaches 165°F.
9. Remove the chicken breast from heat and let them rest for a few minutes. Serve.

Nutrition: Calories 903 Fat: 34g Carbs: 9.9g Protein 131.5g

Maple Bourbon Turkey

Preparation Time: 15 minutes
Cooking Time: 3 hours **Servings:** 8
Ingredients:

- 1 (12 pounds) turkey
- 8 cup chicken broth
- 1 stick butter (softened)
- 1 teaspoon thyme
- 2 garlic clove (minced)
- 1 teaspoon dried basil
- 1 teaspoon pepper
- 1 teaspoon salt
- 1 tablespoon minced rosemary
- 1 teaspoon paprika
- 1 lemon (wedged)
- 1 onion
- 1 orange (wedged)

- 1 apple (wedged)
- Maple Bourbon Glaze:
- ¾ cup bourbon
- 1/2 cup maple syrup
- 1 stick butter (melted)
- 1 tablespoon lime

Directions:

1. Wash the turkey meat inside and out under cold running water.
2. Insert the onion, lemon, orange and apple into the turkey cavity.
3. In a mixing bowl, combine the butter, paprika, thyme, garlic, basil, pepper, salt, basil and rosemary.
4. Brush the turkey generously with the herb butter mixture.
5. Set a rack into a roasting pan and place the turkey on the rack. Put a 5 cups of chicken broth into the bottom of the roasting pan.
6. Preheat the griddle to 350°F with lid closed for 15 minutes.
7. Place the roasting pan in the griddle and cook for 1 hour.
8. Meanwhile, combine all the maple bourbon glaze ingredients in a mixing bowl. Mix until well combined.
9. Baste the turkey with glaze mixture. Continue cooking, basting turkey every 30 minutes and adding more broth as needed for 2 hours, or until the internal temperature of the turkey reaches 165°F.
10. Take off the turkey from the griddle and let it rest for a few minutes. Cut into slices and serve.

Nutrition: Calories 1536 Fat 58.6g Carbs: 24g Protein 20.1g

Thanksgiving Turkey

Preparation Time: 15 minutes
Cooking Time: 4 hours **Servings:** 6
Ingredients:

- 2 cups butter (softened)
- 1 tablespoon cracked black pepper
- 2 teaspoons kosher salt
- 2 tablespoons freshly chopped rosemary
- 2 tablespoons freshly chopped parsley
- 2 tablespoons freshly chopped sage - 2 teaspoons dried thyme
- 6 garlic cloves (minced)
- 1 (18 pound) turkey

Directions:

1. In a mixing bowl, combine the butter, sage, rosemary, 1 teaspoon black pepper, 1 teaspoon salt, thyme, parsley and garlic.
2. Use your fingers to loosen the skin from the turkey.
3. Generously, Rub butter mixture under the turkey skin and all over the turkey as well. 4. Season turkey generously with herb mix. 5. Preheat the griddle to 300°F with lid closed for 15 minutes.
4. Place the turkey on the griddle and roast for about 4 hours, or until the turkey thigh temperature reaches 160°F.

5. Take out the turkey meat from the griddle and let it rest for a few minutes. Cut into sizes and serve.

Nutrition: Calories 278 Fat 30.8g Carbs: 1.6g Protein 0.6g

Spatchcock Smoked Turkey

Preparation Time: 15 minutes
Cooking Time: 4 hours 3 minutes
Servings: 6
Ingredients:

- 1 (18 pounds) turkey
- 2 tablespoons finely chopped fresh parsley
- 1 tablespoon finely chopped fresh rosemary
- 2 tablespoons finely chopped fresh thyme
- ½ cup melted butter
- 1 teaspoon garlic powder
- 1 teaspoon onion powder
- 1 teaspoon ground black pepper
- 2 teaspoons salt or to taste
- 2 tablespoons finely chopped scallions

Directions:

1. Remove the turkey giblets and rinse turkey, in and out, under cold running water.
2. Place the turkey on a working surface, breast side down. Use a poultry shear to cut the turkey along both sides of the backbone to remove the turkey back bone.
3. Flip the turkey over, back side down. Now, press the turkey down to flatten it.
4. In a mixing bowl, combine the parsley, rosemary, scallions, thyme, butter, pepper, salt, garlic and onion powder.
5. Rub butter mixture over all sides of the turkey.
6. Preheat your griddle to HIGH (450°F) with lid closed for 15 minutes.
7. Place the turkey directly on the griddle grate and cook for 30 minutes. Reduce the heat to 300°F and cook for an additional 4 hours, or until the internal temperature of the thickest part of the thigh reaches 165°F. Take out the turkey meat from the griddle and let it rest for a few minutes. Cut into sizes and serve.

Nutrition: Calories: 780 Fat: 19g Carbs: 29.7g Protein 116.4g

Hoisin Turkey Wings

Preparation Time: 15 minutes
Cooking Time: 1 hour **Servings:** 8
Ingredients:

- 2 pounds turkey wings
- ½ cup hoisin sauce
- 1 tablespoon honey
- 2 teaspoons soy sauce
- 2 garlic cloves (minced)
- 1 teaspoons freshly grated ginger
- 2 teaspoons sesame oil
- 1 teaspoons pepper or to taste
- 1 teaspoons salt or to taste
- ¼ cup pineapple juice
- 1 tablespoon chopped green onions
- 1 tablespoon sesame seeds

- 1 lemon (cut into wedges)

Directions:

1. In a huge container, combine the honey, garlic, ginger, soy, hoisin sauce, sesame oil, pepper and salt. Put all the mixture into a zip lock bag and add the wings. Refrigerate for 2 hours.
2. Remove turkey from the marinade and reserve the marinade. Let the turkey rest for a few minutes, until it is at room temperature. Preheat your griddle to 300°F with the lid closed for 15 minutes.
3. Arrange the wings into a griddleing basket and place the basket on the griddle.
4. Griddle for 1 hour or until the internal temperature of the wings reaches 165°F.
5. Meanwhile, pour the reserved marinade into a saucepan over medium-high heat. Stir in the pineapple juice. Wait to boil then reduce heat and simmer for until the sauce thickens. Brush the wings with sauce and cook for 6 minutes more. Remove the wings from heat. Serve and garnish it with green onions, sesame seeds and lemon wedges.

Nutrition: Calories: 115 Fat: 4.8g Carbs: 11.9g Protein 6.8g

Turkey Jerky

Preparation Time: 15 minutes
Cooking Time: 4 hours **Servings:** 6
Ingredients:

- Marinade:
- 1 cup pineapple juice
- ½ cup brown sugar
- 2 tablespoons sriracha
- 2 teaspoons onion powder
- 2 tablespoons minced garlic
- 2 tablespoons rice wine vinegar
- 2 tablespoons hoisin
- 1 tablespoon red pepper flakes
- 1 tablespoon coarsely ground black pepper flakes
- 2 cups coconut amino
- 2 jalapenos (thinly sliced)
- Meat:
- 3 pounds turkey boneless skinless breasts (sliced to ¼ inch thick)

Directions:

1. Pour the marinade mixture ingredients in a container and mix until the ingredients are well combined. Put the turkey slices in a gallon sized zip lock bag and pour the marinade into the bag. Massage the marinade into the turkey. Seal the bag and refrigerate for 8 hours.
2. Remove the turkey slices from the marinade.
3. Activate the griddle for smoking for 5 minutes until fire starts.
4. Close the lid and preheat your griddle to 180°F,.
5. Remove the turkey slices from the marinade and pat them dry with a paper towel.
6. Arrange the turkey slices on the griddle in a single layer. Smoke the turkey for about 3 to 4 hours, turning often after the first 2 hours of smoking. The jerky should be dark and dry when it is done.

7. Remove the jerky from the griddle and let it sit for about 1 hour to cool. Serve immediately or store in refrigerator.

Nutrition: Calories: 109 Carbs: 12g Fat: 1g Protein: 14g

Smoked Turkey Breast

Preparation Time: 10 Minutes
Cooking Time: 1 Hour 30 minutes
Servings: 6
Ingredients:

- For The Brine
- 1 Cup of kosher salt
- 1 Cup of maple syrup
- ¼ Cup of brown sugar
- ¼ Cup of whole black peppercorns
- 4 Cups of cold bourbon
- 1 and ½ gallons of cold water
- 1 Turkey breast of about 7 pounds
- For The Turkey
- 3 Tablespoons of brown sugar
- 1 and ½ tablespoons of smoked paprika
- 1 ½ teaspoons of chipotle chili powder
- 1 ½ teaspoons of garlic powder
- 1 ½ teaspoons of salt
- 1 and ½ teaspoons of black pepper
- 1 Teaspoon of onion powder
- ½ teaspoon of ground cumin
- 6 Tablespoons of melted unsalted butter

Directions:

1. Before beginning; make sure that the bourbon; the water and the chicken stock are all cold
2. Now to make the brine, combine altogether the salt, the syrup, the sugar, the peppercorns, the bourbon, and the water in a large bucket.
3. Remove any pieces that are left on the turkey, like the neck or the giblets
4. Refrigerate the turkey meat in the brine for about 8 to 12 hours in a reseal able bag
5. Remove the turkey breast from the brine and pat dry with clean paper towels; then place it over a baking sheet and refrigerate for about 1 hour
6. Preheat your griddle to about 300°F;
7. In a bowl, mix the paprika with the sugar, the chili powder, the garlic powder, the salt, the pepper, the onion powder and the cumin, mixing very well to combine.
8. Carefully lift the skin of the turkey; then rub the melted butter over the meat
9. Rub the spice over the meat very well and over the skin
10. Smoke the turkey breast for about 1 ½ hours at a temperature of about 375°

Nutrition: Calories: 94 Fat: 2g Carbs: 1g Protein: 18g

Whole Turkey

Preparation Time: 10 Minutes
Cooking Time: 7 Hours And 30 Minutes
Servings: 10
Ingredients:

- 1 frozen whole turkey, giblets removed, thawed

- 2 tablespoons orange zest
- 2 tablespoons chopped fresh parsley
- 1 teaspoon salt
- 2 tablespoons chopped fresh rosemary
- 1 teaspoon ground black pepper
- 2 tablespoons chopped fresh sage
- 1 cup butter, unsalted, softened, divided
- 2 tablespoons chopped fresh thyme
- ½ cup water
- 14.5-ounce chicken broth

Directions:

1. Open hopper of the griddle, add dry pallets, make sure ash-can is in place, then open the ash damper, power on the griddle and close the ash damper.
2. Set the temperature of the griddle to 180 degrees F, let preheat for 30 minutes or until the green light on the dial blinks that indicate griddle has reached to set temperature.
3. Meanwhile, **Prepa**re the turkey and for this, tuck its wings under it by using kitchen twine.
4. Place ½ cup butter in a bowl, add thyme, parsley, and sage, orange zest, and rosemary, stir well until combined and then brush this mixture generously on the inside and outside of the turkey and season the external of turkey with salt and black pepper.
5. Place turkey on a roasting pan, breast side up, pour in broth and water, add the remaining butter in the pan, then place the pan on the griddle and shut with lid.
6. Smoke the turkey for 3 hours, then increase the temperature to 350 degrees F and continue smoking the turkey for 4 hours or until thoroughly cooked and the internal temperature of the turkey reaches to 165 degrees F, basting turkey with the dripping every 30 minutes, but not in the last hour.
7. When you are done, take off the roasting pan from the griddle and let the turkey rest for 20 minutes.
8. Carve turkey into pieces and serve.

Nutrition: Calories: 146 Fat: 8 g Protein: 18 g Carbs: 1 g

Turkey Recipes

Herbed Turkey Breast

Preparation Time: 8 Hours And 10 Minutes

Cooking Time: 3 Hours

Servings: 12

Ingredients:

- 7 pounds turkey breast, bone-in, skin-on, fat trimmed
- 3/4 cup salt
- 1/3 cup brown sugar
- 4 quarts water, cold
- For Herbed Butter:
- 1 tablespoon chopped parsley
- ½ teaspoon ground black pepper
- 8 tablespoons butter, unsalted, softened
- 1 tablespoon chopped sage

- ½ tablespoon minced garlic
- 1 tablespoon chopped rosemary
- 1 teaspoon lemon zest
- 1 tablespoon chopped oregano
- 1 tablespoon lemon juice

Directions:

1. **Prepa**re the brine and for this, pour water in a large container, add salt and sugar and stir well until salt and sugar has completely dissolved.
2. Add turkey breast in the brine, cover with the lid and let soak in the refrigerator for a minimum of 8 hours.
3. Then remove turkey breast from the brine, rinse well and pat dry with paper towels.
4. Open hopper of the griddle, add dry pallets, make sure ash-can is in place, then open the ash damper, power on the griddle and close the ash damper.
5. Set the temperature of the griddle to 350 degrees F, let preheat for 30 minutes or until the green light on the dial blinks that indicate griddle has reached to set temperature.
6. Meanwhile, take a roasting pan, pour in 1 cup water, then place a wire rack in it and place turkey breast on it. **Prepa**re the herb butter and for this, place butter in a heatproof bowl, add remaining ingredients for the butter and stir until just mix.
7. Loosen the skin of the turkey from its breast by using your fingers, then insert 2 tablespoons of **Prepa**red herb butter on each side of the skin of the breastbone and spread it evenly, pushing out all the air pockets.
8. Place the remaining herb butter in the bowl into the microwave wave and heat for 1 minute or more at high heat setting or until melted. Then brush melted herb butter on the outside of the turkey breast and place roasting pan containing turkey on the griddle.
9. Shut the griddle with lid and smoke for 2 hours and 30 minutes or until the turkey breast is nicely golden brown and the internal temperature of turkey reach to 165 degrees F, flipping the turkey and basting with melted herb butter after 1 hour and 30 minutes smoking.
10. When done, transfer the turkey breast to a cutting board, let it rest for 15 minutes, then carve it into pieces and serve.

Nutrition: Calories: 97 Fat: 4 g Protein: 13 g Carbs: 1 g

Jalapeno Injection Turkey

Preparation Time: 15 Minutes
Cooking Time: 4 Hours And 10 Minutes
Servings: 4
Ingredients:

- 15 pounds whole turkey, giblet removed
- ½ of medium red onion, peeled and minced
- 8 jalapeño peppers
- 2 tablespoons minced garlic
- 4 tablespoons garlic powder
- 6 tablespoons Italian seasoning

- 1 cup butter, softened, unsalted
- ¼ cup olive oil
- 1 cup chicken broth

Directions:

1. Open hopper of the griddle, add dry pallets, make sure ash-can is in place, then open the ash damper, power on the griddle and close the ash damper.
2. Make the temperature of the griddle up to 200 degrees F, let preheat for 30 minutes or until the green light on the dial blinks that indicate griddle has reached to set temperature.
3. Meanwhile, place a large saucepan over medium-high heat, add oil and butter and when the butter melts, add onion, garlic, and peppers and cook for 3 to 5 minutes or until nicely golden brown.
4. Pour in broth, stir well, let the mixture boil for 5 minutes, then remove pan from the heat and strain the mixture to get just liquid.
5. Inject turkey generously with **Prepa**red liquid, then spray the outside of turkey with butter spray and season well with garlic and Italian seasoning.
6. Place turkey on the griddle, shut with lid, and smoke for 30 minutes, then increase the temperature to 325 degrees F and continue smoking the turkey for 3 hours or until the internal temperature of turkey reach to 165 degrees F.
7. When done, transfer turkey to a cutting board, let rest for 5 minutes, then carve into slices and serve.

Nutrition: Calories: 131 Fat: 7 g Protein: 13 g Carbs: 3 g

Smoked Turkey Mayo with Green Apple

Preparation Time: 20 minutes
Cooking Time: 4 hours 10 minutes
Servings: 10
Ingredients:

- Whole turkey (4-lbs., 1.8-kg.)
- The Rub
- Mayonnaise – ½ cup
- Salt – ¾ teaspoon
- Brown sugar – ¼ cup
- Ground mustard – 2 tablespoons
- Black pepper – 1 teaspoon
- Onion powder – 1 ½ tablespoons
- Ground cumin – 1 ½ tablespoons
- Chili powder – 2 tablespoons
- Cayenne pepper – ½ tablespoon
- Old Bay Seasoning – ½ teaspoon
- The Filling
- Sliced green apples – 3 cups

Directions:

1. Place salt, brown sugar, brown mustard, black pepper, onion powder, ground cumin, chili powder, cayenne pepper, and old bay seasoning in a bowl then mix well. Set aside.

2. Next, fill the turkey cavity with sliced green apples then baste mayonnaise over the turkey skin. Sprinkle the dry spice mixture over the turkey then wrap with aluminum foil.
3. Marinate the turkey for at least 4 hours or overnight and store in the fridge to keep it fresh.
4. On the next day, remove the turkey from the fridge and thaw at room temperature.
5. Set the griddle for indirect heat then adjust the temperature to 275°F (135°C). Unwrap the turkey and place in the griddle. Smoke the turkey for 4 hours or until the internal temperature has reached 170°F (77°C). Remove the smoked turkey from the griddle and serve.

Nutrition: Calories: 340 Carbs: 40g Fat: 10g Protein: 21g

Buttery Smoked Turkey Beer

Preparation Time: 15 minutes
Cooking Time: 4 hours **Servings:** 6
Ingredients:

- Whole turkey (4-lbs., 1.8-kg.)
- The Brine
- Beer – 2 cans
- Salt – 1 tablespoon
- White sugar – 2 tablespoons
- Soy sauce – ¼ cup
- Cold water – 1 quart
- The Rub
- Unsalted butter – 3 tablespoons
- Smoked paprika – 1 teaspoon
- Garlic powder – 1 ½ teaspoons
- Pepper – 1 teaspoon
- Cayenne pepper – ¼ teaspoon

Directions:

1. Pour beer into a container then add salt, white sugar, and soy sauce then stir well. Put the turkey into the brine mixture cold water over the turkey. Make sure that the turkey is completely soaked. Soak the turkey in the brine for at least 6 hours or overnight and store in the fridge to keep it fresh. On the next day, remove the turkey from the fridge and take it out of the brine mixture.
2. Wash and rinse the turkey then pat it dry. Set the griddle for indirect heat then adjust the temperature to 275°F (135°C). Open the beer can then push it in the turkey cavity. Place the seasoned turkey in the griddle and make a tripod using the beer can and the two turkey-legs. Smoke the turkey for 4 hours or until the internal temperature has reached 170°F (77°C). Once it is done, remove the smoked turkey from the griddle and transfer it to a serving dish.

Nutrition: Calories: 229 Carbs: 34g Fat: 8g Protein: 3g

Barbecue Chili Smoked Turkey Breast

Preparation Time: 15 minutes
Cooking Time: 4 hours 20 minutes
Servings: 8
Ingredients:

- Turkey breast (3-lb., 1.4-kg.)

- The Rub
- Salt – ¾ teaspoon
- Pepper – ½ teaspoon
- The Glaze
- Olive oil – 1 tablespoon
- Ketchup – ¾ cup
- White vinegar – 3 tablespoons
- Brown sugar – 3 tablespoons
- Smoked paprika – 1 tablespoons
- Chili powder – ¾ teaspoon
- Cayenne powder – ¼ teaspoon

Directions:

1. Score the turkey breast at several places then sprinkle salt and pepper over it.
2. Let the seasoned turkey breast rest for approximately 10 minutes. Set the griddle for indirect heat then adjust the temperature to 275°F (135°C).
3. Place the seasoned turkey breast in the griddle and smoke for 2 hours.
4. In the meantime, combine olive oil, ketchup, white vinegar, brown sugar, smoked paprika; chili powder, garlic powder, and cayenne pepper in a saucepan then stir until incorporated. Wait to simmer then remove from heat.
5. After 2 hours of smoking, baste the sauce over the turkey breast and continue smoking for another 2 hours.
6. Once the internal temperature of the smoked turkey breast has reached 170°F (77°C) remove from the griddle and wrap with aluminum foil.
7. Let the smoked turkey breast rest for approximately 15 minutes to 30 minutes then unwrap it. Cut the smoked turkey breast into thick slices then serve.

Nutrition: Calories: 290 Carbs: 2g Fat: 3g Protein: 63g

Hot Sauce Smoked Turkey Tabasco

Preparation Time: 20 minutes **Cooking Time:** 4 hours 15 minutes **Servings:** 8

Ingredients:

- Whole turkey (4-lbs., 1.8-kg.)
- The Rub
- Brown sugar – ¼ cup
- Smoked paprika – 2 teaspoons
- Salt – 1 teaspoon
- Onion powder – 1 ½ teaspoons
- Oregano – 2 teaspoons
- Garlic powder – 2 teaspoons
- Dried thyme – ½ teaspoon
- White pepper – ½ teaspoon
- Cayenne pepper – ½ teaspoon
- The Glaze
- Ketchup – ½ cup
- Hot sauce – ½ cup
- Cider vinegar – 1 tablespoon
- Tabasco – 2 teaspoons
- Cajun spices – ½ teaspoon
- Unsalted butter – 3 tablespoons

Directions:

1. Rub the turkey with 2 tablespoons of brown sugar, smoked paprika, salt, onion powder, garlic powder, dried thyme, white pepper, and cayenne pepper. Let the turkey rest for an hour.

2. Set the griddle for indirect heat then adjust the temperature to 275°F (135°C).
3. Place the seasoned turkey in the griddle and smoke for 4 hours.
4. In the meantime, place ketchup, hot sauce, cider vinegar, Tabasco, and Cajun spices in a saucepan then bring to a simmer.
5. Remove the sauce from heat and quickly add unsalted butter to the saucepan. Stir until melted.
6. After 4 hours of smoking, baste the Tabasco sauce over the turkey then continue smoking for 15 minutes.
7. Once the internal temperature of the smoked turkey has reached 170°F (77°C), remove from the griddle and place it on a serving dish.

Nutrition: Calories: 160 Carbs: 2g Fat: 14g Protein: 7g

Cured Turkey Drumstick

Preparation Time: 20 minutes **Cooking Time:** 2.5 hours to 3 hours **Servings:** 3

Ingredients:

- 3 fresh or thawed frozen turkey drumsticks
- 3 tablespoons extra virgin olive oil
- Brine component
- 4 cups of filtered water
- ¼Cup kosher salt
- ¼ cup brown sugar
- 1 teaspoon garlic powder
- Poultry seasoning 1 teaspoon
- 1/2 teaspoon red pepper flakes
- 1 teaspoon pink hardened salt

Directions:

1. Put the salt water ingredients in a 1 gallon sealable bag. Add the turkey drumstick to the salt water and refrigerate for 12 hours. After 12 hours, remove the drumstick from the saline, rinse with cold water, and pat dry with a paper towel.
2. Air dry the drumstick in the refrigerator without a cover for 2 hours. Remove the drumsticks from the refrigerator and rub a tablespoon of extra virgin olive oil under and over each drumstick.
3. Set the griddle for indirect cooking and preheat to 250 degrees
4. Place the drumstick on the griddle and smoke at 250 ° F for 2 hours. After 2 hours, increase griddle temperature to 325 ° F.
5. Cook the turkey drumstick at 325 ° F until the internal temperature of the thickest part of each drumstick is 180 ° F with an instant reading digital thermometer.
6. Place a smoked turkey drumstick under a loose foil tent for 15 minutes before eating.

Nutrition: Calories: 278 Carbs: 0g Fat: 13g Protein: 37g

Tailgate Smoked Young Turkey

Preparation Time: 20 Minutes
Cooking Time: 4 To 4 Hours 30 Minutes
Servings: 6
Ingredients:

- 1 fresh or thawed frozen young turkey

- 6 glasses of extra virgin olive oil with roasted garlic flavor
- 6 original Yang dry lab or poultry seasonings

Directions:

1. Remove excess fat and skin from turkey breasts and cavities.
2. Slowly separate the skin of the turkey to its breast and a quarter of the leg, leaving the skin intact.
3. Apply olive oil to the chest, under the skin and on the skin.
4. Gently rub or season to the chest cavity, under the skin and on the skin.
5. Set up tailgate griddle for indirect cooking and smoking. Preheat to 225 ° F.
6. Put the turkey meat on the griddle with the chest up.
7. Suck the turkey for 4-4 hours at 225 ° F until the thickest part of the turkey's chest reaches an internal temperature of 170 ° F and the juice is clear.
8. Before engraving, place the turkey under a loose foil tent for 20 minutes

Nutrition: Calories: 240 Carbs: 27g Fat: 9g Protein: 15g

Roast Turkey Orange

Preparation Time: 30 Minutes
Cooking Time: 2 hours 30 minutes
Servings:
Ingredients:

- 1 Frozen Long Island turkey
- 3 tablespoons west
- 1 large orange, cut into wedges
- Three celery stems chopped into large chunks
- Half a small red onion, a quarter
- Orange sauce:
- 2 orange cups
- 2 tablespoons soy sauce
- 2 tablespoons orange marmalade
- 2 tablespoons honey
- 3 teaspoons grated raw

Directions:

1. Remove the jibble from the turkey's cavity and neck and retain or discard for another use. Wash the duck and pat some dry paper towel.
2. Remove excess fat from tail, neck and cavity. Use a sharp scalpel knife tip to pierce the turkey's skin entirely, so that it does not penetrate the duck's meat, to help dissolve the fat layer beneath the skin.
3. Add the seasoning inside the cavity with one cup of rub or seasoning.
4. Season the outside of the turkey with the remaining friction or seasoning.
5. Fill the cavity with orange wedges, celery and onion. Duck legs are tied with butcher twine to make filling easier. Place the turkey's breast up on a small rack of shallow roast bread.
6. To make the sauce, mix the ingredients in the saucepan over low heat and cook until the sauce is thick and syrupy. Set aside and let cool.
7. Set the griddle for indirect cooking and preheat to 350 ° F.

8. Roast the turkey at 350 ° F for 2 hours.
9. After 2 hours, brush the turkey freely with orange sauce.
10. Roast the orange glass turkey for another 30 minutes, making sure that the inside temperature of the thickest part of the leg reaches 165 ° F.
11. Place turkey under loose foil tent for 20 minutes before serving.
12. Discard the orange wedge, celery and onion. Serve with a quarter of turkey with poultry scissors.

Nutrition: Calories: 216 Carbs: 2g Fat: 11g Protein: 34g

CHAPTER 9
Pork Recipes

Herb-Crusted Mediterranean Pork Tenderloin

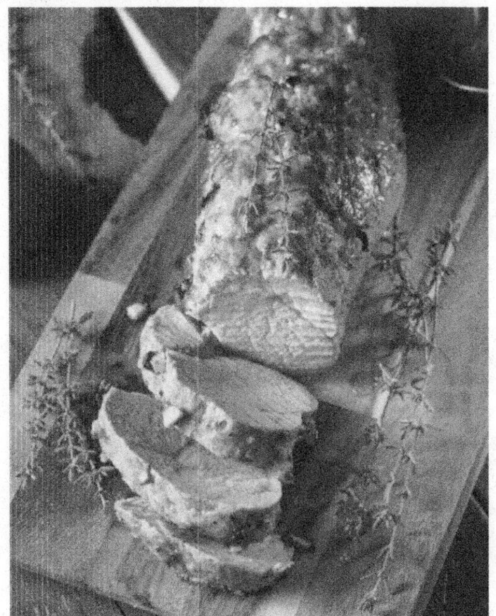

Herb-Crusted Tenderloin with Mediterranean style spices is one great way to griddle up juicy tenderloin. My favorite way to serve this dish is alongside lemon chili pasta and salad with a glass of Pinot Grigio.

Servings: 4 Preparation time: 2 hours Cooking Time: 30 minutes

Ingredients:

1 pound pork tenderloin
1 tablespoon olive oil
2 teaspoons dried oregano
3/4 teaspoon lemon pepper
1 teaspoon garlic powder
1/4 cup parmesan cheese, grated
3 tablespoons olive tapenade

Directions:

1. Place pork on a large piece of plastic wrap.
2. Rub tenderloin with oil, and sprinkle oregano, garlic powder, and lemon pepper evenly over entire tenderloin.
3. Wrap tightly in the plastic wrap and refrigerate for 2 hours.
4. Preheat griddle to medium-high heat.
5. Transfer pork to cutting board, remove plastic wrap, and make a lengthwise cut through center of tenderloin, opening meat so it lies flat, but do not cut all the way through.
6. Combine tapenade and parmesan in a small mixing bowl; rub into the center of the tenderloin and fold meat back together.
7. Tie together with twine in 2-inch intervals.
8. Sear tenderloin for 20 minutes, turning tenderloin once during griddleing, or until internal temperature reaches 145°F.
9. Transfer tenderloin to cutting board.
10. Tent with foil; let rest for 10 minutes.
11. Remove string and cut into 1/4-inch-thick slices and serve.

Nutrition: Calories: 413, Sodium: 1279mg, Dietary Fiber: 0.5g, Fat: 30.5g, Carbs: 2.4g, Protein: 31.4g.

Paprika Dijon Pork Tenderloin

This tender pork loin is paired perfectly with the earthy flavor of mustard for a dish that is sure to please guests or you family. The addition of a little smoked paprika compliments the robust mustard and delicate pork tenderloin.

Servings: 6 Preparation time: 10 minutes Cooking Time: 4 hours

Ingredients:

2 1 lb pork tenderloins
2 tablespoons Dijon mustard
1-1/2 teaspoons smoked paprika
1 teaspoon salt
2 tablespoons olive oil

Directions:

1. In a small bowl, combine the mustard and paprika.

2.Set your griddle to medium heat.
3.Rub the tenderloins with the mustard mixture, making sure they are evenly coated.
4.Place the tenderloins on the griddle and cook until all sides are well browned, and the internal temperature is 135°F.
5.Remove the tenderloins from the griddle and rest 5 minutes before slicing and serving.

Nutrition: Calories: 484, Sodium: 755mg, Dietary Fiber: 4.2g, Fat: 24.7g, Carbs: 13.8g, Protein: 50.9g.

Moroccan Spiced Pork Tenderloin with Creamy Harissa Sauce

Moroccan spice and creamy harissa make for one delicious way to serve up tender pork any night of the week. Enjoy this yummy dish with collard greens and potato salad for a taste twist on your next cookout.

Servings: 6 Preparation time: 40 minutes Cooking Time: 20 minutes

Ingredients:

2 (1 lb.) pork tenderloins
1 teaspoon ground cinnamon
1 teaspoon ground cilantro
1 teaspoon ground cumin
1 teaspoon paprika
1 teaspoon sea salt
2 tablespoons olive oil
For Creamy Harissa Sauce:
1 cup Greek yogurt (8 ounces)
1 tablespoon fresh lemon juice
1 tablespoon extra-virgin olive oil
1 teaspoon harissa sauce
1 clove garlic, minced
Kosher salt and cracked black pepper

Directions:

1.Combine harissa ingredients in a small mixing bowl and set aside.
2.Combine the cinnamon, coriander, cumin, paprika, salt and olive oil.
3.Rub the seasonings evenly over the pork tenderloins; cover and refrigerate for 30 minutes.
4.Preheat griddle to high heat and cook tenderloins until browned; about 8 to 10 minutes.
5.Turn and cook an additional 8 to 10 minutes. Transfer the tenderloins to a cutting board, tent with foil and rest for 10 minutes.
6.Slice and serve with creamy harissa sauce.

Nutrition: Calories: 376, Sodium: 458mg, Dietary Fiber: 0.4g, Fat: 17.9g, Carbs: 2.6g, Protein: 48.7g.

Sticky-Sweet Pork Shoulder

Sweet and sticky sauce is the perfect complement to savory Griddle pork. Serve this delicious dish with your favorite sides or as a delicious stuffing for steamed buns or Griddle bread.

Servings: 6 – 8 Preparation time: 8 hours Cooking Time: 8 minutes

Ingredients:

1 (5 lbs.) Boston Butt pork shoulder
For the marinade:
2 tablespoons garlic, minced
1 large piece ginger, peeled and chopped
1 cup hoisin sauce
3/4 cup fish sauce
2/3 cup honey
2/3 cup Shaoxing
1/2 cup chili oil
1/3 cup oyster sauce
1/3 cup sesame oil
For the glaze:
3/4 cup dark brown sugar
1 tablespoon light molasses

Directions:

1.Place pork shoulder, fat side down, on a cutting board with a short end facing you. Holding a long sharp knife about 1"–1½" above cutting board, make a shallow cut along the entire length of a long side of shoulder.

2.Continue cutting deeper into meat, lifting and unfurling with your free hand, until it lies flat.

3.Purée marinade in a blender and reserve 1 ½ cups for glaze, cover and refrigerate.

4.Pour remaining marinade in a large sealable plastic bag.

5.Add pork shoulder to bag and marinate in the refrigerator for 8 hours.

6.Preheat griddle to medium heat (with cover closed, thermometer should register 350°). Remove pork from marinade, letting excess drip off.

7.Add glaze ingredients to reserved marinade until sugar is dissolved.

8.Griddle pork, for 8 minutes, basting and turning with tongs every minute or so, until thick coated with glaze, lightly charred in spots, and warmed through; an instant-read thermometer inserted into the thickest part should register 145°F.

9.Transfer to a cutting board and slice against the grain, ¼" thick, to serve.

Nutrition: Calories: 1286, Sodium: 2875mg, Dietary Fiber: 1g, Fat: 84.8g, Carbs: 58.3g, Protein: 68.7g.

Griddle Pork Chops with Herb Apple Compote

Apples are one of my absolute favorite ingredients to pair with pork chops, and I hope you love this recipe too! Sweet meets juicy pork for a griddleing flavor that is out of this world.

Servings: 4 Preparation time: 5 minutes Cooking Time: 20 minutes

Ingredients:

4, bone-in pork chops

2 honeycrisp apples, peeled, cored and chopped

1/3 cup orange juice

1 teaspoon chopped fresh rosemary

1 teaspoon chopped fresh sage

Sea salt

Black pepper

Directions:

1.Add the apples, herbs and orange juice to a saucepan and simmer over medium heat until the apples are tender and the juices are thickened to a thin syrup, about 10 to 12 minutes.

2.Season pork chops with salt and pepper.

3.Place on the griddle and cook until the pork chop releases from the griddle, about 4 minutes.

4.Flip and cook on the other side for 3 minutes.

5.Transfer to a cutting board and tent with foil.
6.Top with apple compote and serve!
Nutrition: Calories: 284, Sodium: 173mg, Dietary Fiber: 1g, Fat: 20g, Carbs: 7.2g, Protein: 18.2g.

Yucatan-Style Griddle Pork

Elevate simple Griddle pork with Yucatan citrus combinations to make something different on your outdoor griddle Serve this with a side of Griddle plantains, veggies, and sparkling water.

Servings: 4
Preparation time: 15 minutes
Cooking Time: 8 minutes

Ingredients:

2 pork tenderloins, trimmed
1 teaspoon annatto powder
Olive oil
For the marinade:
2 oranges, juiced
2 lemons, juiced, or more to taste
2 limes, juiced, or more to taste
6 cloves garlic, minced
1 teaspoon ground cumin
1/2 teaspoon cayenne pepper
1/2 teaspoon dried oregano
1/2 teaspoon black pepper

Directions:

1.Combine marinade ingredients in a mixing bowl and whisk until well-blended.
2.Cut the tenderloins in half crosswise; cut each piece in half lengthwise.
3.Place pieces in marinade and thoroughly coat with the mixture.
4.Cover with plastic wrap and refrigerate 4 to 6 hours.
5.Transfer pieces of pork from marinade to a paper-towel-lined bowl to absorb most of the moisture.
6.Discard paper towels. Drizzle olive oil and a bit more annatto powder on the pork.
7.Preheat griddle for medium-high heat and lightly oil.
8.Place pieces evenly spaced on griddle; cook 4 to 5 minutes.
9.Turn and cook on the other side another 4 or 5 minutes.
10. Transfer onto a serving platter and allow meat to rest about 5 minutes before serving.

Nutrition: Calories: 439, Sodium: 1382mg, Dietary Fiber: 1.5g, Fat: 33.1g, Carbs: 11.4g, Protein: 23.9g.

Glazed Country Ribs

Country ribs are full of delicious flavor and make for one great main dish on weeknights or weekends with friends. Serve these ribs with your favorite sides and cold, crisp beer on summer holidays for traditional griddleing fun.

Servings: 6 Preparation time: 10 minutes
Cooking Time: 4 hours

Ingredients:

3 pounds country-style pork ribs
1 cup low-sugar ketchup
1/2 cup water

1/4 cup onion, finely chopped
1/4 cup cider vinegar or wine vinegar
1/4 cup light molasses
2 tablespoons Worcestershire sauce
2 teaspoons chili powder
2 cloves garlic, minced

Directions:

1.Combine ketchup, water, onion, vinegar, molasses, Worcestershire sauce, chili powder, and garlic in a saucepan and bring to boil; reduce heat. Simmer, uncovered, for 10 to 15 minutes or until desired thickness is reached, stirring often.

2.Trim fat from ribs.

3.Preheat griddle to medium-high.

4.Place ribs, bone-side down, on griddle and cook for 1-1/2 to 2 hours or until tender, brushing occasionally with sauce during the last 10 minutes of cooking.

5.Serve with remaining sauce and enjoy!

Nutrition: Calories: 404, Sodium: 733mg, Dietary Fiber: 0.4g, Fat: 8.1g, Carbs: 15.2g, Protein: 60.4g.

Pineapple Bacon Pork Chops

Sweet and juicy pineapple compliments savory pork for one incredible dish! You'll love the sweet and spicy kick in this recipe - serve it with your favorite Griddle side dishes and vegetables and a cold glass of beer or iced tea.

Servings: 6 Preparation time: 30 minutes Cooking Time: 1 hour

Ingredients:

1 large whole pineapple
6 pork chops
12 slices thick-cut bacon
Toothpicks, soaked in water
For the glaze:
1/4 cup honey
1/8 teaspoon cayenne pepper

Directions:

1.Turn both burners to medium-high heat; after about 15 minutes, turn off one of the middle burners and turn the remaining burners down to medium.

2. Slice off the top and bottom of the pineapple, and peel the pineapple, cutting the skin off in strips.

3.Cut pineapple flesh into six quarters.

4.Wrap each pineapple section with a bacon slice; secure each end with a toothpick.

5.Brush quarters with honey and sprinkle with cayenne pepper.

6.Put the quarters on the griddle, flipping when bacon is cooked so that both sides are evenly Griddle.

7.While pineapple quarters are cooking, coat pork chops with honey and cayenne pepper. Set on griddle.

8.Tent with foil and cook for 20 minutes. Flip, and continue cooking an additional 10 to 20 minutes or until chops are fully cooked.

9.Serve each chop with a pineapple quarter on the side.

Nutrition: Calories: 380, Sodium: 852mg, Dietary Fiber: 0.5g, Fat: 23.5g, Carbs: 18.2g, Protein: 25.8g.

Baked Egg and Bacon–Stuffed Peppers

Preparation Time: 10 minutes
Cooking Time: 15 minutes
Servings: 4 slices
Ingredients:

- 1 cup shredded Cheddar cheese
- 4 slices bacon, cooked and chopped
- 4 bell peppers, seeded and tops removed
- 4 large eggs
- Sea salt
- Freshly ground black pepper
- Chopped fresh parsley, for garnish

Directions:

1. Preheat the griddle to medium high.
2. Divide the cheese and bacon between the bell peppers. Crack one of the eggs into each bell pepper, and season with salt and pepper.
3. Place each bell pepper to the grill and cook for 10 to 15 minutes, until the egg whites are cooked and the yolks are slightly runny.
4. Remove the peppers, garnish with parsley, and serve.

Nutrition:
Calories: 326kcal; Fat: 23g; Carbs: 10g; Protein: 22g

Sausage Mixed Grill

Preparation Time: 5 minutes
Cooking Time: 22 minutes
Servings: 4 slices
Ingredients:

- 8 mini bell peppers
- 2 heads radicchio, each cut into 6 wedges
- Canola oil, for brushing
- Sea salt
- Freshly ground black pepper
- 6 breakfast sausage links
- 6 hot or sweet Italian sausage links

Directions:

1. Preheat the griddle to medium high.
2. Brush the bell peppers and radicchio with the oil. Season with salt and black pepper.
3. Place the bell peppers and radicchio on the Grill and cook for 10 minutes, without flipping.
4. Meanwhile, poke the sausages with a fork or knife and brush them with some of the oil.
5. After 10 minutes, remove the vegetables and set aside. Decrease the heat to medium. Place the sausages on the Grill and cook for 6 minutes.
6. Flip the sausages and cook for 6 minutes more. Remove the sausages from the Grill.

7. Serve the sausages and vegetables on a large cutting board or serving tray.

Nutrition:
Calories: 473kcal; Fat: 34g; Carbs: 14g; Protein: 28g

Habanero-Marinated Pork Chops

Kick things up a notch on your outdoor griddle with this spicy recipe. These yummy pork chops pair perfectly with yellow rice, black beans, and your favorite salad.

Servings: 4 Preparation time: 30 minutes Cooking Time: 13 minutes

Ingredients:

4-1/2-inch-thick bone-in pork chops
3 tablespoons olive oil, plus more for griddle
Kosher salt and freshly ground black pepper
For the marinade:
1 habanero chili, seeded, chopped fine
2 garlic cloves, minced
1/2 cup fresh orange juice
2 tablespoons brown sugar
1 tablespoon apple cider vinegar

Directions:

1.Combine marinade ingredients in a large sealable plastic bag.
2.Pierce pork chops all over with a fork and add to bag, seal, and turn to coat.
3.Marinate at room temperature, turning occasionally, for 30 minutes.
4.**Prepa**re griddle for medium-high heat.
5.Brush the griddle with oil.
6.Remove pork chops from marinade and pat dry.
7.Sear for 8 minutes, turning occasionally, until charred and cooked through.
8.Transfer to a plate and let rest 5 minutes.
9.Serve with your favorite sides.

Nutrition: Calories: 490, Sodium: 171mg, Dietary Fiber: 1.1g, Fat: 39.2g, Carbs: 10.9g, Protein: 23.3g.

Garlic Soy Pork Chops

Sweet and spicy ribs are a great way to griddle out with the whole family on the weekends. Serve these sticky ribs with mashed potatoes and Griddle vegetables for some decadent weekend backyard fun.

Servings: 4 – 6 Preparation time: 8 hours Cooking Time: 1 hour

Ingredients:

4 to 6 pork chops
4 cloves garlic, finely chopped
1/2 cup olive oil - 1/2 cup soy sauce
1/2 teaspoon garlic powder
1/2 teaspoon salt - 1/2 black pepper
1/4 cup butter

Directions:

1.In a large zipper lock bag, combine the garlic, olive oil, soy sauce, and garlic powder. Add the pork chops and make sure the marinade coats the chops. Set aside for 30 minutes.
2.Heat your griddle to medium-high heat. Add 2 tablespoons of olive oil and 2 tablespoons of butter to the griddle.
3.Add the chops to the griddle one at a time, making sure they are not crowded. Add another 2 tablespoons of butter to the griddle and cook the chops for 4 minutes. Cook an additional 4 minutes.
4.Remove the chops from the griddle and spread the remaining butter over them. Serve after resting for 5 minutes.

Nutrition: Calories: 398, Sodium: 1484mg, Dietary Fiber: 0.2g, Fat: 37.7g, Carbs: 2.5g, Protein: 13.6g.

Honey Soy Pork Chops

Sweet and tangy Griddle pork is absolutely delicious when Griddle to perfection on your outdoor griddle. Simply serve this dish with rice and Griddle vegetables for one delicious meal.

Servings: 6 Preparation time: 1 hour Cooking Time: 25 minutes

Ingredients:

6 (4 ounce) boneless pork chops
1/4 cup organic honey
1 to 2 tablespoons low sodium soy sauce
2 tablespoons olive oil
1 tablespoon rice mirin

Directions:

1.Combine honey, soy sauce, oil, and white vinegar and whisk until well-combined. Add sauce and pork chops to a large sealable plastic bag and marinate for 1 hour.
2.Preheat the griddle to medium-high heat and cook for 4 to 5 minutes, or until the pork chop easily releases from the griddle.
3.Flip and continue to cook for 5 additional minutes, or until internal temperature reaches 145°F.
4.Serve and enjoy!

Nutrition: Calories: 251, Sodium: 187mg, Dietary Fiber: 0.1g, Fat: 8.7g, Carbs: 13.1g, Protein: 29.9g.

Cuban Pork Chops

These authentic Cuban pork chops are easy to make are a packed with exotic flavors. Thanks to your outdoor griddle they are sure to cook to perfection.

Servings: 4 Preparation time: 30 minutes Cooking Time: 1 hour 30 minutes

Ingredients:

4 pork chops
4 cloves garlic, smashed
2 tablespoons olive oil
1/3 cup lime juice
1/4 cup water
1 teaspoon ground cumin
Salt and black pepper

Directions:

1.Set your griddle to medium. Salt the pork chops on both side and cook the chops until lightly browned.
2.Combine the water, garlic, and lime juice in a bowl and whisk until even.
3.Continue cooking the pork chops while basting them with the lime juice mixture.
4.When the pork chops have finished cooking, remove from the griddle and top with additional sauce and black pepper before serving.

Nutrition: Calories: 323, Sodium: 58mg, Dietary Fiber: 0.1g, Fat: 27g, Carbs: 1.5g, Protein: 18.3g.

Spicy Cajun Pork Chops

Packed with flavor and a nice amount of heat, these Cajun pork chops are perfect for outdoor cooking any time of year. For best results, serve with a nice, rich coleslaw.

Servings: 4 Preparation time: 10 minutes Cooking Time: 15 minutes

Ingredients:

4 pork chops - 1 tablespoon paprika
1/2 teaspoon ground cumin
1/2 teaspoon dried sage
1/2 teaspoon salt
1/2 teaspoon black pepper
1/2 teaspoon garlic powder
1/4 teaspoon cayenne pepper
1 tablespoon butter
1 tablespoon vegetable oil

Directions:

1.In a medium bowl, combine the paprika, cumin, sage, salt, pepper, garlic, and cayenne pepper. 2.Heat your griddle to medium-high heat and add the butter and oil.
3.Rub the pork chops with a generous amount of the seasoning rub.

4. Place the chops on the griddle and cook for 4 to 5 minutes. Turn the pork chops and continue cooking an additional 4 minutes.
5. Remove the pork chops from the griddle and allow to rest 5 minutes before serving.

Nutrition: Calories: 320, Sodium: 368mg, Dietary Fiber: 0.8g, Fat: 26.5g, Carbs: 1.6g, Protein: 18.4g.

Teriyaki-Marinated Pork Sirloin Tip Roast

Preparation Time: 45 minutes
Cooking Time: 2 hours 30 minutes
Servings: 4
Ingredients:

- 1 (1½ to 2 pounds) pork sirloin tip roast
- Teriyaki marinade, for example, Mr. Yoshida's Original Gourmet Marinade

Directions:

1. Dry the roast with a piece of paper
2. Utilizing a 1-gallon cooler stockpiling sack or a sealable compartment, spread the roast with the teriyaki marinade.
3. Refrigerate medium-term, turning at regular intervals whenever the situation allows.
4. Smoke the meat for 1 hour at 180°F.
5. After 60 minutes, increase your pit temperature to 325°F.
6. Cook the roast until the internal temperature, at the thickest part of the roast, arrives at 145°F, around 1 to 1½ hours.
7. Rest the roast under a free foil tent for 15 minutes.
8. Remove the cooking groups or twine and cut the roast contrary to what would be expected.

Nutrition:
Calories: 214 kCal
Protein: 17 g
Fat: 19 g

Pork Sirloin Tip Roast

Preparation Time: 30 minutes
Cooking Time: 3 hours
Servings: 3
Ingredients:

- 1 (1½ to 2 pounds) pork sirloin tip roast
- 2 tablespoons roasted garlic–seasoned extra-virgin olive oil
- 5 tablespoons Jan's Original Dry Rub, Pork Dry Rub, or your preferred pork rub

Directions:

1. Pat the roast dry with a paper towel.
2. Rub the whole roast with the olive oil. Coat the roast with the rub.
3. Support the roast utilizing 2 to 3 silicone nourishment grade cooking groups or butcher's twine to ensure the roast keeps up its shape during cooking.
4. Wrap the tip roast in plastic wrap and refrigerate medium-term.
5. Place the roast directly on the griddle grates and smoke the roast until the internal temperature, at the thickest part of the roast, arrives at 145°F, around 3 hours.
6. Rest the roast under a free foil tent for 15 minutes.

7. Remove the cooking groups or twine and cut the roast contrary to what would be expected.

Nutrition:
Calories: 276 kCal
Protein: 28 g
Fat: 12 g

Double-Smoked Ham

Preparation Time: 15 minutes
Cooking Time: 2½ to 3 hours
Servings: 8 to 12
Ingredients:

- 1 (10-pound) smoked, boneless, wholly cooked, ready-to-eat ham or bone-in smoked ham

Directions:

1. Remove the ham from its bundling and let sit at room temperature for 30 minutes.
2. Arrange the griddle for a non-direct cooking and preheat to 180°F.
3. Place the ham directly on the griddle grates and smoke the ham for 1 hour at 180°F.
4. After 60 minutes, increase pit temperature to 350°F.
5. Cooking Time the ham until the internal temperature arrives at 140°F, about 1½ to 2 additional hours.
6. Remove the ham and wrap in foil for 15 minutes before cutting contrary to what would be expected.

Nutrition:
Calories: 215 kCal
Protein: 21 g
Fat: 19 g

Prime Rib of Pork

Preparation Time: 30 minutes
Cooking Time: 3 hours **Servings:** 6
Ingredients:

- 1 (5-pound) rack of pork, around 6 ribs
- ¼ cup roasted garlic–enhanced extra-virgin olive oil
- 6 tablespoons Jan's Original Dry Rub, Pork Dry Rub, or your preferred pork roast rub

Directions:

1. Trim of the fat cap and silver skin from the rack of pork. Much the same as a chunk of ribs a rack of pork has a membrane on the bones. Remove the membrane from the bones by working a spoon handle under the bone membrane until you can get the membrane with a paper towel to pull it off. Rub the olive oil generously on all sides of the meat. Season with the rub, covering all sides of the meat. Double wrap the seasoned rack of pork in plastic wrap and refrigerate for 2 to 4 hours or medium-term.
2. Remove the seasoned rack of pork from the refrigerator and let sit at room temperature for 30 minutes before cooking. Arrange the griddle for a non-direct cooking and preheat to 225°F. Add your griddle meat probe or a remote meat probe into the thickest part of the rack of pork. On the off chance that your griddle doesn't have meat probe capabilities or you don't claim a remote meat probe at that point, utilize a moment read computerized thermometer during the cook for internal temperature readings.

3. Place the rack rib-side down directly on the griddle grates.
4. Smoke the rack of pork for 3 to 3½ hours, until the internal temperature arrives at 140°F.
5. Remove from the meat from the griddle, and let it rest under a free foil tent for 15 minutes before cutting.

Nutrition:
Calories: 189 kCal Protein: 17 g Fat: 12 g

Tender Griddle Loin Chops

Preparation Time: 10 minutes
Cooking Time: 12 to 15 minutes **Servings:** 6
Ingredients:

- 6 boneless focus cut midsection pork cleaves, 1 to 1½ inches thick 2 quarts Pork Brine
- 2 tablespoons roasted garlic–seasoned extra-virgin olive oil
- 2 teaspoons black pepper

Directions:

1. Trim abundance fat and silver skin from the pork slashes.
2. Place the pork slashes and brine in a 1-gallon sealable pack and refrigerate for in any event 12 hours or medium-term.
3. Remove the pork slashes from the brine and pat them dry with paper towels.
4. Brined pork hacks cook quicker than un-brined cleaves, so be mindful so as to screen internal temperatures.
5. Rest the pork slashes under a foil tent for 5 minutes before serving.

Nutrition: Calories: 211 kCal
Protein: 17 g Fat: 21 g

Florentine Ribeye Pork Loin

Preparation Time: 30 minutes
Cooking Time: 60 to 75 minutes
Servings: 6 to 8
Ingredients:

- 1 (3-pound) boneless ribeye pork loin roast
- 4 tablespoons extra-virgin olive oil, divided
- 2 tablespoons Pork Dry Rub or your favorite pork seasoning
- 4 bacon slices
- 6 cups fresh spinach
- 1 small red onion, diced
- 6 cloves garlic, cut into thin slivers
- ¾ cup shredded mozzarella cheese

Directions:

1. Trim away any abundance fat and silver skin.
2. Butterfly the pork loin or approach your butcher to butterfly it for you. There are numerous phenomenal recordings online with nitty gritty directions on the various systems for butterflying a loin roast.
3. Rub 2 tablespoons of the olive oil on each side of the butterflied roast and season the two sides with the rub.
4. Cook the bacon in a large griddle over medium heat. Disintegrate and set aside. Reserve the bacon fat.
5. Griddle the pork loin for 60 to 75 minutes, or until the internal temperature at the thickest part arrives at 140°F.

6. Rest the pork loin under a free foil tent for 15 minutes before cutting contrary to what would be expected.

Nutrition:

Calories: 365 kCal Protein: 32.1 g
Fat: 22 g

Naked St. Louis Ribs

Preparation Time: 30 minutes
Cooking Time: 5 to 6 hours **Servings:** 6 to 8

Ingredients:

- 3 St. Louis–style pork rib racks
- 1 cup in addition to 1 tablespoon Jan's Original Dry Rub or your preferred pork rub

Directions:

1. Remove the membrane on the underside of the rib racks by embedding a spoon handle between the membrane and rib bones. Get the membrane with a paper towel and gradually dismantle it down the rack to remove.
2. Rub the two sides of the ribs with a liberal measure of the rub.
3. Arrange the griddle for a non-direct cooking and preheat to 225°F.In the event of utilizing a rib rack, place the ribs in the rack on the griddle grates. Else you can utilize Teflon-covered fiberglass tangles or place the ribs directly on the griddle grates.
4. Smoke the ribs at 225°F for 5 to 6 hours until the internal temperature, at the thickest part of the ribs, arrives at 185°F to190°F.
5. Rest the ribs under a free foil tent for 10 minutes before cutting and serving.

Nutrition:

Calories: 241kCal
Protein: 23.6 g Fat: 13 g

Buttermilk Pork Sirloin Roast

Preparation Time: 20 minutes
Cooking Time: 3 to 3½ hours
Servings: 4 to 6

Ingredients:

- 1 (3 to 3½-pound) pork sirloin roast

Directions:

1. Trim all fat and silver skin from the pork roast.
2. Place the roast and buttermilk brine in a 1-gallon sealable plastic sack or brining holder.
3. Refrigerate medium-term, turning the roast like clockwork whenever the situation allows.
4. Remove the brined pork sirloin roast from the brine and pat dry with a paper towel.
5. Supplement a meat probe into the thickest part of the roast.
6. Design the griddle for a non-direct cooking and preheat to 225°F.
7. Smoke the roast until the internal temperature arrives at 145°F, 3 to 3½ hours.
8. Rest the roast under a free foil tent for 15 minutes, at that point cut contrary to what would be expected.

Nutrition:

Calories: 311 kCal Protein: 25 g
Fat: 18 g

Pierna Criolla

Preparation Time: 12 Hours
Cooking Time: 2.5 Hours
Servings: 18
Ingredients:

- 1 - 8 lbs. pork shoulder
- 8 slices bacon
- 1/2 lb. ham
- 1 bottle Malta
- 1 cup guava shells
- 1 cup Mojo (pg. 125)
- 1 cup prunes
- 4 Tbsp. Adobo Spices
- 2 cups brown sugar
- 2 Tbsp. sea salt

Directions:

1. Debone and flatten meat so that it may be rolled.
2. If the pork shoulder is very fatty, a small amount may be removed.
3. Score fat well and marinate for a minimum of 12 hours in the Mojo, and Adobo.
4. Sear both sides of roast on a very hot grate until dark brown and charred in spots.
5. Remove roast to cutting board, and line unrolled roast with ham slices, bacon slices, prunes and guava shells. Roll meat carefully to keep the filling inside. Tie firmly with a butcher cord.
6. Cover with brown sugar and 1/2 bottle of Malta.
7. Cook for one hour in the griddle at 325. At this point, turn the meat, cover with the remaining Malta and cook for an extra hour, or until you reach a meat temperature of 180.
8. Allow to cool at least 30 minutes and cut into fine slices. Pour the drippings over the meat after slicing the meat.
9. These ingredients can be found at most Hispanic grocery stores.

Nutrition:
Calories: 83
Carbs: 19g Fat: 0g Protein: 3g

Sweet & Spicy Pork Kabobs

Preparation Time: 24 Hours
Cooking Time: 10 minutes **Servings:** 6
Ingredients:

- 2lbs. boneless pork, 1-inch cubes
- ¾ C olive oil
- 1 Tbsp. Worcestershire sauce
- 1 tsp dried thyme
- 2 tsp black pepper
- ½ tsp cayenne
- ¾ C cider vinegar
- ¼ C sugar
- 4 Tbsp. lemon juice
- 1 Tbsp. oregano
- 2 cloves garlic, minced
- 1 tsp salt

Directions:

1. Mix together first 11 ingredients, place in sealable bag and refrigerate 24 hours: thread onto skewers.
2. Griddle on high heat, basting with reserved marinade, for 4-5 minutes; turn and griddle another 4-5 minutes.
3. Sprinkle with salt and serve.

Nutrition:
Calories: 160
Carbs: 2g Fat: 5g
Protein: 28g

Big Island Pork Kabobs

Preparation Time: 24 Hours
Cooking Time: 15 minutes **Servings:** 6
Ingredients:

- 3 lbs. Pork tenderloin
- 3 C margarita mix
- 3 clove garlic – minced
- 2 lg bell peppers
- 4 lbs. whole mushrooms
- ¼ C butter - softened
- 4 tsp lime juice
- 1 teaspoon sugar
- 3 Tbsp. minced parsley

Directions:

1. Cut pork into 1-inch cubes, place in a sealable plastic bag; pour marinade over to cover. Marinate overnight.
2. Blend together the butter, lime juice, Splenda, and parsley; set aside.
3. Thread pork cubes onto skewers, alternating with mushrooms and pepper, cut into eighths.
4. Griddle over high heat, basting with butter mixture, for 10-15 minutes, turning frequently.
5. If you're using bamboo skewers, soak them in water 20-30 minutes before using.

Nutrition:
Calories: 160 Carbs: 2g Fat: 5g
Protein: 28g

Asian Pork Sliders

Preparation Time: 24 Hours
Cooking Time: 15 minutes
Servings: 8
Ingredients:

- 2 lbs. ground pork
- 1 C diced green onion
- 2 tsp garlic powder
- 2 Tbsp. soy sauce
- 2 tsp brown sugar
- 1 C shredded lettuce
- 1 tsp cornstarch
- Honey-mustard dressing
- 16 sesame rolls, split

Directions:

1. Mix all ingredients (except soy sauce) and form 16 equal patties. Brush each patty with soy sauce, and griddle over high heat, turning once.
2. Serve with honey mustard and cucumber spears.
3. I like to chill the seasoned meat and then spread it on an oiled cutting board, using a rolling pin for an even 1/4-inch thickness.
4. Then, I just grab a biscuit cutter, and voila...perfectly round sliders!

Nutrition:
Calories: 280
Carbs: 31g
Fat: 9g
Protein: 26g

Luau Pork

Preparation Time: 12 Hours
Cooking Time: 12 Hours
Servings:50
Ingredients:

- 2 - boneless pork shoulders (6 lbs.)
- 2 C hot water
- 3 Qtrs. gal Hawaiian Mojo
- 2 Tbsp. seasoned salt
- ¼ C Stubbs liquid smoke
- 4 Tbsp. garlic powder

- ½ C Adobo Criollo spices

Directions:

1. Marinate pork in Hawaiian Mojo overnight. Remove from marinade, pat dry, and inject each shoulder with 6-8ozs of remaining marinade.
2. Score pork on all sides, rub with salt, then brush with liquid smoke, and sprinkle with garlic. Wrap entirely in banana leaves, tie with string.
3. Heat one side of your griddle to high, covered.
4. Once pre-heated, place the butts on the "cool" side of the griddle, roast 3 hours, and then remove banana leaves. Baste with mojo every 45 minutes throughout the rest of the cooking time. The shoulders should not be over any exposed flame.
5. Cover the griddle and vent slightly. Slow cook the shoulders for a total of 6 to 8 hours, until the meat is very tender, or you reach 195 F on the meat thermometer.
6. Chop the meat and then mix with a wash of 1/2 cup liquid smoke, 4 cups hot water, 1/4 cup Adobo Criollo spices, and 2 Tbsp. seasoned salt.
7. Let that sit about 15 minutes, drain remaining liquid, and serve with Sweet Hawaiian Pork Sauce

Nutrition:

Calories: 116

Carbs: 4g

Fat: 5g

Protein: 12g

Carolina Pork Ribs

Preparation Time: 12 Hours

Cooking Time: 3 Hours

Servings: 6

Ingredients:

- 2 racks of pork spareribs
- ½ C of "Burning' Love" Rub
- 1 C Carolina Basting Sauce
- 1 C Carolina BBQ Sauce

Directions:

1. **Prepa**re ribs by removing the membrane from the underside. Trim off any loose fat, and season ribs with rub, wrap in plastic wrap and refrigerate overnight.
2. Allow ribs to warm 1 hour. Preheat griddle to 280F.
3. If you want to sauce the ribs, do so 5 minutes before they're done, turning ever minute, and observe.

Nutrition:

Calories: 290

Carbs: 5g

Fat: 23g

Protein: 15g

Italian Pancetta Sandwiches

Preparation Time: 48 Hours

Cooking Time: 8 Hours

Servings: 24

Ingredients:

- 2 - 8lbs. pork shoulders, butterflied
- 6 Tbsp. fennel Seeds
- 24 cloves garlic, peeled
- Salt & pepper
- 12 Tbsp. fresh rosemary
- 2 C red wine
- 32 oz sliced pancetta

- 24 crusty Italian rolls
- 4 C caramelized onions
- 6 C Italian parsley

Directions:

1. Place the fennel, garlic, rosemary, salt, pepper, wine, and pancetta in a food processor and pulse until well mixed.
2. Spread the pancetta mixture evenly over the opened pork butt. Roll the pork up firmly, and tie with kitchen twine in four places to hold the pork together.
3. The pork is done when it reaches an internal temperature of 195 degrees.
4. If you don't have an instant read thermometer (you should really get one) the meat is done when it pulls apart quickly with a fork.
5. Heat the rolls. Place ¼ cup of meat on the warm roll and spoon over a little of the pan juices onto the sandwich.
6. Top meat with caramelized onions, the ¼ cup of fresh chopped parsley.

Nutrition:

Calories: 324
Carbs: 0g
Fat: 28g
Protein: 18g

Bourbon Pork Tenderloin

Preparation Time: 24 Hours
Cooking Time: 1 Hour
Servings: 10
Ingredients:

- 2 C white sugar
- ½ C Jim Beam® Bourbon
- 2 C water
- 2 tsp vanilla extract
- 3 to 4 lbs. pork tenderloin
- 2 tsp black pepper
- 2 tsp garlic powder
- 2 Tbsp. salt

Directions:

1. In medium bowl, combine sugar, Jim Beam® Bourbon, water, salt and vanilla. Mix well. Place tenderloin in a large zip bag and pour ½ of marinade over the top. Refrigerate 24 hours. Season tenderloin with garlic and pepper.
2. Heat your griddle for two-zone griddling and brush the rack with vegetable oil.
3. Remove to a cutting board and slice against the grain.

Nutrition:

Calories: 100
Carbs: 5g
Fat: 2g
Protein: 15g

Carolina Pulled Pork Sandwiches

Preparation Time: 24 Hours
Cooking Time: 12 Hour
Servings: 30
Ingredients:

- 1 boneless pork butt (5-6 pounds)
- 2 Tbsp. smoked paprika
- 2 Tbsp. hickory salt
- 1 Tbsp. black pepper
- 2 cups cider vinegar
- 1 cup Southern Comfort
- 1 cup water
- 2 Tbsp. molasses
- 2 Tbsp. salt

- ¼ cup hot sauce
- 1 Tbsp. red pepper flakes
- 1 Tbsp. black pepper
- 2 teaspoons ground cayenne

Directions:

1. In a bowl, combine paprika, hickory salt, 1 Tbsp. black pepper, and cayenne. Coat pork shoulder with seasonings and cover with plastic wrap. Refrigerate 24 hours.
2. Preheat griddle to medium heat. Place pork shoulder on griddle and smoke. Place a thermometer on the grate to track temperature. Combine remaining ingredients for baste.
3. Remove from heat and allow to rest 20 minutes (still in foil) and then unwrap and rest another 10 minutes. Shred pork, tossing with reserved pan juices.
4. Serve on soft white rolls, topped with your favorite coleslaw.

Nutrition:

Calories: 692 Carbs: 6g
Fat: 42g Protein: 70g

BBQ Sauce Pork Chops

Preparation Time: 4 Hours
Cooking Time: 15 minutes
Servings: 6
Ingredients:

- 6 boneless pork chops, thick
- 1 Tbsp. salt and sugar
- Pepper to taste
- 1 cup water
- 1 cup sweet barbecue sauce
- 1/4 cup cider vinegar

Directions:

1. Place chops in a baggie with 1 cup of water and sugar (boiled and cooled), and brine 4 hours.
2. Preheat your griddle for high heat.
3. In a small saucepan, combine barbecue sauce and vinegar. Bring to a simmer and allow to cook 20-30 minutes, uncovered, stirring often. Brush grate lightly with oil before placing pork chops on the griddle. Cook over high heat for 10 to 12 minutes, turning once. Brush with sauce just before removing chops from griddle. Serve with remaining sauce.

Nutrition:

Calories: 220 Carbs: 12g Fat: 9g Protein: 22g

Peach Mojo Pork Shoulder

Preparation Time: 1 Hours
Cooking Time: 6 hours **Servings:** 12
Ingredients:

- 1 - 6lbs. pork shoulder
- 1 qt Hawaiian Mojo
- ½ cup sea-salt
- 1 can peach slices, in syrup
- 2 Tbsp. garlic powder
- 2 Tbsp. red pepper flakes
- 15 oz sliced peaches in syrup
- 16 oz peach preserves
- 12oz apricot & pineapple preserves
- ½ cup Stubbs Mesquite Liquid Smoke

Directions:

1. Inject the pork with mojo and marinate overnight. Then, allow pork to come to room temp just before roasting. Smoke pork shoulder for 5-6 hours or until internal temperatures reach 185°F.

2. Slice the pork and pile in a pan, slather the top with a generous layer of peach-pineapple glaze and then place pans under a hot broiler for another 5-10 minutes to brown the glaze.
3. Serve with sweet Hawaiian rolls and white rice.

Nutrition: Calories: 210 Carbs: 18g Fat: 6g Protein: 23g

Sweet & Savory Bacon Wrapped Dates

Preparation Time: 30 minutes
Cooking Time: 30 minutes **Servings:** 16
Ingredients:

- 1 lb. thick-sliced bacon, cut in half
- 1 lb. pitted dates
- 4 ounces gorgonzola cheese
- 32 toothpicks

Directions:

1. Slice dates up one side and open them up. Pinch off a piece of cheese and place it into the center of the date. Close the halves of the dates and wrap a half-slice of bacon around the outside, secure with a toothpick. Lay a single sheet of foil over griddle grates and add the wraps in a single layer. Griddle until bacon starts to crisp, then flip each wrap over.
2. When the second side is crisped, remove to a platter lined with paper towels, allow to cool slightly before serving.

Nutrition: Calories: 248 Carbs: 33g Fat: 10g Protein: 10g

Jalapeño Pepper Bombs

Preparation Time: 10 minutes
Cooking Time: 15 minutes
Servings: 10
Ingredients:

- 10 fresh jalapenos
- 20 Cheddar Little Smokies
- 8oz. Cream Cheese
- 2 lbs. Bacon (½ strip each)
- 1/8 Sweet Onion (diced)
- 1 Tbsp. Sugar

Directions:

1. Soften cream cheese and blend in sugar and onions.
2. Slice Jalapenos in half, lengthwise, and trim away all seeds and membranes, rinse.
3. Spoon 1 teaspoon of cream cheese mixture into each side. Place 1 smokie on each half and press it into the cream cheese.
4. Add the bombs in a single layer. Griddle until bacon starts to crisp, moving to cool side of the griddle starts flaring up, and then remove to a platter lined with paper towels.
5. Allow to cool slightly and serve.

Nutrition:
Calories: 281
Carbs: 10g
Fat: 24g
Protein: 6g

CHAPTER 10
Beef Recipes

Basic Juicy NY Strip Steak

Servings 1 Preparation time: 45 minutes
Cooking Time: 8 minutes
Ingredients:

- (8 ounce) NY strip steak
- Olive oil - Sea salt
- Fresh ground black pepper

Directions:

1. Remove the steak from the refrigerator and let it come to room temperature, about 30 to 45 minutes.
2. Preheat griddle to medium-high heat and brush with olive oil.
3. Season the steak on all sides with salt and pepper.
4. Cook steak about 4 to 5 minutes.
5. Flip and cook about 4 minutes more for medium rare steak; between 125°F and 130°F on a meat thermometer.
6. Transfer the steak to a plate and let it rest for 5 minutes before serving.

Nutrition: Calories:1560, Sodium: 8468 mg, Dietary Fiber: 0.g, Fat: 86g, Carbs: 0.1g Protein: 184g

High-Low Strip Steak

Servings: 2 Preparation time: 8 - 12 hours
Cooking Time: 15 minutes
Ingredients:

- 2 (1-pound) New York strip steaks, trimmed
- For the rub:
- 1 bunch thyme sprigs
- 1 bunch rosemary sprigs
- 1 bunch sage sprigs
- 1 1/2 teaspoons black pepper, divided
- 3/4 teaspoon sea salt, divided
- 1/2 teaspoon garlic powder
- 2 tablespoons chopped fresh flat-leaf parsley
- 2 tablespoons extra-virgin olive oil

Directions:

1. Preheat griddle to high heat.
2. Combine rub ingredients in a small mixing bowl and rub steaks with spice mixture; let rest 10 minutes.
3. Place steaks on grill and cook 1 minute per side.
4. Turn griddle down to medium heat.
5. Turn steaks and grill 3 additional minutes per side; or until thermometer registers 135°F for medium rare.
6. Remove steaks to a platter.
7. Let rest 5 minutes. Cut steaks across grain into thin slices.

Nutrition: Calories: 347, Sodium: 831 mg, Dietary Fiber: 1.9g, Fat: 20.4g, Carbs:3.7g Protein: 38.7g

Teppanyaki Beef with Vegetables

Servings: 6
Preparation time: 10 minutes
Cooking Time: 15 minutes
Ingredients:
Steak:

- 2- 1 lb. sirloin steaks
- 1 tablespoon garlic powder
- 2 tablespoons soy sauce
- 1 white onion, sliced into large rounds
- 1 zucchini, sliced into 1/4 inch thick flats
- 2 cups snap peas

- 3 tablespoons vegetable oil
- 3 tablespoons butter
- Salt and black pepper

Directions:

1. Season the steak with salt, pepper, and garlic powder.
2. Set your griddle to high heat on one side and medium-high heat on the other side.
3. Add some vegetable oil to the medium-hot side and add the onion rings, zucchini, and snap peas. Season with a little salt and pepper.
4. Add the steaks to the hot side and cook for 3 minutes. Flip, top with butter and add soy sauce to the steaks. Continue cooking an additional 4 minutes.
5. Remove the steak and vegetables from the griddle and slice the steak across the grain before serving.

Nutrition: Calories: 484, Sodium: 755 mg, Dietary Fiber: 4.2g, Fat: 24.7g, Carbs: 13.8g Protein: 50.9g

Tuscan-Style Steak with Crispy Potatoes

Servings: 4
Preparation time: 30 minutes
Cooking Time: 35 minutes
Ingredients:

- 2 bone-in porterhouse steaks
- 1 1/2 lb. small potatoes, like Yukon Gold, scrubbed but skins left on, halved
- 3 tablespoons extra-virgin olive oil, divided
- Sea salt and freshly ground pepper, to taste
- 2 teaspoons red wine, like Sangiovese or Montepulciano
- 1 teaspoon balsamic vinegar
- pinch red pepper flakes
- 2 fresh rosemary sprigs, needles removed (discard stems)

Directions:

2. Add potatoes to a large pot and cover with water, bring to a boil over high heat, then reduce the heat to medium-high and cook until the potatoes are almost tender, about 10 minutes. Drain, add to a medium mixing bowl, coat with 2 tablespoons olive oil, and set aside. Preheat griddle to medium heat. Whisk 2 tablespoons olive oil, rosemary, red wine, vinegar, and pepper flakes; add steaks to marinade and set aside until ready to cook.
3. Sprinkle potatoes with salt and pepper.
4. Add steaks to one side of the griddle and potatoes to the other.
5. Cook steak for 5 minutes, flip and 4 minutes on the other side for medium rare.
6. Add the potatoes to cook for 5 minutes.
7. Transfer steaks to a cutting board and tent with aluminum foil and let rest for 5 minutes while potatoes are cooking.
8. Divide each steak into 2 pieces and divide among 4 dinner plates. Spoon some potatoes around the steak and serve hot!

Nutrition: Calories:366, Sodium: 153 mg, Dietary Fiber: 4.5g, Fat: 23.3g, Carbs: 27.3g Protein: 13.4g

Caprese Grilled Filet Mignon

Servings: 4
Preparation time: 10 minutes
Cooking Time: 10 minutes Ingredients:

- (6 ounce) filets
- 2 teaspoon garlic salt
- Italian Olive oil
- 2 roma tomatoes, sliced
- 2 ounces fresh buffalo mozzarella, cut into four slices
- 8 fresh basil leaves
- Balsamic vinegar glaze, for drizzling
- Sea salt, for seasoning
- Fresh ground pepper

Directions:

2. Lightly brush each filet, on all sides, with olive oil and rub with garlic salt. Preheat griddle to high. Place steaks on griddle, reduce heat to medium, tent with foil and cook for 5 minutes.
3. Flip, re-tent, and cook for an additional 5 minutes; during the last 2 minutes of grilling top each with a slice of mozzarella.
4. Remove steaks from the griddle and top each with a few tomato slices, 2 basil leafs. Drizzle with balsamic, sprinkle with sea salt and black pepper and serve.

Nutrition: Calories: 406, Sodium: 688 mg, Dietary Fiber: 0.8g, Fat: 21.8g, Carbs: 7.2g Protein: 45.1g

Rib-Eye Steak with Herbed Steak Butter

Servings: 2 - 4 Preparation time: 12 hours
Cooking Time: 50 minutes Ingredients:

- 1 (24-ounce) bone-in Tomahawk rib-eye, about 2 1/2 inches thick
- Olive oil - Sea salt
- Fresh cracked pepper
- 2 tablespoons premium French butter
- ½ teaspoon Herbes de Provence

Directions:

1. Beat butter with herbs in a small mixing bowl, cover and refrigerate until ready to grill rib-eye.
2. Rub the rib-eye liberally with olive oil, salt and pepper until entire steak is covered.
3. Wrap lightly with cling wrap and place in the refrigerator to marinate for 12 hours.
4. Preheat the griddle to high heat on one side and medium low on the other side, at least one hour prior to cooking.
5. Remove the steak from the refrigerator and leave at room temperature during the hour that the griddle is preheating.
6. Place the steak on the center of the hottest side of the griddle. Do this for both sides, about 10 minutes.
7. Move the rib-eye to the cooler side of the griddle and cook to rare, about 25 to 30 minutes.
8. Transfer rib-eye to a grill rack, add herbed butter on top, and lightly tent it with tin foil to rest for at least 15 minutes before carving.
9. Serve with your favorite sides!

Nutrition: Calories: 549 , Sodium: 607 mg, Dietary Fiber: 1.5g, Fat: 40.3g, Carbs: 3.5g Protein: 40.9g

Texas-Style Brisket

Servings: 6
Preparation time: 10 minutes
Cooking Time: 6 hours 20 minutes
Ingredients:

- 1 (4 1/2 lb) flat cut beef brisket (about 3 inches thick)
- For the rub:
- 1 tablespoon sea salt
- 1 tablespoon dark brown sugar
- 2 teaspoons smoked paprika
- 2 teaspoons chili powder
- 1 teaspoon garlic powder
- 1 teaspoon onion powder
- 1 teaspoon ground black pepper
- 1 teaspoon mesquite liquid smoke, like Colgin

Directions:

1. Combine the rub ingredients in a small mixing bowl.
2. Rinse and pat brisket dry and rub with coffee mix.
3. Preheat the griddle for two zone cooking; heat one side to high and leaving one side with low heat.
4. Sear on high heat side for 3 - 5 minutes on each side or until nicely charred.
5. Move to low heat side, tent with foil, and cook for 6 hours or until a meat thermometer registers 195°F.
6. Remove from griddle. Let stand, covered, 30 minutes.
7. Cut brisket across grain into thin slices and serve.

Nutrition: Calories:591, Sodium: 3953 mg, Dietary Fiber: 0.7g, Fat: 42.8g, Carbs: 3.2g Protein: 45.9g

Tender Steak with Pineapple Rice

Servings: 4
Preparation time: 10 minutes
Cooking Time: 10 minutes
Ingredients:

- (4-ounce) beef fillets
- ¼ cup soy sauce
- ½ teaspoon black pepper
- ½ teaspoon garlic powder
- (8-ounce) can pineapple chunks, in juice, drained
- 2 scallions, thin sliced
- 1 (8.8-ounce) packages pre-cooked brown rice, like Uncle Ben's
- 7/8 teaspoon kosher salt
- Olive oil, for brushing

Directions:

1. Combine soy sauce, pepper, garlic powder, and beef in a large sealable plastic bag.
2. Seal and massage sauce into beef; let stand at room temperature for 7 minutes, turning bag occasionally.
3. Preheat griddle to medium-high heat and brush with olive oil.
4. Add pineapple and green onions to grill and cook 5 minutes or until well charred, turning to char evenly.
5. Remove pineapple mix and brush with additional olive oil.
6. Add steaks and cook 3 minutes on each side, for rare, or until desired temperature is reached.
7. Cook rice according to package instructions.
8. Add rice, pineapple, onions, and salt to a bowl and stir gently to combine.

9. Plate steaks with pineapple rice and serve!

Nutrition: Calories: 369, Sodium: 1408 mg, Dietary Fiber: 2.1g, Fat: 12.4g, Carbs: 37g Protein: 27.9g

Caprese Flank Steak

Servings: 4
Preparation time: 10 minutes
Cooking Time: 10 minutes Ingredients:

- (6 ounce) flank steaks
- Sea salt, for seasoning
- Flakey sea salt, for serving
- Fresh ground pepper
- Olive oil
- 2 roma tomatoes, sliced
- ounces fresh buffalo mozzarella, cut into four slices
- 8 fresh basil leaves
- Balsamic vinegar glaze, for drizzling

Directions:

1. Lightly brush each filet, on all sides, with olive oil and season with salt and pepper.
2. Preheat griddle to high. Place steaks on griddle, reduce heat to medium, tent with foil and cook for 5 minutes.Flip, re-tent, and cook for an additional 5 minutes; during the last 2 minutes of cooking, top each with a slice of mozzarella.
3. Remove steaks from the griddle and top each with a few tomato slices, 2 basil leafs. Drizzle with balsamic glaze, and sprinkle with flakey salt and a little more black pepper.

Nutrition: Calories: 461, Sodium:485 mg, Dietary Fiber: 0.8g, Fat: 22.8g, Carbs: 5.7g Protein: 55.9g

Flank Steak with Garlic and Rosemary

Servings: 4
Preparation time: 10 minutes
Cooking Time: 20 minutes
Ingredients:

- 2 (8 ounce) flank steaks
- For the marinade:
- 1 tablespoon extra virgin olive oil, plus more for brushing
- 2 tablespoons fresh rosemary, chopped
- 2 cloves garlic, minced
- 2 teaspoons sea salt
- 1/4 teaspoon black pepper

Directions:

1. Add marinade ingredients to a food processor or blender and pulse until garlic and rosemary are pulverized.
2. Use a fork to pierce the steaks 10 times on each side.
3. Rub each evenly with the marinade on both sides.
4. Place in a covered dish and refrigerate for at least 1 hour or overnight.
5. Preheat griddle to high and brush with olive oil and preheat to high.
6. Cook steaks for 5 minutes, flip, tent with foil, and cook for about 3-4 minutes more.
7. Transfer meat to rest on a cutting board, cover with aluminum foil, for about 15 minutes.
8. Slice very thin against the grain and serve immediately.

Nutrition: Calories: 260, Sodium: 1001 mg, Dietary Fiber: 0.8g, Fat: 13.2g, Carbs:

Greek Flank Steak Gyros

Servings: 4
Preparation time: 5 minutes
Cooking Time: 20 minutes
Ingredients:

- 1 pound flank steak
- 1 white onion, thinly sliced
- 1 roma tomato, thinly sliced
- 1 cucumber, peeled and thinly sliced
- 1/4 cup crumbled feta cheese
- 6-inch pita pockets
- For the marinade:
- 1/4 cup olive oil, plus more for brushing
- 1 teaspoon dried oregano
- 1 teaspoon balsamic vinegar
- 1 teaspoon garlic powder
- Sea salt and freshly ground pepper, to taste
- For the sauce:
- 1 cup plain yogurt
- 2 tablespoons fresh dill (can use dried), chopped
- 1 teaspoon garlic, minced
- 2 tablespoons lemon juice

Directions:

1. Cut the flank steak into thin strips against the grain. Add the marinade ingredients to a large sealable plastic bag, add the sliced meat, seal, and turn to coat.
2. Place in the refrigerator to marinate for 2 hours or overnight.
3. Preheat the griddle to medium-high heat, and an oven to 250°F.
4. Combine the sauce ingredients in small mixing bowl and set aside.
5. Spritz the pitas with a little water, wrap in foil and place in the oven to warm.
6. Brush griddle with olive oil.
7. Add meat to grill and discard marinade. Cook until brown and cooked through, about 5 minutes.
8. Remove the pitas from the oven, and cut in half.
9. Arrange the pitas on plates and stuff with cucumber, tomato, onions, and beef. Spoon some yogurt sauce over the meat and top with feta and serve.

Nutrition: Calories:901, Sodium: 1221 mg, Dietary Fiber: 5.7g, Fat: 27.2g, Carbs:107.8g Protein: 53.5g

Flash-Marinated Skirt Steak

Servings: 4
Preparation time: 30 minutes
Cooking Time: 45 minutes
Ingredients:

- 2 (8 ounce) skirt steaks
- For the marinade:
- 2 tablespoons balsamic vinegar
- 2 teaspoons olive oil, more for brushing
- 2 garlic cloves, minced
- Sea salt, to taste
- Black pepper, to taste

Directions:

1. Combine marinade ingredients in a sealable plastic bag, add steaks, seal bag, turn to coat; let stand at room temperature for 30 minutes.
2. Preheat griddle to medium-high heat.

3. Remove steaks and discard marinade, place on griddle and cook about 3 minutes per side. Transfer steaks to cutting board and rest for 5 Minutes. Cut across the grain into slices and serve with your favorite sides.

Nutrition: Calories: 256, Sodium: 204 mg, Dietary Fiber: 0g, Fat: 13.8g, Carbs: 0.6g Protein: 30.3g

Coffee Crusted Skirt Steak

Servings: 8 Preparation time: 10 minutes
Cooking Time: 20 minutes
Ingredients:

- 1/4 cup coffee beans, finely ground
- 1/4 cup dark brown sugar, firmly packed - 1/2 teaspoon sea salt
- 1/8 teaspoon ground cinnamon
- Pinch cayenne pepper
- 1/2 lb. skirt steak, cut into 4 pieces
- 1 tablespoon olive oil

Directions:

1. Heat griddle to high.
2. Combine coffee, brown sugar, salt, cinnamon, and cayenne pepper in a bowl to make rub.
3. Remove steak from refrigerator and let come to room temperature, about 15 minutes. Rub steak with oil, and sprinkle with spice rub. Massage spice rub into meat. Sear until charred and medium-rare, 2 to 4 minutes per side. Transfer to a cutting board, cover with foil and let rest 5 minutes before thinly slicing against the grain.

Nutrition: Calories:324, Sodium: 461 mg, Dietary Fiber: 0.1g, Fat: 16g, Carbs: 4.6g Protein: 37.9g

Carne Asada

Servings: 4 Preparation time: 1 - 2 hours
Cooking Time: 15 minutes
Ingredients:

- 1 lb. hanger steak or shirt steak
- 1/4 cup olive oil
- 1 lime, juiced
- 1 orange, juiced
- 1 garlic clove, finely chopped
- 1/2 teaspoon cumin
- 1/4 teaspoon salt
- 1/4 teaspoon ground pepper
- handful of fresh cilantro, chopped

Directions:

1. Combine all of the ingredients in a large sealable plastic bag. Marinate in the refrigerator for 1 to 2 hours.
2. Preheat to medium/high heat, cook for 3 minutes on each side or until just cooked through.
3. Transfer to cutting board to rest for 10 minutes.
4. Slice against the grain and serve.

Nutrition: Calories: 363, Sodium: 200mg, Dietary Fiber: 1.7g, Fat: 18.4g, Carbs: 7.7g Protein: 41.6g

Mexican Steak Salad

Servings: 2 Preparation time: 10 minutes
Cooking Time: 10 minutes
Ingredients:
Steak marinade:

- 2 tablespoons olive oil
- 3 garlic cloves, minced
- 2 teaspoons chili powder
- 1 teaspoon ground cumin
- 1 teaspoon kosher salt
- 1 teaspoon freshly ground pepper

- 1 1/2 pounds skirt or flap steak, cut into 4-inch lengths
- ½ cup lager beer
- Salad:
- 12 ounces romaine hearts, trimmed and chopped
- 1 can black beans, drained and rinsed
- 1 pint cherry tomatoes, halved
- 1 large ripe avocado, pitted, peeled, and cut into chunks
- About 1/3 cup crumbled queso fresco
- Chopped fresh cilantro, for garnish
- Kosher salt
- Dressing:
- ½ cup plain whole milk yogurt
- 1/3 cup chopped fresh cilantro
- Zest of 1 lime
- Juice of 2 limes

Directions:

1. Make marinade, then marinate steak for 4 hours to overnight.
2. Combine salad ingredients in a large bowl; add dressing and mix well. Place salad on separate plates. Preheat griddle to high. Place marinated steak on griddle, reduce heat to medium, tent with foil and cook for 5 minutes.
3. Flip, re-tent, and cook for an additional 5 minutes.
4. Remove steak from the griddle and slice into 2 inch strips.
5. Place steak strips on individual salads, and sprinkle with flakey salt and a little black pepper. Garnish with cilantro.

Nutrition: Calories:1332, Sodium: 2011 mg, Dietary Fiber: 13.3g, Fat: 65.1g, Carbs:29.4g Protein: 152.3g

Easy Sirloin Steaks

Preparation Time: 10 minutes
Cooking Time: 15 minutes
Serve: 4
Ingredients:

- 4 top sirloin steaks
- 1 tbsp Montreal steak seasoning
- Pepper
- Salt

Directions:

1. Season steaks with Montreal steak seasoning, pepper, and salt.
2. Preheat the griddle to medium heat.
3. Spray griddle top with cooking spray.
4. Place steaks on a hot griddle top and cook for 3-5 minutes on each side or until the internal temperature reaches 145 F.
5. Serve and enjoy.

Nutrition:

- Calories 163 Fat 5.3 g
- Carbohydrates 0 g
- Sugar 0 g Protein 25.8 g
- Cholesterol 76 mg

Juicy Beef Burger Patties

Preparation Time: 10 minutes
Cooking Time: 12 minutes Serve: 6
Ingredients:

- 2 lbs ground beef
- 2 tbsp Worcestershire sauce
- 3/4 cup onion, chopped
- 1/2 tsp pepper
- 1/2 tsp salt

Directions:

1. Add all ingredients into the bowl and mix until well combined.
2. Preheat the griddle to high heat.

3. Spray griddle top with cooking spray.
4. Make patties from mixture and place on hot griddle top and cook for 5 minutes on each side.
5. Serve and enjoy.

Nutrition:

- Calories 292 Fat 9.4 g
- Carbohydrates 2.5 g
- Sugar 1.6 g
- Protein 46.1 g
- Cholesterol 135 mg

Beef Skewers

Preparation Time: 10 minutes
Cooking Time: 15 minutes
Serve: 4
Ingredients:

- 1 lb beef sirloin tips
- 1 zucchini, cut into chunks

For marinade:

- 1/4 cup olive oil
- 1 jalapeno pepper
- 1/2 tbsp lime juice
- 1 1/2 tbsp red wine vinegar
- 1 tsp dried oregano
- 2 garlic cloves
- 1 cup cilantro

Directions:

1. Add all marinade ingredients into the blender and blend until smooth.
2. Pour the blended mixture into the mixing bowl. Add beef tips and mix well and let it marinate for 30 minutes.
3. Thread marinated beef tips and zucchini chunks onto the skewers.
4. Preheat the griddle to high heat.
5. Spray griddle top with cooking spray.
6. Place skewers on a hot griddle top and cooks for 7-8 minutes or until beef tips are cooked.
7. Serve and enjoy.

Nutrition:

- Calories 179
- Fat 14.3 g
- Carbohydrates 3.3 g
- Sugar 1.2 g
- Protein 11.4 g
- Cholesterol 0 mg

Pineapple Beef Burger Patties

Preparation Time: 10 minutes
Cooking Time: 8 minutes Serve: 4
Ingredients:

- 1 1/4 lbs ground beef
- 2 pineapple slices, chopped
- 1/4 tsp pepper
- 1 garlic clove, minced
- 1 tsp ginger, grated
- 1/4 cup green onions, chopped
- 1/4 cup soy sauce
- Salt

Directions:

1. Add all ingredients into the bowl and mix until well combined.
2. Preheat the griddle to high heat.
3. Spray griddle top with cooking spray.
4. Make patties from mixture and place on hot griddle top and cook for 4 minutes on each side.
5. Serve and enjoy.

Nutrition: Calories 135 Fat 5.3 g Carbohydrates 13.1 g Sugar 8.6 g Protein 9.8 g Cholesterol 28 mg

Steak Sandwich

Preparation Time: 10 minutes
Cooking Time: 10 minutes
Serve: 2
Ingredients:

- 1/4 lb steaks, cooked & sliced
- 2 tbsp chimichurri sauce
- 1 tbsp butter
- 4 bread slices
- 4 cheese slices

Directions:

1. Spread butter on one side of each bread slice.
2. Take 2 bread slices and spread with chimichurri sauce and top with steak and cheese.
3. Cover with remaining bread slices.
4. Preheat the griddle to high heat.
5. Spray griddle top with cooking spray.
6. Place sandwich on hot griddle top and cook for 5 minutes or until golden brown from both sides.
7. Serve and enjoy.

Nutrition: Calories 617 Fat 46.8 g Carbohydrates 11.8 g Sugar 1.6 g Protein 36.4 g Cholesterol 125 mg

Roast Beef Sandwich

Preparation Time: 10 minutes
Cooking Time: 5 minutes
Serve: 1
Ingredients:

- 2 bread slices
- 2 cheese slices
- 4 deli roast beef, sliced
- 2 tsp butter
- 1 tbsp mayonnaise
- 1/4 cup caramelized onions, sliced

Directions:

1. Spread butter on one side of each bread slice.
2. Take 1 bread slice and spread with mayo top with beef, onion, and cheese.
3. Cover with remaining bread slice.
4. Preheat the griddle to high heat.
5. Spray griddle top with cooking spray.
6. Place sandwich on hot griddle top and cook for 5 minutes or until golden brown from both sides.
7. Serve and enjoy.

Nutrition:

- Calories 859 Fat 44.6 g
- Carbohydrates 25.4 g
- Sugar 5.5 g Protein 83.4 g
- Cholesterol 265 mg

Tomato Roast Beef Sandwich

Preparation Time: 10 minutes
Cooking Time: 10 minutes
Serve: 2
Ingredients:

- 4 bread slices
- 1/2 lb deli roast beef slices
- 2 tbsp mayonnaise
- 1 tbsp butter
- 1/2 onion, sliced
- 1 tomato, sliced
- 4 cheese slices

Directions:

1. Spread butter on one side of each bread slice.

2. Take 4 bread slices and spread with mayo and top with beef, cheese, tomatoes, and onion.
3. Cover with remaining bread slices.
4. Preheat the griddle to high heat.
5. Spray griddle top with cooking spray.
6. Place sandwich on hot griddle top and cook for 5 minutes or until golden brown from both sides.
7. Serve and enjoy.

Nutrition:

- Calories 617
- Fat 35.9 g
- Carbohydrates 17.1 g
- Sugar 4 g
- Protein 53.9 g
- Cholesterol 177 mg

Dijon Beef Burger Patties

Preparation Time: 10 minutes
Cooking Time: 10 minutes
Serve: 4
Ingredients:

- 1 lb ground beef
- 1/2 tsp pepper
- 3/4 tbsp Worcestershire sauce
- 1 tbsp Dijon mustard
- 1/8 tsp cayenne
- 1/8 tsp chili flakes
- 1 tbsp parsley, chopped
- 1/2 tsp kosher salt

Directions:

1. Add all ingredients into the bowl and mix until well combined.
2. Preheat the griddle to high heat.
3. Spray griddle top with cooking spray.
4. Make patties from mixture and place on hot griddle top and cook for 5 minutes on each side.
5. Serve and enjoy.

Nutrition:

- Calories 217
- Fat 7.3 g
- Carbohydrates 1 g
- Sugar 0.6 g
- Protein 34.6 g
- Cholesterol 101 mg

CHAPTER 11
Seafood Recipes

Salmon Fillets with Basil Butter & Broccolini

Servings: 2 Preparation time: 10 minutes Cooking Time: 12 minutes

Ingredients:

2 (6 ounce) salmon fillets, skin removed
2 tablespoons butter, unsalted
2 basil leaves, minced
1 garlic clove, minced
6 ounces broccolini
2 teaspoons olive oil - Sea salt, to taste

Directions:

1. Blend butter, basil, and garlic together until well-incorporated. Form into a ball and place in refrigerator until ready to serve.
2. Preheat griddle to medium-high heat.
3. Season both sides of the salmon fillets with salt and set aside.
4. Add broccolini, a pinch of salt, and olive oil to a bowl, toss to coat, and set aside.
5. Brush griddle with olive oil, and cook salmon, skin side down, for 12 minutes. Turn the salmon and cook for an additional 4 minutes. Remove from the griddle and allow to rest while the broccolini cooks.
6. Add the broccolini to the griddle, turning occasionally, until slightly charred, about 6 minutes.
7. Top each salmon fillet with a slice of basil butter and serve with a side of broccolini.

Nutrition: Calories: 398, Sodium: 303mg, Dietary Fiber: 2.2g, Fat: 26.7g, Carbs: 6.2g, Protein: 35.6g.

Spiced Snapper with Mango and Red Onion Salad

Servings: 4 Preparation time: 10 minutes Cooking Time: 20 minutes

Ingredients:

2 red snappers, cleaned
Sea salt
1/3 cup tandoori spice
Olive oil, plus more for griddle
Extra-virgin olive oil, for drizzling
Lime wedges, for serving
For the salsa:
1 ripe but firm mango, peeled and chopped
1 small red onion, thinly sliced
1 bunch cilantro, coarsely chopped
3 tablespoons fresh lime juice

Directions:

1. Toss mango, onion, cilantro, lime juice, and a big pinch of salt in a medium mixing bowl; drizzle with a bit of olive oil and toss again to coat.
2. Place snapper on a cutting board and pat dry with paper towels. Cut slashes crosswise on a diagonal along the body every 2" on both sides, with a sharp knife, cutting all the way down to the bones.
3. Season fish generously inside and out with salt. Coat fish with tandoori spice.
4. Preheat griddle medium-high heat and brush with oil.
5. Griddle fish for 10 minutes, undisturbed, until skin is puffed and charred.
6. Flip and griddle fish until the other side is lightly charred and skin is puffed, about 8 to 12 minutes.
7. Transfer to a platter. Top with mango salad and serve with lime wedges.

Nutrition: Calories: 211, Sodium: 170mg, Dietary Fiber: 2.5g, Fat: 5.4g, Carbs: 18.9g, Protein: 23.6g.

Honey-Lime Tilapia and Corn Foil Pack

Servings: 4 Preparation time: 10 minutes Cooking Time: 10 minutes

Ingredients:

4 fillets tilapia
2 tablespoons honey
4 limes, thinly sliced
2 ears corn, shucked
2 tablespoons fresh cilantro leaves
1/4 cup olive oil
Kosher salt
Freshly ground black pepper

Directions:

1.Preheat griddle to high.
2.Cut 4 squares of foil about 12" long.
3.Top each piece of foil with a piece of tilapia.
4.Brush tilapia with honey and top with lime, corn and cilantro.
5.Drizzle with olive oil and season with sea salt and pepper.
6.Cook until tilapia is cooked through and corn tender, about 15 minutes.

Nutrition: Calories: 319, Sodium: 92mg, Dietary Fiber: 4g, Fat: 14.7g, Carbs: 30.3g, Protein: 24g.

Halibut Fillets with Spinach and Olives

Servings: 4 Preparation time: 10 minutes Cooking Time: 10 minutes

Ingredients:

4 (6 ounce) halibut fillets
1/3 cup olive oil
4 cups baby spinach
1/4 cup lemon juice
2 ounces pitted black olives, halved
2 tablespoons flat leaf parsley, chopped
2 teaspoons fresh dill, chopped
Lemon wedges, to serve

Directions:

1.Preheat griddle to medium heat.
2.Toss spinach with lemon juice in a mixing bowl and set aside.
3.Brush fish with olive oil and cook for 3-4 minutes per side, or until cooked through.
4.Remove from heat, cover with foil and let rest for 5 minutes.
5.Add remaining oil and cook spinach for 2 minutes, or until just wilted. Remove from heat.
6.Toss with olives and herbs, then transfer to serving plates with fish, and serve with lemon wedges.

Nutrition: Calories: 773, Sodium: 1112mg, Dietary Fiber: 1.4g, Fat: 36.6g, Carbs: 2.9g, Protein: 109.3g.

Gremolata Swordfish Skewers

Servings: 4 Preparation time: 20 minutes Cooking Time: 10 minutes

Ingredients:

1-1/2 lb. skinless swordfish fillet
2 teaspoons lemon zest
3 tablespoons lemon juice
1/2 cup finely chopped parsley
2 teaspoons garlic, minced
3/4 teaspoon sea salt
1/4 teaspoon black pepper
2 tablespoons extra-virgin olive oil, plus extra for serving
1/2 teaspoon red pepper flakes
3 lemons, cut into slices

Directions:

1.Preheat griddle to medium-high.
2.Combine lemon zest, parsley, garlic, 1/4 teaspoon of the salt, and pepper in a small bowl with a fork to make gremolata and set aside.

3.Mix swordfish pieces with reserved lemon juice, olive oil, red pepper flakes, and remaining salt.
4.Thread swordfish and lemon slices, alternating each, onto the metal skewers.
5.Griddle skewers 8 to 10 minutes, flipping halfway through, or until fish is cooked through.
6.Place skewers on a serving platter and sprinkle with gremolata.
7.Drizzle with olive oil and serve.

Nutrition: Calories: 333, Sodium: 554mg, Dietary Fiber: 0.5g, Fat: 16g, Carbs: 1.6g, Protein: 43.7g.

Lobster Tails with Lime Basil Butter

Servings: 4 Preparation time: 5 minutes Cooking Time: 6 minutes

Ingredients:

4 lobster tails (cut in half lengthwise)
3 tablespoons olive oil
Lime wedges (to serve) - Sea salt, to taste
For the lime basil butter:
1 stick unsalted butter, softened
1/2 bunch basil, roughly chopped
1 lime, zested and juiced
2 cloves garlic, minced
1/4 teaspoon red pepper flakes

Directions:

1.Add the butter ingredients to a mixing bowl and combine; set aside until ready to use.
2.Preheat griddle to medium-high heat.
3.Drizzle the lobster tail halves with olive oil and season with salt and pepper.
4.Place the lobster tails, flesh-side down, on the griddle.
5.Allow to cook until opaque, about 3 minutes, flip and cook another 3 minutes.
6.Add a dollop of the lime basil butter during the last minute of cooking .Serve immediately.

Nutrition: Calories: 430, Sodium: 926mg, Dietary Fiber: 0.5g, Fat: 34.7g, Carbs: 2.4g, Protein: 28g.

Spiced Crab Legs

Servings: 4 Preparation time: 5 minutes Cooking Time: 5 minutes

Ingredients:

4 lbs king crab legs, cooked
2 tablespoons chili oil

Directions:

1.Preheat griddle to high.
2.Brush both sides of crab legs with chili oil and place on griddle. Tent with foil.
3.Cook 4 to 5 minutes, turning once.
4.Transfer to plates and serve with drawn butter.

Nutrition: Calories: 518, Sodium: 4857mg, Dietary Fiber: 0g, Fat: 13.9g, Carbs: 0g, Protein: 87.1g.

Lump Crab Cakes

Servings: 4 Preparation time: 10 minutes Cooking Time: 15 minutes

Ingredients:

1 lb lump crab meat
1/2 cup panko breadcrumbs
1/3 cup mayonnaise
1 egg, beaten
2 tablespoons Dijon mustard
2 teaspoons Worcestershire sauce
1/2 teaspoon paprika
1/2 teaspoon salt
1/4 teaspoon black pepper
3 tablespoons vegetable oil

Directions:

1.Preheat griddle to medium heat.

2.In a large bowl, combine the crab, breadcrumbs, mayo, egg, mustard Worcestershire sauce, paprika, salt and pepper. Mix well to combine.
3.Form the crab mixture into 4 large balls and flatten them slightly.
4.Add the oil to the griddle and cook the crab cakes for approximately 5 minutes per side or until browned and crispy. Serve immediately.

Nutrition: Calories: 282, Sodium: 1205mg, Dietary Fiber: 0.6g, Fat: 27.4g, Carbs: 9.5g, Protein: 18.8g.

Spicy Griddle Jumbo Shrimp

Servings: 6 Preparation time: 15 minutes
Cooking Time: 8 minutes

Ingredients:

1-1/2 pounds uncooked jumbo shrimp, peeled and deveined
For the marinade:
2 tablespoons fresh parsley
1 bay leaf, dried
1 teaspoon chili powder
1 teaspoon garlic powder
1/4 teaspoon cayenne pepper
1/4 cup olive oil
1/4 teaspoon salt
1/8 teaspoon pepper

Directions:

1.Add marinade ingredients to a food processor and process until smooth.
2.Transfer marinade to a large mixing bowl.
3.Fold in shrimp and toss to coat; refrigerate, covered, 30 minutes.
4.Thread shrimp onto metal skewers.
5.Preheat griddle to medium heat.
6.Cook 5-6 minutes, flipping once, until shrimp turn opaque pink.
7.Serve immediately.

Nutrition: Calories: 131, Sodium: 980mg, Dietary Fiber: 0.4g, Fat: 8.5g, Carbs: 1g, Protein: 13.7g.

Coconut Pineapple Shrimp Skewers

Servings: 4 Preparation time: 1 hour 20 minutes
Cooking Time: 5 minutes

Ingredients:

1-1/2 pounds uncooked jumbo shrimp, peeled and deveined
1/2 cup light coconut milk
1 tablespoon cilantro, chopped
4 teaspoons Tabasco Original Red Sauce
2 teaspoons soy sauce
1/4 cup freshly squeezed orange juice
1/4 cup freshly squeezed lime juice (from about 2 large limes)
3/4 pound pineapple, cut into 1 inch chunks
Olive oil, for griddleing

Directions:

1.Combine the coconut milk, cilantro, Tabasco sauce, soy sauce, orange juice, lime juice. Add the shrimp and toss to coat.
2.Cover and place in the refrigerator to marinate for 1 hour.
3.Thread shrimp and pineapple onto metal skewers, alternating each.
4.Preheat griddle to medium heat.
5.Cook 5-6 minutes, flipping once, until shrimp turn opaque pink.
6.Serve immediately.

Nutrition: Calories: 150, Sodium: 190mg, Dietary Fiber: 1.9g, Fat: 10.8g, Carbs: 14.9g, Protein: 1.5g.

Mexican Shrimp Tacos

Servings: 4 Preparation time: 10 minutes
Cooking Time: 10 minutes

Ingredients:

2 lbs. medium shrimp, peeled and deveined
8 flour tortillas, warmed
1 bag cabbage slaw
1 cup salsa

1 cup Mexican crema
For marinade:
2 tablespoons olive oil
1 tablespoon chili powder
1 tablespoon cumin
1 tablespoon garlic powder
1 tablespoon fresh lime juice
1/4 teaspoon sea salt
1/8 teaspoon fresh ground pepper

Directions:

1.Preheat a griddle to medium-high.
2.Combine oil marinade in a large sealable plastic bag. Add shrimp and toss coat; let marinate in the refrigerator for 30 minutes.
3.Cook shrimp for 3 minutes, on each side, until cooked through.
4.Transfer to a plate.
5.Lay two tortillas on each plate. Evenly divide the shrimp, cabbage slaw, salsa in the middle of each tortilla.
6.Drizzle with Mexican crema and serve.

Nutrition: Calories: 400, Sodium: 92mg, Dietary Fiber: 4g, Fat: 14.7g, Carbs: 30.3g, Protein: 24g.

Bacon Wrapped Scallops

Servings: 4 Preparation time: 15 minutes Cooking Time: 4 minutes

Ingredients:

12 large sea scallops, side muscle removed
8 slices of bacon
1 tablespoon vegetable oil
12 toothpicks

Directions:

1.Heat your griddle to medium heat and cook the bacon until fat has rendered but bacon is still flexible. Remove bacon from the griddle and place on paper towels.
2.Raise griddle heat to medium-high.
3.Wrap each scallop with a half slice of bacon and skewer with a toothpick to keep the bacon in place.
4.Place the scallops on the griddle and cook for 90 seconds per side. They should be lightly browned on both sides.
5.Remove from the griddle and serve immediately.

Nutrition: Calories: 315, Sodium: 1023mg, Dietary Fiber: 0g, Fat: 20g, Carbs: 2.7g, Protein: 29.2g.

Griddle Oysters with Spiced Tequila Butter

Servings: 6 Preparation time: 5 minutes Cooking Time: 25 minutes

Ingredients:

3 dozen medium oysters, scrubbed and shucked
Flakey sea salt, for serving
For the butter:
1/4 teaspoon crushed red pepper
7 tablespoons unsalted butter
1/4 teaspoon chili oil
1 teaspoon dried oregano
2 tablespoons freshly squeezed lemon juice
2 tablespoons Tequila Blanco, like Espolon

Directions:

1.Combine butter ingredients in a small mixing bowl until well-incorporated and set aside.
2.Preheat griddle to high.
3.Griddle the oysters about 1 to 2 minutes.
4.Sprinkle the oysters with salt flakes.
5.Warm the butter in a microwave for 30 seconds, and spoon the warm Tequila butter over the oysters and serve.

Nutrition: Calories: 184, Sodium: 300mg, Dietary Fiber: 0.2g, Fat: 15g, Carbs: 3.8g, Protein: 0.2g.

Pop-Open Clams with Horseradish-Tabasco Sauce

Servings: 4 Preparation time: 5 minutes Cooking Time: 10 minutes

Ingredients:

2 dozen littleneck clams, scrubbed
4 tablespoons unsalted butter, softened
2 tablespoons horseradish, drained
1 tablespoon hot sauce, like Tabasco
1/4 teaspoon lemon zest, finely grated
1 tablespoon fresh lemon juice
1/4 teaspoon smoked paprika
Sea salt

Directions:

1.Preheat the griddle to high.
2.Blend the butter with the horseradish, hot sauce, lemon zest, lemon juice, paprika, and pinch of salt.
3.Arrange the clams over high heat and griddle until they pop open, about 25 seconds.
4.Carefully turn the clams over using tongs, so the meat side is down.
5.Griddle for about 20 seconds longer, until the clam juices start to simmer.
6.Transfer the clams to a serving bowl.
7.Top each with about 1/2 teaspoon of the sauce and serve.

Nutrition: Calories: 191, Sodium: 382mg, Dietary Fiber: 0.3g, Fat: 12.7g, Carbs: 4g, Protein: 14.8g.

Spicy Griddle Squid

Servings: 4 Preparation time: 5 minutes Cooking Time: 5 minutes

Ingredients:

1-1/2 lbs. Squid, red - Olive oil
For the marinade:
2 cloves garlic cloves, minced
1/2 teaspoon ginger, minced
3 tablespoons gochujang
3 tablespoons corn syrup
1 teaspoon yellow mustard
1 teaspoon soy sauce
2 teaspoons sesame oil
1 teaspoon sesame seeds
2 green onions, chopped

Directions:

1.Preheat griddle to medium high heat and brush with olive oil. Add the squid and tentacles to the griddle and cook for 1 minute until the bottom looks firm and opaque..Turn them over and cook for another minute; straighten out the body with tongs if it curls.Baste with sauce on top of the squid and cook 2 additional minutes.
2.Flip and baste the other side, cook 1 minute until the sauce evaporates and the squid turns red and shiny.

Nutrition: Calories: 292, Sodium: 466mg, Dietary Fiber: 2.7g, Fat: 8.6g, Carbs: 25.1g, Protein: 27.8g.

Salmon Zucchini Patties

10 minutes **Cooking Time:** 10 minutes
Servings: 6

Ingredients:

- 2 eggs
- 1 1/2 lbs salmon, cooked
- 2 cups zucchini, shredded
- 2 tbsp onion, minced
- 1/4 cup fresh cilantro, chopped
- 1/4 cup olive oil
- 3/4 cup almond flour
- 3 tbsp fresh lime juice
- 2 tbsp jalapeno, minced
- 2 tsp salt

Directions:

1. Add salmon, lime juice, cilantro, zucchini, jalapenos, onion, eggs, and salt into the food processor

and process until the mixture is combined.

2. Add almond flour to a shallow dish. Preheat the griddle to high heat. Add oil to griddle.
3. Take 1/4 cup salmon mixture and form patties, coat patties with almond flour then place onto the hot griddle top and cook for 5 minutes per side.
4. Serve and enjoy.

Nutrition:

- Calories 330
- Fat 24 g
- Carbohydrates 5 g
- Sugar 1.5 g
- Protein 27.4 g
- Cholesterol 105 mg

Lemon Garlic Shrimp

Preparation Time: 10 minutes
Cooking Time: 15 minutes
Servings: 4
Ingredients:

- 1 1/2 lbs shrimp, peeled and deveined
- 1 tbsp garlic, minced
- 1/4 cup butter
- 1/4 cup fresh parsley, chopped
- 1/4 cup fresh lemon juice
- Pepper
- Salt

Directions:

1. Preheat the griddle to high heat.
2. Melt butter on the griddle top.
3. Add garlic and sauté for 30 seconds.
4. Add shrimp and season with pepper and salt and cook for 4-5 minutes or until it turns to pink.
5. Add lemon juice and parsley and stir well and cook for 2 minutes.
6. Serve and enjoy.

Nutrition:

- Calories 312 Fat 14.6 g
- Carbohydrates 3.9 g
- Sugar 0.4 g Protein 39.2 g
- Cholesterol 389 mg

Flavorful Mexican Shrimp

Preparation Time: 10 minutes
Cooking Time: 12 minutes **Servings:** 4
Ingredients:

- 1 lb shrimp, cleaned
- 3 tbsp fresh parsley, chopped
- 1 tbsp garlic, minced
- 1/4 onion, sliced
- 1/4 tsp paprika
- 1/4 tsp ground cumin
- 2 fresh lime juice
- 2 tbsp olive oil
- 1/4 cup butter
- Pepper - Salt

Directions:

1. Season shrimp with paprika, cumin, pepper, and salt.
2. Preheat the griddle to high heat.
3. Add oil and butter to the griddle top.
4. Add onion and garlic and sauté for 5 minutes.
5. Add shrimp and cook for 5-8 minutes or until cooked.
6. Add parsley and lime juice.
7. Stir well and serve.

Nutrition:

- Calories 311 Fat 20.5 g
- Carbohydrates 5 g Sugar 0.7 g
- Protein 26.4 g
- Cholesterol 269 mg

Pesto Shrimp

Preparation Time: 10 minutes
Cooking Time: 5 minutes **Servings:** 4
Ingredients:

- 1 lb shrimp, remove shells and tails
- 1/2 cup basil pesto
- Pepper
- Salt

Directions:

1. Add shrimp, pesto, pepper, and salt into the large bowl and toss well. Set aside for 15 minutes.
2. Heat griddle over medium-high heat.
3. Thread marinated shrimp onto the skewers and place onto the hot griddle top and cook for 1-2 minutes on each side.
4. Serve and enjoy.

Nutrition:

- Calories 270
- Fat 15 g
- Carbohydrates 3.7 g
- Sugar 2 g Protein 28.8 g
- Cholesterol 246 mg

Healthy Salmon Patties

Preparation Time: 10 minutes
Cooking Time: 10 minutes
Servings: 2
Ingredients:

- 6 oz can salmon, drained, remove bones, and pat dry
- 2 tbsp mayonnaise
- 1/2 cup almond flour
- 1/4 tsp thyme
- 1 egg, lightly beaten
- 2 tbsp olive oil
- Pepper - Salt

Directions:

1. Add salmon, thyme, egg, mayonnaise, almond flour, pepper, and salt into the mixing bowl and mix until well combined.
2. Preheat the griddle to high heat.
3. Add oil to the griddle top.
4. Make small patties from salmon mixture and place onto the hot griddle top and cook for 5-6 minutes.
5. Turn patties and cook for 3-4 minutes more. Serve and enjoy.

Nutrition:

- Calories 530 Fat 41 g
- Carbohydrates 9.8 g Sugar 1.1 g
- Protein 30.6 g Cholesterol 146 mg

Blackened Salmon

Preparation Time: 10 minutes
Cooking Time: 10 minutes **Servings:** 5
Ingredients:

- 1 1/4 lbs salmon fillets
- 2 tbsp blackened seasoning
- 2 tbsp butter

Directions:

1. Season salmon fillets with blackened seasoning.
2. Preheat the griddle to high heat.
3. Melt butter on the griddle top.
4. Place salmon fillets onto the hot griddle top and cook for 4-5 minutes.
5. Turn salmon and cook for 4-5 minutes more. Serve and enjoy.

Nutrition:

- Calories 190 Fat 11 g
- Carbohydrates 0 g Sugar 0 g
- Protein 21.1 g Cholesterol 62 mg

Blackened Tilapia

Preparation Time: 10 minutes
Cooking Time: 6 minutes **Servings:** 4
Ingredients:

- 4 tilapia fillets
- 2 tbsp butter
- 1 tbsp olive oil
- For seasoning:
- 1 1/2 tsp paprika
- 1 lemon, sliced
- 1/2 tsp ground cumin
- 1 tsp oregano
- 1/2 tsp garlic powder
- Pepper
- Salt

Directions:

1. In a small bowl, mix together all seasoning ingredients and rub over fish fillets.
2. Preheat the griddle to high heat.
3. Add butter and oil on the hot griddle top.
4. Place fish fillets onto the griddle top and cook for 3 minutes.
5. Turn fish fillets and cook for 3 minutes more or until cooked through. Serve and enjoy.

Nutrition:

- Calories 181 Fat 10.5 g
- Carbohydrates 1.2 g
- Sugar 0.2 g Protein 21.4 g
- Cholesterol 70 mg

Italian Shrimp

Preparation Time: 10 minutes
Cooking Time: 5 minutes **Servings:** 4
Ingredients:

- 1 lb shrimp, deveined
- 1 tsp Italian seasoning
- 1 tsp paprika
- 1 1/2 tsp garlic, minced
- 1 stick butter
- 1 fresh lemon juice
- 1/4 tsp pepper
- 1/2 tsp salt

Directions:

1. Preheat the griddle to high heat.
2. Melt butter on the hot griddle top.
3. Add garlic and cook for 30 seconds.
4. Toss shrimp with paprika, Italian seasoning, pepper, and salt.
5. Add shrimp into the pan and cook for 2-3 minutes per side.
6. Drizzle lemon juice over shrimp.
7. Stir and serve.

Nutrition:

- Calories 346
- Fat 25 g
- Carbohydrates 2.6 g
- Sugar 0.2 g
- Protein 26.2 g
- Cholesterol 300 mg

Shrimp Veggie Stir Fry

Preparation Time: 10 minutes
Cooking Time: 10 minutes
Servings: 2
Ingredients:

- 1/2 lb shrimp, peeled and deveined
- 1 tbsp garlic, minced
- 1/3 cup olives
- 1 cup mushrooms, sliced
- 2 tbsp olive oil
- 1 cup tomatoes, diced
- 1 small onion, chopped

- Pepper
- Salt

Directions:

1. Preheat the griddle to high heat. Add oil.
2. Add onion, mushrooms, and garlic and sauté until onion soften.
3. Add shrimp and tomatoes and stir until shrimp is cooked through.
4. Add olives and stir well.
5. Remove pan from heat and set aside for 5 minutes. Season with pepper and salt.
6. Serve and enjoy.

Nutrition:

- Calories 325
- Fat 18.7 g
- Carbohydrates 12.5 g
- Sugar 4.5 g
- Protein 28.6 g
- Cholesterol 239 mg

Lemon Garlic Scallops

Preparation Time: 10 minutes
Cooking Time: 5 minutes
Servings: 2
Ingredients:

- 1 lb frozen bay scallops, thawed, rinsed & pat dry
- 1 tsp garlic, minced
- 2 tbsp olive oil
- 1 tsp parsley, chopped
- 1 tsp lemon juice
- Pepper
- Salt

Directions:

1. Preheat the griddle to high heat.
2. Add oil to the griddle top.
3. Add garlic and sauté for 30 seconds.
4. Add scallops, lemon juice, pepper, and salt, and sauté until scallops turn opaque.
5. Garnish with parsley and serve.

Nutrition:

- Calories 123
- Fat 14 g
- Carbohydrates 0.6 g
- Sugar 0.1 g
- Protein 0.1 g
- Cholesterol 0 mg

Tasty Shrimp Skewers

Preparation Time: 10 minutes
Cooking Time: 7 minutes
Servings: 6
Ingredients:

- 1 1/2 lbs shrimp, peeled and deveined
- 1 tbsp dried oregano
- 2 tsp garlic paste
- 2 lemon juice
- 1/4 cup olive oil
- 1 tsp paprika
- Pepper
- Salt

Directions:

1. Add all ingredients into the mixing bowl and mix well and place in the refrigerator for 1 hour.
2. Remove marinated shrimp from refrigerator and thread onto the skewers.
3. Preheat the griddle to high heat.
4. Place skewers onto the griddle top and cook for 5-7 minutes.

5. Serve and enjoy.

Nutrition:

- Calories 212
- Fat 10.5 g
- Carbohydrates 2.7 g
- Sugar 0.1 g
- Protein 26 g
- Cholesterol 239 mg

Balsamic Salmon

Preparation Time: 10 minutes
Cooking Time: 10 minutes
Servings: 6
Ingredients:

- 6 salmon fillets
- 5 tbsp balsamic vinaigrette
- 2 tbsp olive oil
- 1 1/2 tsp garlic powder
- Pepper
- Salt

Directions:

1. In a mixing bowl, add salmon, garlic powder, balsamic vinaigrette, pepper, and salt and mix well. Set aside.
2. Preheat the griddle to high heat.
3. Add oil to the hot griddle top.
4. Place salmon onto the griddle top and cook for 3-5 minutes on each side or until cooked through.
5. Serve and enjoy.

Nutrition:

- Calories 328
- Fat 20.7 g
- Carbohydrates 1.4 g
- Sugar 1 g
- Protein 34.7 g
- Cholesterol 78 mg

Paprika Garlic Shrimp

Preparation Time: 10 minutes
Cooking Time: 5 minutes
Servings: 4
Ingredients:

- 1 lb shrimp, peeled and cleaned
- 5 garlic cloves, chopped
- 2 tbsp olive oil
- 1 tbsp fresh parsley, chopped
- 1 tsp paprika
- 2 tbsp butter
- 1/2 tsp sea salt

Directions:

1. Add shrimp, 1 tbsp oil, garlic, and salt in a large bowl and toss well and place in the refrigerator for 1 hour.
2. Preheat the griddle to high heat.
3. Add remaining oil and butter on the hot griddle top.
4. Once butter is melted then add marinated shrimp and paprika and stir constantly for 2-3 minutes or until shrimp is cooked.
5. Garnish with parsley and serve.

Nutrition:

- Calories 253 Fat 15 g
- Carbohydrates 3.3 g
- Sugar 0.1 g
- Protein 26.2 g
- Cholesterol 254 mg

Spicy Lemon Butter Shrimp

Preparation Time: 10 minutes
Cooking Time: 10 minutes
Servings: 4
Ingredients:

- 1 1/2 lbs shrimp, peeled and deveined

- 3 garlic cloves, minced
- 1 small onion, minced
- 1/2 cup butter
- 1 1/2 tbsp fresh parsley, chopped
- 1 tbsp fresh lemon juice
- 1/4 tsp red pepper flakes
- Pepper
- Salt

Directions:

1. Preheat the griddle to high heat.
2. Melt butter on the griddle top.
3. Add garlic, onion, red chili flakes, pepper, and salt and stir for 2 minutes.
4. Season shrimp with pepper and salt and thread onto skewers.
5. Brush shrimp skewers with butter mixture.
6. Place shrimp skewers on griddle top and cook until shrimp turns to pink, about 3-4 minutes.
7. Transfer shrimp to the serving plate.
8. Drizzle lemon juice over shrimp and garnish with parsley.
9. Serve and enjoy.

Nutrition:

- Calories 419 Fat 25 g
- Carbohydrates 5.2 g
- Sugar 0.9 g Protein 39.4 g
- Cholesterol 419 mg

Greek Salmon

Preparation Time: 10 minutes
Cooking Time: 6 minutes **Servings:** 2
Ingredients:

- 12 oz salmon, cut into two pieces
- 1 tsp Greek seasoning
- 1 tbsp olive oil
- 1/2 tsp lemon zest
- 1 garlic clove, minced
- Pepper - Salt

Directions:

1. In a large bowl, mix olive oil, lemon zest, garlic, pepper, salt, and greek seasoning.
2. Add salmon in a bowl and coat well with marinade and set aside for 15 minutes.
3. Preheat the griddle to high heat.
4. Place marinated salmon on hot griddle top and cook for 2-3 minutes. Turn salmon to the other side and cook for 2-3 minutes more.
5. Serve and enjoy.

Nutrition:

- Calories 290 - Fat 17.6 g
- Carbohydrates 1.4 g
- Sugar 0.1 g - Protein 33.2 g
- Cholesterol 75 mg

Garlic Butter Tilapia

Preparation Time: 10 minutes
Cooking Time: 8 minutes
Servings: 6
Ingredients:

- 2 lbs tilapia fillets
- 1 tsp garlic powder
- 1/2 fresh lemon juice
- 1 tbsp butter, melted
- Pepper - Salt

Directions:

1. In a small bowl, combine together lemon juice, garlic powder, and butter and microwave for 10 seconds.

2. Brush both the side of the fish fillet with lemon mixture. Season fillet with pepper and salt.
3. Preheat the griddle to high heat.
4. Spray griddle top with cooking spray.
5. Place fillets on hot griddle top and cook for 4 minutes on each side.
6. Serve and enjoy.

Nutrition:

- Calories 143
- Fat 3 g
- Carbohydrates 0.4 g
- Sugar 0.1 g
- Protein 28.2 g
- Cholesterol 79 mg

Caper Basil Halibut

Preparation Time: 10 minutes
Cooking Time: 8 minutes
Servings: 4
Ingredients:

- 24 oz halibut fillets
- 2 garlic cloves, crushed
- 2 tbsp olive oil
- 2 tsp capers, drained
- 3 tbsp fresh basil, sliced
- 2 1/2 tbsp fresh lemon juice

Directions:

1. In a small bowl, whisk together garlic, olive oil, and lemon juice. Stir in 2 tbsp basil.
2. Season garlic mixture with pepper and salt.
3. Season fish fillets with pepper and salt and brush with garlic mixture.
4. Preheat the griddle to high heat.
5. Place fish fillets on hot griddle and cook for 4 minutes on each side.
6. Transfer fish fillets on serving plate and top with remaining garlic mixture and basil.
7. Serve and enjoy.

Nutrition:

- Calories 250
- Fat 10.5 g
- Carbohydrates 0.8 g
- Sugar 0.2 g
- Protein 39.1 g
- Cholesterol 59 mg

Greek Salmon Fillets

Preparation Time: 10 minutes
Cooking Time: 6 minutes **Servings:** 2
Ingredients:

- 2 salmon fillets
- 1 tbsp fresh basil, minced
- 1 tbsp butter, melted
- 1 tbsp fresh lemon juice
- 1/8 tsp salt

Directions:

1. Preheat the griddle to high heat.
2. In a small bowl, mix together lemon juice, basil, butter, and salt.
3. Brush salmon fillets with lemon mixture and place them on the hot griddle top.
4. Cook salmon for 2-3 minutes. Flip salmon and cook for 2-3 minutes more. Serve and enjoy.

Nutrition:

- Calories 290 Fat 16.8 g
- Carbohydrates 0.3 g
- Sugar 0.2 g Protein 34.7 g
- Cholesterol 46 mg

Salmon Skewers

Preparation Time: 10 minutes
Cooking Time: 10 minutes
Servings: 4
Ingredients:

- 1 lb salmon fillets, cut into 1-inch cubes
- 2 tbsp soy sauce
- 1 tbsp toasted sesame seeds
- 1 lime zest
- 2 tsp olive oil
- 1 1/2 tbsp maple syrup
- 1 tsp ginger, crushed
- 1 lime juice

Directions:

1. In a bowl, mix together olive oil, soy sauce, lime zest, lime juice, maple syrup, and ginger.
2. Add salmon and stir to coat. Set aside for 10 minutes.
3. Preheat the griddle to high heat.
4. Slide marinated salmon pieces onto the skewers and cook on a hot griddle top for 8-10 minutes or until cooked through.
5. Sprinkle salmon skewers with sesame seeds and serve.

Nutrition:

- Calories 209
- Fat 10 g
- Carbohydrates 6.5 g
- Sugar 4.6 g
- Protein 22.9 g
- Cholesterol 50 mg

Parmesan Shrimp

Preparation Time: 10 minutes
Cooking Time: 6 minutes **Servings:** 4
Ingredients:

- 1 lb shrimp, peeled and deveined
- 2 tbsp parmesan cheese, grated
- 1 tbsp fresh lemon juice
- 1 tbsp pine nuts, toasted
- 1 garlic clove
- 1/2 cup basil
- 1 tbsp olive oil
- Pepper
- Salt

Directions:

1. Add basil, lemon juice, cheese, pine nuts, garlic, pepper, and salt in a blender and blend until smooth.
2. Add shrimp and basil paste in a bowl and mix well.
3. Place shrimp bowl in the fridge for 20 minutes.
4. Preheat the griddle to high heat.
5. Spray griddle top with cooking spray.
6. Thread marinated shrimp onto skewers and place skewers on the hot griddle top.
7. Cook shrimp for 3 minutes on each side or until cooked.
8. Serve and enjoy.

Nutrition:

- Calories 225
- Fat 11.2 g
- Carbohydrates 2.2 g
- Sugar 0.2 g
- Protein 27.2 g
- Cholesterol 241 mg

Roasted Yellowtail

Preparation Time: 10 minutes
Cooking Time: 30 minutes
Servings: 4
Ingredients:

- 4 Yellowtail Filets (6 oz.)

- 1 lb. new Potatoes -2 tbsp. Olive oil
- 1 lb. Mushrooms, oyster
- 1 tsp. ground Black pepper
- 4 tbsp. of olive oil

Salsa Verde:

- 1 tbsp. Cilantro, chopped
- 2 tbsp. Mint, chopped
- ½ cup Parsley, chopped
- 2 cloves of garlic, minced
- 1 tbsp. Oregano, chopped
- 1 Lemon, the juice
- 1 cup of Olive oil
- 1/8 tsp. Pepper Flake
- Salt

Directions:

1. Preheat the griddle to high with closed lid.
2. Place an iron pan directly on the griddle. Let it heat for 10 minutes.
3. Rub the fish with oil. Season with black pepper and salt.
4. In a 2 different bowls place the mushrooms and potatoes, drizzle with oil and season with black pepper and salt. Toss. Place the potatoes in the pan. Cook 10 minutes. Add the mushrooms.
5. Place the fillets on the grate with the skin down. Cook for 6 minutes and flip. Cook for 4 minutes more.
6. While the potatoes, mushrooms, and fish are cooking make the Salsa Verde. In a bowl combine all the ingredients and stir to combine.
7. Place the mushrooms and potatoes on a plate, top with a fillet and drizzle with the Salsa Verde. Serve and Enjoy!

Nutrition: Calories: 398 Protein: 52g Carbs: 20g Fat: 18gg

Baked Steelhead

Preparation Time: 15 minutes
Cooking Time: 20 minutes
Servings: 4 - 6
Ingredients:

- 1 Lemon
- 2 Garlic cloves, minced
- ½ Shallot, minced
- 3 tbsp. Butter, unsalted
- Saskatchewan seasoning, blackened
- Italian Dressing
- 1 Steelhead, (a fillet)

Directions:

1. Preheat the griddle to 350F with closed lid.
2. In an iron pan place the butter. Place the pan in the griddle while preheating so that the butter melts. Coat the fillet with Italian dressing. Rub with Saskatchewan rub. Make sure the layer is thin.
3. Mince the garlic and shallot. Remove the pan from the griddle and add the garlic and shallots.
4. Spread the mixture on the fillet. Slice the lemon into slices. Place the slice on the butter mix.
5. Place the fish on the grate. Cook 20 - 30 minutes.
6. Remove from the griddle and serve. Enjoy!

Nutrition: Calories: 230 Protein: 28g Carbs 2g: Fat: 14g

Wine Brined Salmon

Preparation Time: 15 minutes
Cooking Time: 5 hours
Servings: 4
Ingredients:

- 2 cups low-sodium soy sauce
- 1 cup dry white wine

- 1 cup water
- ½ teaspoon Tabasco sauce
- 1/3 cup sugar
- ¼ cup salt
- ½ teaspoon garlic powder
- ½ teaspoon onion powder
- Ground black pepper, as required
- 4 (6-ounce) salmon fillets

Directions:

1. In a large bowl, add all ingredients except salmon and stir until sugar is dissolved.
2. Add salmon fillets and coat with brine well.
3. Refrigerate, covered overnight.
4. Remove salmon from bowl and rinse under cold running water.
5. With paper towels, pat dry the salmon fillets.
6. Arrange a wire rack in a sheet pan.
7. Place the salmon fillets onto wire rack, skin side down and set aside to cool for about 1 hour.
8. Preheat the Griddle to 165 degrees F.
9. Arrange the salmon fillets onto the griddle, skin side down and cook for about 3-5 hours or until desired doneness.
10. Remove the salmon fillets from griddle and serve hot.

Nutrition:

Calories 379 Total Fat 10.5 g
Saturated Fat 1.5 g
Cholesterol 75 mg
Sodium 14000 mg
Total Carbs 26.8 g Fiber 0.1 g
Sugar 25.3 g Protein 41.1 g

Citrus Salmon

Preparation Time: 15 minutes
Cooking Time: 30 minutes
Servings: 6
Ingredients:

- 2 (1-pound) salmon fillets
- Salt and ground black pepper, as required
- 1 tablespoon seafood seasoning
- 2 lemons, sliced
- 2 limes, sliced

Directions:

1. Preheat the griddle to 225 degrees F.
2. Season the salmon fillets with salt, black pepper and seafood seasoning evenly.
3. Place the salmon fillets onto the griddle and top each with lemon and lime slices evenly.
4. Cook for about 30 minutes.
5. Remove the salmon fillets from griddle and serve hot.

Nutrition:

Calories 327
Total Fat 19.8 g
Saturated Fat 3.6 g
Cholesterol 81 mg
Sodium 237 mg
Total Carbs 1 g
Fiber 0.3 g
Sugar 0.2 g
Protein 36.1 g

Simple Mahi-Mahi

Preparation Time: 10 minutes
Cooking Time: 10 minutes
Servings: 4
Ingredients:

- 4 (6-ounce) mahi-mahi fillets
- 2 tablespoons olive oil

- Salt and ground black pepper, as required

Directions:

1. Preheat the griddle to 350 degrees F.
2. Coat fish fillets with olive oil and season with salt and black pepper evenly.
3. Place the fish fillets onto the griddle and cook for about 5 minutes per side.
4. Remove the fish fillets from griddle and serve hot.

Nutrition:

Calories 195
Total Fat 7 g
Saturated Fat 1 g
Cholesterol 60 mg
Sodium 182 mg
Total Carbs 0 g
Fiber 0 g
Sugar 0 g
Protein 31.6g

Rosemary Trout

Preparation Time: 10 minutes
Cooking Time: 5 hours
Servings: 8
Ingredients:

- 1 (7-pound) whole lake trout, butterflied
- ½ cup kosher salt
- ½ cup fresh rosemary, chopped
- 2 teaspoons lemon zest, grated finely

Directions:

1. Rub the trout with salt generously and then, sprinkle with rosemary and lemon zest.
2. Arrange the trout in a large baking dish and refrigerate for about 7-8 hours.
3. Remove the trout from baking dish and rinse under cold running water to remove the salt.
4. With paper towels, pat dry the trout completely.
5. Arrange a wire rack in a sheet pan.
6. Place the trout onto the wire rack, skin side down and refrigerate for about 24 hours.
7. Preheat the griddle to 180 degrees F, using charcoal.
8. Place the trout onto the griddle and cook for about 2-4 hours or until desired doneness.
9. Remove the trout from griddle and place onto a cutting board for about 5 minutes before serving.

Nutrition:

Calories 633
Total Fat 31.8 g
Saturated Fat 7.9 g
Cholesterol 153 mg
Sodium 5000 mg
Total Carbs 2.4 g
Fiber 1.6 g
Sugar 0 g
Protein 85.2 g

Sesame Seeds Flounder

Preparation Time: 15 minutes
Cooking Time: 2½ hours
Servings: 4
Ingredients:

- ½ cup sesame seeds, toasted
- ½ teaspoon kosher salt flakes
- 1 tablespoon canola oil

- 1 teaspoon sesame oil
- 4 (6-ounce) flounder fillets

Directions:

1. Preheat the griddle to 225 degrees F.
2. With a mortar and pestle, crush sesame seeds with kosher salt slightly.
3. In a small bowl, mix together both oils.
4. Coat fish fillets with oil mixture generously and then, rub with sesame seeds mixture.
5. Place fish fillets onto the lower rack of griddle and cook for about 2-2½ hours.
6. Remove the fish fillets from griddle and serve hot.

Nutrition:

Calories 343
Total Fat 16.2 g
Saturated Fat 2.3 g
Cholesterol 116 mg
Sodium 476 mg
Total Carbs 4.2 g
Fiber 2.1 g Sugar 0.1 g
Protein 44.3 g

Parsley Prawn Skewers

Preparation Time: 15 minutes
Cooking Time: 8 minutes
Servings: 5
Ingredients:

- ¼ cup fresh parsley leaves, minced
- 1 tablespoon garlic, crushed
- 2½ tablespoons olive oil
- 2 tablespoons Thai chili sauce
- 1 tablespoon fresh lime juice
- 1½ pounds prawns, peeled and deveined

Directions:

1. In a large bowl, add all ingredients except for prawns and mix well.
2. In a resealable plastic bag, add marinade and prawns.
3. Seal the bag and shake to coat well
4. Refrigerate for about 20-30 minutes.
5. Preheat the griddle to 450 degrees F.
6. Remove the prawns from marinade and thread onto metal skewers.
7. Arrange the skewers onto the griddle and cook for about 4 minutes per side.
8. Remove the skewers from griddle and serve hot.

Nutrition:

Calories 234
Total Fat 9.3 g
Saturated Fat 1.7 g
Cholesterol 287 mg
Sodium 562 mg
Total Carbs 4.9 g
Fiber 0.1 g
Sugar 1.7 g
Protein 31.2 g

Buttered Shrimp

Preparation Time: 15 minutes
Cooking Time: 30 minutes
Servings: 6
Ingredients:

- 8 ounces salted butter, melted
- ¼ cup Worcestershire sauce
- ¼ cup fresh parsley, chopped
- 1 lemon, quartered

- 2 pounds jumbo shrimp, peeled and deveined
- 3 tablespoons BBQ rub

Directions:

1. In a metal baking pan, add all ingredients except for shrimp and BBQ rub and mix well.
2. Season the shrimp with BBQ rub evenly.
3. Add shrimp in the pan with butter mixture and coat well.
4. Set aside for about 20-30 minutes.
5. Preheat the griddle to 250 degrees F.
6. Place the pan onto the griddle and cook for about 25-30 minutes.
7. Remove the pan from griddle and serve hot.

Nutrition:
Calories 462
Total Fat 33.3 g
Saturated Fat 20.2 g
Cholesterol 400 mg
Sodium 485 mg
Total Carbs 4.7 g Fiber 0.2 g
Sugar 2.1 g Protein 34.9 g

Prosciutto Wrapped Scallops

Preparation Time: 15 minutes
Cooking Time: 40 minutes **Servings:** 4
Ingredients:

- 8 large scallops, shelled and cleaned
- 8 extra-thin prosciutto slices

Directions:

1. Preheat the griddle to 225-250 degrees F.
2. Arrange the prosciutto slices onto a smooth surface.
3. Place 1 scallop on the edge of 1 prosciutto slice and roll it up tucking in the sides of the prosciutto to cover completely.
4. Repeat with remaining scallops and prosciutto slices
5. Arrange the wrapped scallops onto a small wire rack.
6. Place the wire rack onto the griddle and cook for about 40 minutes.
7. Remove the scallops from griddle and serve hot.

Nutrition:
Calories 160
Total Fat 6.7 g
Saturated Fat 2.3 g
Cholesterol 64 mg
Sodium 1000 mg
Total Carbs 1.4 g
Fiber 0 g
Sugar 0 g
Protein 23.5 g

Buttered Clams

Preparation Time: 15 minutes
Cooking Time: 8 minutes
Servings: 6
Ingredients:

- 24 littleneck clams
- ½ cup cold butter, chopped
- 2 tablespoons fresh parsley, minced
- 3 garlic cloves, minced
- 1 teaspoon fresh lemon juice

Directions:

1. Preheat the griddle to 450 degrees F.
2. Scrub the clams under cold running water.

3. In a large casserole dish, mix together remaining ingredients.
4. Place the casserole dish onto the griddle.
5. Now, arrange the clams directly onto the griddle and cook for about 5-8 minutes or until they are opened. (Discard any that fail to open).
6. With tongs, carefully transfer the opened clams into the casserole dish and remove from the griddle.
7. Serve immediately.

Nutrition:
Calories 306
Total Fat 17.6 g
Saturated Fat 9.9 g
Cholesterol 118 mg
Sodium 237 mg
Total Carbs 6.4 g
Fiber 0.1 g
Sugar 0.1 g
Protein 29.3 g

Lemony Lobster Tails

Preparation Time: 15 minutes
Cooking Time: 25 hours
Servings: 4
Ingredients:

- ½ cup butter, melted
- 2 garlic cloves, minced
- 2 teaspoons fresh lemon juice
- Salt and ground black pepper, as required
- 4 (8-ounce) lobster tails

Directions:

1. Preheat the griddle to 450 degrees F.
2. In a metal pan, add all ingredients except for lobster tails and mix well.
3. Place the pan onto the griddle and cook for about 10 minutes.
4. Meanwhile, cut down the top of the shell and expose lobster meat.
5. Remove pan of butter mixture rom griddle.
6. Coat the lobster meat with butter mixture.
7. Place the lobster tails onto the griddle and cook for about 15 minutes, coating with butter mixture once halfway through.
8. Remove from the griddle and serve hot.

Nutrition:
Calories 409
Total Fat 24.9 g
Saturated Fat 15.1 g
Cholesterol 392 mg
Sodium 1305 mg
Total Carbs 0.6 g
Fiber 0 g
Sugar 0.1 g
Protein 43.5 g

Chile Lime Clams with Tomatoes and Griddle Bread

Preparation Time: 10 minutes
Cooking Time: 25 minutes
Servings: 4
Ingredients:

- 6 tbsp unsalted pieces of butter
- 2 large shallots, chopped
- 4 thinly sliced garlic cloves
- 1 tbsp of tomato paste
- 1 cup of beer
- 1 cup cherry tomatoes

- 1 1/2 ounce can-chickpeas, rinsed
- 2 tbsp sambal oelek
- 24 scrubbed littleneck clams
- 1 tbsp fresh lime juice
- 4 thick slices of country-style bread
- 2 tbsp olive oil
- Kosher salt
- ½ cup cilantro leaves
- lime wedges

Intolerances:

- Gluten-Free
- Egg-Free

Directions:

1. Set up the griddle for medium, indirect heat. Put a large griddle on the griddle over direct heat and melt 4 tbsp of butter in it.
2. Add the shallots and garlic and keep cooking, often stirring, until they soften, about 4 minutes.
3. Add the tomato paste and keep cooking, continually stirring, until paste darkens to a rich brick red color. Add the beer and tomatoes.
4. Cook until the beer is reduced nearly by half, about 4 minutes. Add in the chickpeas and sambal oelek, then the clams.
5. Cover and keep cooking until clams have opened, maybe from 5 to 10 minutes depending on the size of clams and the heat. Discard any clams that don't open. Pour in the lime juice and the remaining 2 tbsp of butter.
6. While griddling the clams, you can sprinkle the bread with oil and season with salt. Griddle until it becomes golden brown and crisp.
7. Put the toasts onto plates and spoon with clam mixture, then top with cilantro. Serve with lime wedges.

Nutrition:
Calories: 400
Fat: 21g
Carbs: 33g
Protein: 17g

Fish with Salsa Verde

Preparation Time: 15 minutes
Cooking Time: 30 minutes
Servings: 4
Ingredients:

- 2 garlic cloves
- 3 tbsp fresh orange juice
- 1 tsp dried oregano
- 2 cups of chopped white onion
- ¾ cup chopped cilantro
- ¼ cup extra virgin olive oil and more for the griddle
- 5 tbsp fresh lime juice
- 1 lb. of tilapia, striped bass or sturgeon fillets
- Kosher salt and grounded pepper
- 1 cup of mayonnaise
- 1 tbsp of milk
- 4 corn tortillas
- 2 avocados, peeled and sliced
- ½ small head of cabbage, cored and thinly sliced
- Salsa Verde - Lime wedges

Intolerances:

- Gluten-Free
- Egg-Free

Directions:

1. Mix the garlic, orange juice, oregano, one cup onion, ¼ cup cilantro, ¼ cup oil, and 3 tbsp of lime juice in a medium bowl.
2. Season the fish with salt and grounded pepper. Spoon the 1/2 onion mixture on a glass baking dish then put the fish on it.
3. Spoon the remaining onion mixture over the fish and chill for half hour. Turn the fish , cover and chill for another half hour.
4. Mix the mayo, milk, and the remaining two tbsp of lime juice in a little bowl.
5. Set up the griddle for medium-high heat and brush the grate with oil.
6. Griddle the fish, with some marinade on, till opaque in the center, about 3–5 minutes for each side.
7. Griddle the tortillas till slightly burned, about ten seconds per side. Coarsely chop the fish and put it onto a platter.
8. Serve with lime mayonnaise, tortillas, avocados, cabbage, Salsa Verde, lime wedges and the remaining cup of sliced onion and ½ cup cilantro.

Nutrition:

Calories: 270
Fat: 22g
Cholesterol: 11mg
Carbs: 2g
Protein: 20g

Salmon Steaks with Cilantro Yogurt Sauce

Preparation Time: 10 minutes
Cooking Time: 20 minutes **Servings:** 4
Ingredients:

- Vegetable oil (for the griddle)
- 2 serrano chilis
- 2 garlic cloves
- 1 cup cilantro leaves
- ½ cup plain whole-milk Greek yogurt
- 1 tbsp of extra virgin olive oil
- 1 tsp honey
- Kosher salt
- 2 12oz bone-in salmon steaks

Intolerances:

- Gluten-Free
- Egg-Free

Directions:

1. Set up the griddle for medium-high heat, then oil the grate.
2. Expel and dispose of seeds from one chili. Mix the two chilis, garlic, cilantro, the yogurt, oil, the nectar, and ¼ cup water in a blender until it becomes smooth, then season well with salt.
3. Move half of the sauce to a little bowl and put it aside. Season the salmon steaks with salt.
4. Griddle it, turning more than once, until it's beginning to turn dark, about 4 minutes.
5. Keep on griddleing, turning frequently, and seasoning with residual sauce for at least 4 minutes longer.

Nutrition:

Calories: 290 Fat: 14g Cholesterol: 80g Carbs: 1g Protein: 38g

Scallops with Lemony Salsa Verde

Preparation Time: 15 minutes
Cooking Time: 15 minutes
Servings: 2
Ingredients:

- 2 tbsp of vegetable oil and more for the griddle
- 12 large sea scallops, side muscle removed
- Kosher salt and grounded black pepper
- Lemony Salsa Verde

Intolerances:

- Gluten-Free - Egg-Free - Lactose-Free

Directions:

1. Set up the griddle for medium-high heat, then oil the grate. Toss the scallops with 2 tbsp of oil on a rimmed baking sheet and season with salt and pepper.
2. Utilizing a fish spatula or your hands, place the scallops on the griddle.
3. Griddle them, occasionally turning, until gently singed and cooked through, around 2 minutes for each side.
4. Serve the scallops with Lemony Salsa Verde.

Nutrition:
Calories: 30 Fat: 1g Cholesterol: 17mg Carbs: 1g Protein: 6g

Shrimp with Shrimp Butter

Preparation Time: 15 minutes
Cooking Time: 15 minutes **Servings:** 4
Ingredients:

- 6 tbsp unsalted butter
- 1/2 cup finely chopped red onion
- 1 1/2 tsp crushed red pepper
- 1 tsp Malaysian shrimp paste
- 1 1/2 tsp lime juice
- salt
- grounded black pepper
- 24 shelled and deveined large shrimp
- 6 wooden skewers(better if soaked in water for 30 minutes)
- Torn mint leaves and assorted sprouts

Intolerances:

- Gluten-Free - Egg-Free

Directions:

1. In a little griddle, liquefy 3 tbsp of butter. Add the onion then cook over moderate heat for about 3 minutes.
2. Add in the squashed red pepper and shrimp paste and cook until fragrant, about 2 minutes.
3. Add in the lime juice and the remaining 3 tbsp of butter and season with salt. Keep the shrimp sauce warm.
4. Set up the griddle. Season the shrimp with salt and pepper and string onto the skewers, not too tightly.
5. Griddle over high heat, turning once until gently singed and cooked through, around 4 minutes.
6. Move onto a platter and spoon with shrimp sauce. Spread on the mint leaves and sprouts and serve.

Nutrition:
Calories: 224 Fat: 10g Cholesterol: 260mg
Carbs: 1g
Protein: 30g

Sea Scallops with Corn Salad

Preparation Time: 25 minutes
Cooking Time: 30 minutes
Servings: 6
Ingredients:

- 6 shucked ears of corn
- 1-pint grape tomatoes, halved
- 3 sliced scallions, white and light green parts only
- 1/3 cup basil leaves, finely shredded
- Salt and grounded pepper
- 1 small shallot, minced
- 2 tbsp balsamic vinegar
- 2 tbsp hot water
- 1 tsp Dijon mustard 1/4 cup
- 3 tbsp sunflower oil
- 1 1/2 pounds sea scallops

Intolerances:

- Gluten-Free
- Egg-Free
- Lactose-Free

Directions:

1. In a pot of boiling salted water, cook the corn for about 5 minutes. Drain and cool.
2. Place the corn into a big bowl and cut off the kernels. Add the tomatoes, the scallions and basil then season with salt and grounded pepper.
3. In a blender, mix the minced shallot with the vinegar, heated water, and mustard. With the blender on, gradually add 6 tbsp of the sunflower oil.
4. Season the vinaigrette with salt and pepper; at that point, add it to the corn salad.
5. In a huge bowl, toss the remaining 1 tbsp of oil with the scallops, then season with salt and grounded pepper.
6. Heat a griddle pan. Put on half of the scallops and griddle over high heat, turning once, until singed, around 4 minutes.
7. Repeat with the other half of the scallops. Place the corn salad on plates, then top with the scallops and serve.

Nutrition:
Calories: 230
Fat: 5g
Cholesterol: 60mg
Carbs: 13g
Protein: 33g

Oysters with Tequila Butter

Preparation Time: 20 minutes
Cooking Time: 25 minutes
Servings: 6
Ingredients:

- 1/2 tsp fennel seeds
- 1/4 tsp crushed red pepper
- 7 tbsp of unsalted butter
- 1/4 cup of sage leaves, plus 36 small leaves for the garnish
- 1 tsp of dried oregano
- 2 tbsp lemon juice
- 2 tbsp of tequila
- Kosher salt
- rock salt, for the serving
- 3 dozen scrubbed medium oysters

Intolerances:

- Gluten-Free
- Egg-Free
- Lactose-Free

Directions:

1. Using a griddle, toast the fennel seeds and squashed red pepper over moderate heat until fragrant for 1 minute.
2. Move onto a mortar and let it cool. With a pestle, pound the spices to a coarse powder, then move into a bowl.
3. Using the same griddle, cook 3 1/2 tbsp of the butter over moderate heat until it becomes dark-colored, about two minutes. Add 1/4 cup of sage and keep cooking, occasionally turning, for about 2 minutes. Move the sage onto a plate. Transfer the butter into the bowl with the spices. Repeat with the remaining butter and sage leaves. Put some aside for decoration.
4. Put the fried sage leaves onto the mortar and squash them with the pestle. Add the squashed sage to the butter along with the oregano, lemon juice, and tequila and season with salt. Keep warm.
5. Set up the griddle. Line a platter with rock salt. Griddle the oysters over high heat until they open, about 1 to 2 minutes.
6. Dispose of the top shell and spot the oysters on the rock salt, being careful not to spill their juice. Spoon the warm tequila sauce over the oysters, decorate with a fresh sage leaf, and serve.

Nutrition:

Calories: 68 Fat: 3g Carbs: 4g Protein: 10g

Citrus Soy Squid

Preparation Time: 15 minutes
Cooking Time: 45 minutes
Servings: 4
Ingredients:

- 1 cup mirin
- 1 cup of soy sauce
- 1/3 cup yuzu juice or fresh lemon juice
- 2 cups of water
- 2 pounds squid tentacles left whole; bodies cut crosswise 1 inch thick

Intolerances:

- Gluten-Free
- Egg-Free
- Lactose-Free

Directions:

1. In a bowl, mix the mirin, soy sauce, the yuzu juice, and water.
2. Put a bit of the marinade in a container and refrigerate it for later use.
3. Add the squid to the bowl with the rest of the marinade and let it sit for about 30 minutes or refrigerate for 4 hours.
4. Set up the griddle. Drain the squid.
5. Griddle over medium-high heat, turning once until white all through for 3 minutes.
6. Serve hot.

Nutrition:

Calories: 110
Fat: 6g
Carbs: 6g
Protein: 8g

Spiced Salmon Kebabs

Preparation Time: 20 minutes
Cooking Time: 25 minutes
Servings: 4
Ingredients:

- 2 tbsp of chopped fresh oregano
- 2 tsp of sesame seeds
- 1 tsp ground cumin
- 1 tsp Kosher salt
- 1/4 tsp crushed red pepper flakes
- 1 1/2 pounds of skinless salmon fillets, cut into 1" pieces
- 2 lemons, thinly sliced into rounds
- 2 tbsp of olive oil
- 16 bamboo skewers soaked in water for one hour

Intolerances:

- Gluten-Free
- Egg-Free
- Lactose-Free

Directions:

1. Set up the griddle for medium heat. Mix the oregano, sesame seeds, cumin, salt, and red pepper flakes in a little bowl. Put the spice blend aside.
2. String the salmon and the lemon slices onto 8 sets of parallel skewers in order to make 8 kebabs.
3. Spoon with oil and season with the spice blend.
4. Griddle and turn at times until the fish is cooked.

Nutrition:
Calories: 230
Fat: 10g Carbs: 1g
Protein: 30g

Onion Butter Cod

Preparation Time: 10 minutes
Cooking Time: 15 minutes
Servings: 4
Ingredients:

- 1/4 cup butter
- 1 finely chopped small onion
- 1/4 cup white wine
- 4 (6ounce) cod fillets
- 1 tbsp of extra virgin olive oil
- 1/2 tsp salt (or to taste)
- 1/2 tsp black pepper
- Lemon wedges

Intolerances:

- Gluten-Free - Egg-Free

Directions:

1. Set up the griddle for medium-high heat.
2. In a little griddle liquefy the butter. Add the onion and cook for 1or 2 minutes.
3. Add the white wine and let stew for an extra 3 minutes. Take away and let it cool for 5 minutes.
4. Spoon the fillets with extra virgin olive oil and sprinkle with salt and pepper. Put the fish on a well-oiled rack and cook for 8 minutes.
5. Season it with sauce and cautiously flip it over. Cook for 6 to 7 minutes more, turning more times or until the fish arrives at an inside temperature of 145°F.
6. Take away from the griddle, top with lemon wedges, and serve.

Nutrition:
Calories: 140 Fat: 5g Cholesterol: 46mg
Carbs: 4g Protein: 20g

Calamari with Mustard Oregano and Parsley Sauce

Preparation Time: 10 minutes
Cooking Time: 35 minutes
Servings: 6
Ingredients:

- 8 Calamari, cleaned
- 2 cups of milk
- Sauce
- 4 tsp of sweet mustard
- Juice from 2 lemons
- 1/2 cup of olive oil
- 2 tbsp fresh oregano, finely chopped
- Pepper, ground
- 1/2 bunch of parsley, finely chopped

Intolerances:

- Gluten-Free
- Egg-Free
- Lactose-Free

Directions:

1. Clean calamari well and cut into slices.
2. Place calamari in a large metal bow, cover and marinate with milk overnight.
3. Remove calamari from the milk and drain well on paper towel. Grease the fish lightly with olive oil.
4. In a bowl, combine mustard and the juice from the two lemons.
5. Beat lightly and pour the olive oil very slowly; stir until all the ingredients are combined well.
6. Add the oregano and pepper and stir well.
7. Start the griddle and set the temperature to moderate; preheat, lid closed, for 10 to 15 minutes.
8. Place the calamari on the griddle and cook for 2-3 minutes per side or until it has a bit of char and remove from the griddle.
9. Transfer calamari to serving platter and pour them over with mustard sauce and chopped parsley.

Nutrition:
Calories: 212
Fat: 19g
Cholesterol: 651mg
Carbs: 7g
Protein: 3g

Cuttlefish with Spinach and Pine Nuts Salad

Preparation Time: 15 minutes
Cooking Time: 30 minutes **Servings:** 6
Ingredients:

- 1/2 cup of olive oil
- 1 tbsp of lemon juice
- 1 tsp oregano
- Pinch of salt
- 8 large cuttlefish, cleaned
- Spinach, pine nuts, olive oil and vinegar for serving

Intolerances:

- Gluten-Free
- Egg-Free
- Lactose-Free

Directions:

1. **Prepa**re marinade with olive oil, lemon juice, oregano and a pinch of salt pepper (be careful, cuttlefish do not need too much salt).

2. Place the cuttlefish in the marinade, tossing to cover evenly. Cover and marinate for about 1 hour.
3. Remove the cuttlefish from marinade and pat dry them on paper towel.
4. Start the griddle, and set the temperature to high and preheat, lid closed, for 10 to 15 minutes.
5. Griddle the cuttlefish just 3 - 4 minutes on each side.
6. Serve hot with spinach, pine nuts, olive oil, and vinegar.

Nutrition:
Calories: 299
Fat: 19g
Cholesterol: 186mg
Carbs: 3g
Protein: 28g

Dijon Lemon Catfish Fillets

Preparation Time: 15 minutes
Cooking Time: 25 minutes **Servings:** 6
Ingredients:

- 1/2 cup olive oil
- Juice of 4 lemons
- 2 tbsp Dijon mustard
- 1/2 tsp salt
- 1 tsp paprika
- Fresh rosemary chopped
- 4 (6- to 8-oz.) catfish fillets, 1/2-inch thick

Intolerances:

- Gluten-Free
- Egg-Free
- Lactose-Free

Directions:

1. Set the temperature to Medium and preheat, lid closed, for 10 to 15 minutes.
2. Whisk the olive oil, lemon juice, mustard, salt, paprika and chopped rosemary in a bowl.
3. Brush one side of each fish fillet with half of the olive oil-lemon mixture; season with salt and pepper to taste.
4. Griddle fillets, covered, 4 to 5 minutes. Turn fillets and brush with remaining olive oil-lemon mixture.
5. Griddle 4 to 5 minutes more (do not cover).
6. Remove fish fillets to a serving platter, sprinkle with rosemary and serve.

Nutrition:
Calories: 295 Fat: 24g
Cholesterol: 58mg
Carbs: 3g
Protein: 16g

Halibut Fillets in Chili Rosemary Marinade

Preparation Time: 15 minutes
Cooking Time: 55 minutes **Servings:** 6
Ingredients:

- 1 cup of virgin olive oil
- 2 large red chili peppers, chopped
- 2 cloves garlic, cut into quarters
- 1 bay leaf
- 1 twig of rosemary
- 2 lemons
- 4 tbsp of white vinegar
- 4 halibut fillets

Intolerances:

- Gluten-Free
- Egg-Free
- Lactose-Free

Directions:

1. In a large container, mix olive oil, chopped red chili, garlic, bay leaf, rosemary, lemon juice and white vinegar. Submerge halibut fillets and toss to combine well.
2. Cover and marinate in the refrigerator for several hours or overnight. Remove anchovies from marinade and pat dry on paper towels for 30 minutes.
3. Start the griddle, set the temperature to medium and preheat, lid closed for 10 to 15 minutes. Griddle the anchovies, skin side down for about 10 minutes, or until the flesh of the fish becomes white (thinner cuts and fillets can cook in as little time as 6 minutes).
4. Turn once during cooking to avoid having the halibut fall apart. Transfer to a large serving platter, pour a little lemon juice over the fish, sprinkle with rosemary and serve.

Nutrition:

Calories: 259 Fat: 4g Cholesterol: 133mg Carbs: 5g Protein: 51g

Lobster with Lemon Butter and Parsley

Preparation Time: 15 minutes

Cooking Time: 40 minutes **Servings:** 4

Ingredients:

- 1 lobster (or more)
- 1/2 cup fresh butter
- 2 lemons juice (freshly squeezed)
- 2 tbsp parsley
- Salt and freshly ground pepper to taste

Intolerances:

- Gluten-Free
- Egg-Free

Directions:

1. Use a pot large enough large to hold the lobsters and fill water and salt. Bring to boil and put in lobster. Boil for 4 - 5 minutes.
2. Remove lobster to the working surface.
3. Pull the body to the base of the head and divide the head.
4. Firmly hold the body, with the abdomen upward, and with a sharp knife cut it along in the middle.
5. Start your griddle with the lid open until the fire is established (4 to 5 minutes). Set the temperature to 350°F and preheat, lid closed for 10 to 15 minutes.
6. Melt the butter and beat it with a lemon juice, parsley, salt, and pepper. Spread butter mixture over lobster and put directly on a griddle grate.
7. Griddle lobsters cut side down about 7 - 8 minutes until the shells are bright in color (also, depends on its size).
8. Turn the lobster over and brush with butter mixture. Griddle for another 4 - 5 minutes.
9. Serve hot sprinkled with lemon butter and parsley finely chopped.

Nutrition:

Calories: 385 Fat: 24g
Cholesterol: 346mg
Carbs: 2g
Protein: 37g

Trout in White Wine and Parsley Marinade

Preparation Time: 20 minutes
Cooking Time: 45 minutes
Servings: 4
Ingredients:

- 1/4 cup olive oil
- 1 lemon juice
- 1/2 cup of white wine
- 2 cloves garlic minced
- 2 tbsp fresh parsley, finely chopped
- 1 tsp fresh basil, finely chopped
- Salt and freshly ground black pepper to taste
- 4 trout fish, cleaned
- Lemon slices for garnish

Intolerances:

- Gluten-Free
- Egg-Free
- Lactose-Free

Directions:

1. In a large container, stir olive oil, lemon juice, wine, garlic, parsley, basil and salt and freshly ground black pepper to taste.
2. Submerge fish in sauce and toss to combine well.
3. Cover and marinate in refrigerate overnight.
4. When ready to cook, start the griddle on Smoke with the lid open for 4 to 5 minutes. Set the temperature to 400°F and preheat, lid closed, for 10 to 15 minutes.
5. Remove the fish from marinade and pat dry on paper towel; reserve marinade.
6. Griddle trout for 5 minutes from both sides (be careful not to overcook the fish).
7. Pour fish with marinade and serve hot with lemon slices.

Nutrition:
Calories: 267
Fat: 18g
Carbs: 3g
Protein: 16g

CHAPTER 12
Game Recipes

Flavorful Cornish Game Hen

Preparation Time: 10 minutes
Cooking Time: 60 minutes **Servings:** 2
Ingredients:

- 1 cornish game hen
- 1/2 tbsp olive oil
- 1/4 tbsp poultry seasoning

Directions:

1. Brush hen with oil and rub with poultry seasoning.
2. Preheat the griddle to high heat.
3. Spray griddle top with cooking spray.
4. Place hen on hot griddle top and cook from all the sides until brown.
5. Cover hen with lid or pan and cook for 60 minutes or until the internal temperature of hen reaches 180 F.
6. Slice and serve.

Nutrition:

- Calories 366 Fat 26.9 g
- Carbohydrates 0.3 g
- Sugar 0 g Protein 28 g
- Cholesterol 168 mg

Flavorful Marinated Cornish Hen

Preparation Time: 10 minutes
Cooking Time: 60 minutes **Servings:** 2
Ingredients:

- 1 cornish hen
- 1 cup cold water
- 16 oz apple juice
- 1/8 cup brown sugar
- 1 cinnamon stick
- 1 cup hot water
- 1/4 cup kosher salt

Directions:

1. Add cinnamon, hot water, cold water, apple juice, brown sugar, and salt into the large pot and stir until sugar is dissolved.
2. Add hen in the brine and place in the refrigerator for 4 hours.
3. Preheat the griddle to high heat.
4. Spray griddle top with cooking spray.
5. Remove hens from brine and place on hot griddle top and cook for 60 minutes or until internal temperature reaches 160 F.
6. Slice and serve.

Nutrition:

- Calories 938 Fat 9.5 g
- Carbohydrates 232 g
- Sugar 200 g Protein 10 g
- Cholesterol 51 mg

Montreal Seasoned Spatchcocked Hens

Preparation Time: 10 minutes
Cooking Time: 60 minutes **Servings:** 2
Ingredients:

- 1 cornish hen
- 1 tbsp olive oil

- 1 tbsp Montreal chicken seasoning

Directions:

1. Cut the backbone of hens and flatten the breastplate.
2. Brush hen with oil and rub with Montreal chicken seasoning.
3. Wrap hens in plastic wrap and place in the refrigerator for 4 hours.
4. Preheat the griddle to high heat.
5. Spray griddle top with cooking spray.
6. Place marinated hen on hot griddle top and cook for 60 minutes or until internal temperature reaches 180 F.
7. Serve and enjoy.

Nutrition:

- Calories 228
- Fat 18 g
- Carbohydrates 0 g
- Sugar 0 g
- Protein 14 g
- Cholesterol 85 mg

Rosemary Hen

Preparation Time: 10 minutes
Cooking Time: 60 minutes
Servings: 2
Ingredients:

- 1 cornish game hen
- 1 tbsp butter, melted
- 1/2 tbsp rosemary, minced
- 1 tsp chicken rub

Directions:

1. Brush hens with melted butter.
2. Mix together rosemary and chicken rub.
3. Rub hen with rosemary and chicken rub mixture.
4. Preheat the griddle to high heat.
5. Spray griddle top with cooking spray.
6. Place hen on hot griddle top and cook for 60 minutes or until internal temperature reaches 165 F.
7. Serve and enjoy.

Nutrition:

- Calories 221
- Fat 17 g
- Carbohydrates 0.5 g
- Sugar 0 g
- Protein 14.5 g
- Cholesterol 100 mg

BBQ Hen

Preparation Time: 10 minutes
Cooking Time: 1 hour 30 minutes
Servings: 8
Ingredients:

- 1 cornish hen
- 2 tbsp BBQ rub

Directions:

1. Preheat the griddle to high heat.
2. Spray griddle top with cooking spray.
3. Coat hens with BBQ rub and place on hot griddle top and cook for 1 1/2 hours or until the internal temperature of hens reach 165 F.
4. Slice and serve.

Nutrition:

- Calories 168 Fat 11 g
- Carbohydrates 0 g
- Sugar 0 g Protein 14 g
- Cholesterol 85 mg

Honey Garlic Cornish Hen

Preparation Time: 10 minutes
Cooking Time: 60 minutes **Servings:** 2
Ingredients:

- 1 cornish hen
- 2 garlic cloves, minced
- 1/8 cup honey
- 1/4 cup soy sauce
- 3/4 cup warm water
- 1 tbsp cornstarch
- 1/4 cup brown sugar

Directions:

1. Mix together soy sauce, warm water, brown sugar, garlic, cornstarch, and honey.
2. Place Cornish hen in baking dish and season with pepper and salt.
3. Pour marinade over hen and place in the refrigerator for 10 hours.
4. Preheat the griddle to high heat.
5. Spray griddle top with cooking spray. Place marinated hen on hot griddle top and cook for 60 minutes or until internal temperature reaches 165 F.
6. Serve and enjoy.

Nutrition:

- Calories 338 Fat 11.8 g
- Carbohydrates 42.3 g
- Sugar 35.6 g Protein 16.6 g
- Cholesterol 85 mg

Sage Thyme Cornish Hen

Preparation Time: 10 minutes
Cooking Time: 60 minutes
Servings: 2
Ingredients:

- 1 cornish hen
- 1/2 tbsp paprika
- 1/4 tsp pepper
- 1/4 tsp sage
- 1/2 tsp thyme
- 1/2 tbsp onion powder

Directions:

1. In a small bowl, mix together paprika, onion powder, thyme, sage, and pepper.
2. Rub hen with paprika mixture.
3. Preheat the griddle to high heat.
4. Spray griddle top with cooking spray.
5. Place hen on hot griddle top and cook for 60 minutes or until internal temperature reaches 185 F.
6. Serve and enjoy.

Nutrition:

- Calories 180
- Fat 12 g
- Carbohydrates 2.7 g
- Sugar 0.8 g
- Protein 14.9 g
- Cholesterol 85 mg

Asian Cornish Hen

Preparation Time: 10 minutes
Cooking Time: 60 minutes
Servings: 2
Ingredients:

- 1 cornish hen
- 1 1/2 tsp Chinese five-spice powder
- 1 1/2 tsp rice wine
- 1/2 tsp pepper
- 2 cups of water
- 3 tbsp soy sauce
- 2 tbsp sugar
- Salt

Directions:

1. In a large bowl, mix together water, soy sauce, sugar, rice wine, five-spice, pepper, and salt.
2. Place Cornish hen in the bowl and place in the refrigerator for overnight.
3. Preheat the griddle to high heat.
4. Spray griddle top with cooking spray.
5. Remove Cornish hen from marinade and place on hot griddle top and cook for 60 minutes or until internal temperature reaches 185 F.
6. Slice and serve.

Nutrition:

- Calories 233
- Fat 11.8 g
- Carbohydrates 15.9 g
- Sugar 13.4 g
- Protein 15.9 g
- Cholesterol 85 mg

Orange Cornish Hen

Preparation Time: 10 minutes
Cooking Time: 60 minutes
Servings: 2
Ingredients:

- 1 cornish hen
- 1/4 onion, cut into chunks
- 1/4 orange cut into wedges
- 2 garlic cloves
- 4 fresh sage leaves
- 1 1/2 fresh rosemary sprigs
- For glaze:
- 2-star anise
- 1 tbsp honey
- 1 cup orange juice
- 1/4 fresh orange, sliced
- 1/2 orange zest
- 1.5 oz Grand Marnier
- 1/2 cinnamon stick

Directions:

1. Stuff hen with orange wedges, garlic, onions, and herbs. Season with pepper and salt.
2. Preheat the griddle to high heat.
3. Spray griddle top with cooking spray.
4. Place hen on hot griddle top and cook for 60 minutes or until the internal temperature of hens reaches 165 F.
5. Meanwhile, in a saucepan heat, all glaze ingredients until reduce by half over medium-high heat.
6. Brush hen with glaze.
7. Slice and serve.

Nutrition:

- Calories 351 Fat 12.1 g
- Carbohydrates 29.2 g
- Sugar 40.9 g Protein 16 g
- Cholesterol 85 mg

Rosemary Butter Cornish Hens

Preparation Time: 10 minutes
Cooking Time: 60 minutes
Servings: 2
Ingredients:

- 1 cornish hen, rinse and pat dry with paper towels
- 1 tbsp butter, melted
- 1 rosemary sprigs
- 1 tsp poultry seasoning

Directions:

1. Stuff rosemary sprigs into the hen cavity.

2. Brush hen with melted butter and season with poultry seasoning.
3. Preheat the griddle to high heat.
4. Spray griddle top with cooking spray.
5. Place hen on hot griddle top and cook for 60 minutes or until the internal temperature of hens reaches 165 F.
6. Slice and serve.

Nutrition:

- Calories 127
- Fat 8 g
- Carbohydrates 0.5 g
- Sugar 0 g
- Protein 13 g
- Cholesterol 74 mg

CHAPTER 13
Appetizers and Sides Recipes

Smashed Potato Casserole

Preparation Time: 30 minutes
Cooking Time: 45 - 60 minutes **Servings:** 8
Ingredients:

- 1 small red onion, thinly sliced
- 1 small green bell pepper, thinly sliced
- 1 small red bell pepper, thinly sliced
- 1 small yellow bell pepper, thinly sliced
- 3 cups mashed potatoes
- 8 - 10 bacon slices
- ¼ cup bacon grease or salted butter (½ stick)
- ¾ cup sour cream
- 1 ½ teaspoons barbecue rub
- 3 cups shredded sharp cheddar cheese (divided)
- 4 cups hash brown potatoes (frozen)

Intolerances:

- Gluten-Free Egg-Free

Directions:

1. Get that bacon cooking over medium heat in a large griddle. Cook till nice and crisp. Aim for 5 minutes on both sides. Then set aside your bacon.
2. Pour the bacon grease into a glass container and set aside.
3. Using the same griddle, warm up the butter or bacon grease over medium heat. When warm enough, sauté bell peppers and red onions. You're aiming for al dente. When done, set it all aside.
4. Grab a casserole dish, preferably one that is 9 by 11 inches. Spray with some nonstick cooking spray, then spread the mashed potatoes out, covering the entire bottom of the dish. Add the sour cream to the next layer over the potatoes. When you're done, season it with some of the barbecue rub. Create a new layer with the sautéed veggies over the potatoes, leaving the butter or grease in the pan.
5. Sprinkle your sharp cheddar cheese—just 1½ of the cups. Then add the frozen hash brown potatoes. Scoop out the rest of the bacon grease or butter from the sautéed veggies, all over the hash browns, and then top it all off with some delicious crumbled bacon bits.
6. Add the rest of the sharp cheddar cheese (1½ cups) over the whole thing, and then use some aluminum foil to cover the casserole dish.
7. Set up your griddle for indirect cooking. Preheat to 350°F. Let the whole thing bake for 45 - 60 minutes. Ideally, you want the cheese to bubble. Take it out and let it sit for about 10 minutes. Serve!

Nutrition: Calories: 232 Fat: 2g Carbs: 48g Protein: 9g

Atomic Buffalo Turds

Preparation Time: 30 minutes
Cooking Time: 1 hour and 30 minutes
Servings: 10
Ingredients:

- 8 ounces regular cream cheese (room temp)

- 10 jalapeno peppers (medium)
- ¾ cup cheddar cheese blend and shredded Monterey Jack (not necessary)
- 1 teaspoon smoked paprika
- 1 teaspoon garlic powder
- ½ teaspoon red pepper flakes (not necessary)
- Little Smokies sausages (20)
- 10 bacon strips, thinly sliced and halved

Intolerances:

- Egg-Free

Directions:

1. Wash the jalapenos, then slice them up along the length. Get a spoon, or a paring knife if you prefer, and use that to take out the seeds and the veins.
2. Place the scooped-out jalapenos on a veggie griddleing tray and put it all aside.
3. Get a small bowl and mix the shredded cheese, cream cheese, paprika, cayenne pepper, garlic powder, and red pepper flakes. Mix them thoroughly.
4. Get your jalapenos which you've hollowed out, and then stuff them with the cream cheese mix.
5. Get your little Smokies sausage, and then put it right onto each of the cheese stuffed jalapenos.
6. Grab some of the thinly sliced and halved bacon strips and wrap them around each of the stuffed jalapenos and their sausage.
7. Grab some toothpicks. Use them to keep the bacon nicely secured to the sausage.
8. Set up your griddle so it's ready for indirect cooking. Get it preheated to 250°F.
9. Put your jalapeno peppers in and smoke them at 250°F for anywhere from 90 minutes to 120 minutes. You want to keep it going until the bacon is nice and crispy.
10. Take out the atomic buffalo turds, and then let them rest for about 5 minutes. Serve!

Nutrition:

Calories: 198 Fat: 17g

Cholesterol: 48mg Carbs: 3g Protein: 8g

Brisket Baked Beans

Preparation Time: 20 minutes

Cooking Time: 1 hour and 30 minutes

Servings: 10

Ingredients:

- 1 green bell pepper (medium, diced)
- 1 red bell pepper (medium, diced)
- 1 yellow onion (large, diced)
- 2 - 6 jalapeno peppers (diced)
- 2 tablespoons olive oil (extra-virgin)
- 3 cups brisket flat (chopped)
- 1 can baked beans (28 ounces)
- 1 can red kidney beans (1 4ounces, rinsed, drained)
- 1 cup barbecue sauce
- ½ cup brown sugar (packed)
- 2 teaspoons mustard (ground)
- 3 cloves of garlic (chopped)
- 1 ½ teaspoon black pepper
- 1 ½ teaspoon kosher salt

Intolerances:

- Gluten-Free Egg-Free
- Lactose-Free

Directions:

1. Put a griddle on the fire, on medium heat. Warm up your olive oil. Toss in the diced jalapenos, peppers, and onions. Stir every now and then for 8 minutes.
2. Grab a 4-quart casserole dish. Now, in your dish, mix in the pork and beans, kidney beans, baked beans, chopped brisket, cooked peppers and onions, brown sugar, barbecue sauce, garlic, mustard, salt, and black pepper.
3. Set up your griddle so it's ready for indirect cooking.
4. Preheat your griddle to 325°F.
5. Cook your brisket beans on the griddle, for 90 minutes to 120 minutes. Keep it uncovered as you cook. When it's ready, you'll know, because the beans will get thicker and will have bubbles as well.
6. Rest the food for 15 minutes, before you finally move on to step number 5.
7. Serve!

Nutrition:

Calories: 200 Fat: 2g
Cholesterol: 10mg Carbs: 35g
Protein: 9g

Twice-Baked Spaghetti Squash

Preparation Time: 15 minutes
Cooking Time: 1 hour **Servings:** 2
Ingredients:

- 1 spaghetti squash (medium)
- 1 tablespoon olive oil (extra virgin)
- 1 teaspoon salt
- ½ teaspoon pepper
- ½ cup Parmesan cheese (grated, divided)
- ½ cup mozzarella cheese (shredded, divided)

Intolerances:

- Egg-Free

Directions:

1. Cut the squash along the length in half. Make sure you're using a knife that's large enough, and sharp enough. Once you're done, take out the pulp and the seeds from each half with a spoon.
2. Rub the insides of each half of the squash with some olive oil. When you're done with that, sprinkle the salt and pepper.
3. Set up your griddle for indirect cooking.
4. Preheat your griddle to 375°F.
5. Put each half of the squash on the griddle. Make sure they're both facing upwards on the griddle grates, which should be nice and hot.
6. Bake for 45 minutes, keeping it on the griddle until the internal temperature of the squash hits 170°F. You'll know you're done when you find it easy to pierce the squash with a fork.
7. Move the squash to your cutting board. Let it sit there for 10 minutes so that it can cool a bit.
8. Turn up the temp on your griddle to 425°F.

9. Use a fork to remove the flesh from the squash in strands by raking it back and forth. Do be careful, because you want the shells to remain intact. The strands you rake off should look like spaghetti, if you're doing it right.
10. Put the spaghetti squash strands in a large bowl, and then add in half of your mozzarella and half of your Parmesan cheeses. Combine them by stirring.
11. Take the mix, and stuff it into the squash shells. When you're done, sprinkle them with the rest of the Parmesan and mozzarella cheeses. Optional: You can top these with some bacon bits, if you like.
12. Allow the stuffed spaghetti squash shells you've now stuffed to bake at 435°F for 15 minutes, or however long it takes the cheese to go brown.
13. Serve and enjoy.

Nutrition:
Calories: 214 Fat: 3g Cholesterol: 17mg Carbs: 27g Protein: 16g

Bacon-Wrapped Asparagus

Preparation Time: 15 minutes
Cooking Time: 25 - 30 minutes
Servings: 6
Ingredients:

- 15 - 20 spears of fresh asparagus (1 pound)
- Olive oil (extra virgin)
- 5 slices bacon (thinly sliced)
- 1 teaspoon salt and pepper (or your preferred rub)

Intolerances:

- Gluten-Free
- Egg-Free
- Lactose-Free

Directions:

1. Break off the ends of the asparagus, then trim it all so they're down to the same length.
2. Separate the asparagus into bundles—3 spears per bundle. Then spritz them with some olive oil.
3. Use a piece of bacon to wrap up each bundle. When you're done, lightly dust the wrapped bundle with some salt and pepper to taste, or your preferred rub.
4. Set up your griddle so that it's ready for indirect cooking.
5. Put some fiberglass mats on your grates. Make sure they're the fiberglass kind. This will keep your asparagus from getting stuck on your griddle gates.
6. Preheat your griddle to 400°F.
7. Griddle the wraps for 25 minutes to 30 minutes, tops. The goal is to get your asparagus looking nice and tender, and the bacon deliciously crispy.

Nutrition:
Calories: 71 Fat: 3g
Carbs: 1g Protein: 6g

Garlic Parmesan Wedges

Preparation Time: 15 minutes
Cooking Time: 35 minutes
Servings: 3
Ingredients:

- 3 russet potatoes (large)

- 2 teaspoons of garlic powder
- ¾ teaspoon black pepper
- 1 ½ teaspoons of salt
- ¾ cup Parmesan cheese (grated)
- 3 tablespoons fresh cilantro (chopped, optional. You can replace this with flat-leaf parsley)
- ½ cup blue cheese (per serving, as optional dip. Can be replaced with ranch dressing)

Intolerances:

- Gluten-Free
- Egg-Free

Directions:

1. Use some cold water to scrub your potatoes as gently as you can with a veggie brush. When done, let them dry.
2. Slice your potatoes along the length in half. Cut each half into a third.
3. Get all the extra moisture off your potato by wiping it all away with a paper towel. If you don't do this, then you're not going to have crispy wedges!
4. In a large bowl, throw in your potato wedges, some olive oil, garlic powder, salt, garlic, and pepper, and then toss them with your hands, lightly. You want to make sure the spices and oil get on every wedge.
5. Place your wedges on a nonstick tray, or pan, or basked. The single layer kind. Make sure it's at least 15 x 12 inches.
6. Set up your griddle so it's ready for indirect cooking.
7. Preheat your griddle to 425°F.
8. Set the tray upon your preheated griddle. Roast the wedges for 15 minutes before you flip them. Once you turn them, roast them for another 15 minutes, or 20 tops. The outside should be a nice, crispy, golden brown.
9. Sprinkle your wedges generously with the Parmesan cheese. When you're done, garnish it with some parsley, or cilantro, if you like. Serve these bad boys up with some ranch dressing, or some blue cheese, or just eat them that way!

Nutrition:

Calories: 194 Fat: 5g Cholesterol: 5mg Carbs: 32g Protein: 5g

Smoked Moink Ball Skewers

Preparation Time: 30 minutes
Cooking Time: 1 hour and 15 minutes
Servings: 6
Ingredients:

- ½ pound pork sausage (ground)
- ½ pound ground beef (80% lean)
- 1 egg (large)
- ½ cup red onions (minced)
- ½ cup Parmesan cheese (grated)
- ½ cup Italian breadcrumbs
- ¼ cup parsley (finely chopped)
- ¼ cup milk (whole)
- 2 garlic cloves (minced) or 1 teaspoon garlic (crushed)
- 1 teaspoon oregano
- ½ teaspoon kosher salt
- ½ teaspoon black pepper
- ¼ cup barbecue sauce

- ½ pound bacon slices (thinly sliced, halved)

Intolerances:

- Egg-Free

Directions:

1. Mix up the ground pork sausage, ground beef, breadcrumbs, onion, egg, parsley, Parmesan cheese, garlic, milk, oregano, salt, and pepper in a large bowl. Whatever you do, don't overwork your meat.
2. Make meatballs of 1½ ounces each. They should be about 1½ in width. Put them on your Teflon-coated fiberglass mat.
3. Wrap up each meatball in half a slice of your thinly sliced bacon.
4. Spear your moink balls, three to a skewer.
5. Set up your griddle so that it's nice and ready for indirect cooking.
6. Preheat your griddle to 225°F,.
7. Smoke the skewered moink balls for half an hour.
8. Turn up the temperature to 350°F, and keep it that way until the internal temperature of your skewered moink balls hits 175°F, which should take about 40 to 45 minutes, max.
9. When the bacon gets nice and crispy, brush your moink balls with whatever barbecue sauce you like. Ideally, you should do this in the last five minutes of your cook time.
10. Serve the moink ball skewers while they're hot.

Nutrition:

Calories: 314 Fat: 28g Protein: 15g

Bacon Cheddar Slider

Preparation Time: 30 minutes
Cooking Time: 15 minutes
Servings: 2
Ingredients:

- 1 pound ground beef (80% lean)
- 1/2 teaspoon of garlic salt
- 1/2 teaspoon salt
- 1/2 teaspoon of garlic
- 1/2 teaspoon onion
- 1/2 teaspoon black pepper
- 6 bacon slices, cut in half
- 1/2 Cup mayonnaise
- 2 teaspoons of creamy wasabi (optional)
- 6 (1 oz) sliced sharp cheddar cheese, cut in half (optional)
- Sliced red onion
- 1/2 Cup sliced kosher dill pickles
- 12 mini breads sliced horizontally
- Ketchup

Intolerances:

- Egg-Free

Directions:

1. Place ground beef, garlic salt, seasoned salt, garlic powder, onion powder and black hupe pepper in a medium bowl.
2. Divide the meat mixture into 12 equal parts, shape into small thin round patties (about 2 ounces each) and save.
3. Cook the bacon on medium heat over medium heat for 5-8 minutes until crunchy. Set aside.
4. To make the sauce, mix the mayonnaise and horseradish in a small bowl, if used.

5. Preheat griddle to 350°F. Griddle surface should be approximately 400°F.
6. Spray a cooking spray on the griddle cooking surface for best non-stick results.
7. Griddle the putty for 3-4 minutes each until the internal temperature reaches 160°F.
8. If necessary, place a sharp cheddar cheese slice on each patty while the patty is on the griddle or after the patty is removed from the griddle.
9. Place a small amount of mayonnaise mixture, a slice of red onion, and a hamburger pate in the lower half of each roll.
10. Pickled slices, bacon and ketchup.

Nutrition:

Calories: 160
Fat: 11g
Carbs: 20g
Protein: 10g

Mushrooms Stuffed with Crab Meat

Preparation Time: 20 minutes
Cooking Time: 30 – 45 minutes
Servings: 6
Ingredients:

- 6 medium-sized portobello mushrooms
- Extra virgin olive oil
- 1/3 Grated parmesan cheese cup
- Club Beat Staffing:
- 8 oz fresh crab meat or canned or imitation crab meat
- 2 tablespoons extra virgin olive oil
- 1/3 Chopped celery
- Chopped red peppers
- 1/2 cup chopped green onion
- 1/2 cup Italian breadcrumbs
- 1/2 Cup mayonnaise
- 8 oz cream cheese at room temperature
- 1/2 teaspoon of garlic
- 1 tablespoon dried parsley
- Grated parmesan cheese cup
- 1 1 teaspoon of Old Bay seasoning
- 1/4 teaspoon of kosher salt
- 1/4 teaspoon black pepper

Intolerances:

- Egg-Free

Directions:

1. Clean the mushroom cap with a damp paper towel. Cut off the stem and save it.
2. Remove the brown gills from the bottom of the mushroom cap with a spoon and discard.
3. **Prepa**re crab meat stuffing. If you are using canned crab meat, drain, rinse, and remove shellfish.
4. Heat the olive oil in a frying pan over medium high heat. Add celery, peppers and green onions and fry for 5 minutes. Set aside for cooling.
5. Gently pour the chilled sautéed vegetables and the remaining ingredients into a large bowl.
6. Cover and refrigerate crab meat stuffing until ready to use.

7. Put the crab mixture in each mushroom cap and make a mound in the center.
8. Sprinkle extra virgin olive oil and sprinkle parmesan cheese on each stuffed mushroom cap. Put the mushrooms in a 10 x 15-inch baking dish.
9. Use the griddle to indirect heating and preheat to 375°F.
10. Bake for 30-45 minutes until the filling becomes hot (165°F as measured by an instant-read digital thermometer) and the mushrooms begin to release juice.

Nutrition:
Calories: 60
Fat: 4g
Cholesterol: 20mg
Carbs: 2g
Protein: 2g

Parmesan Tomatoes

Preparation Time: 110 minutes
Cooking Time: 20 minutes
Servings: 6
Ingredients:

- 9 halved Tomatoes
- 1 cup grated Parmesan cheese
- 1/2 tsp. Ground black pepper
- 1/4 tsp. Onion powder
- 1 tbsp. Dried rosemary
- 2 tbsps. Olive oil
- 5 minced Garlic cloves
- 1 tsp. Kosher salt

Intolerances:

- Gluten-Free
- Egg-Free

Directions:

1. Heat a griddle to medium-low heat and oil grates.
2. Place tomatoes halves cut side down, onto the griddle and cook for 5-7 minutes.
3. Heat olive oil in a pan over a medium heat. Add garlic, rosemary, black pepper, onion powder, and salt and cook for 3-5 minutes.
4. Remove from heat and set aside. Flip each tomato half and brush with olive oil garlic mixture and top with grated parmesan cheese.
5. Close griddle and cook for 7-10 minutes more until cheese is melted.
6. Remove tomatoes from the griddle and serve immediately.

Nutrition:
Calories: 130
Fat: 8g
Carbs: 9g
Protein: 6g

Feta Spinach Turkey Burgers

Preparation Time: 10 minutes
Cooking Time: 10 minutes
Servings: 4
Ingredients:

- 1 lb. Ground turkey
- 1 tbsp. Breadcrumbs
- 1/4 tsp. Crushed red pepper
- 1 tsp. Parsley
- 1 tsp. Oregano
- 1 tsp. Garlic powder
- 1/3 cup. Sun-dried tomatoes
- 1/2 cup, crumbled Feta cheese
- 1/2 cup, chopped Baby spinach

- 1/2 tsp. Pepper
- 1/2 tsp. Sea salt

Intolerances:

- Egg-Free

Directions:

1. Add all ingredients into the mixing bowl and mix until just combined.
2. Make four equal shaped patties from the mixture.
3. Preheat the griddle to high heat.
4. Place patties on a hot griddle and cook for 3-5 minutes on each side or until internal temperature reaches to 165°F. Serve

Nutrition:

Calories: 215 Fat: 6g Carbs: 9g
Protein: 30g

Griddle Potato Skewers

Preparation Time: 15 minutes
Cooking Time: 25 minutes
Servings: 8
Ingredients:

- 2 lbs. quartered Potatoes
- 1 tsp. Garlic powder
- 2 tsps. Crushed dried rosemary
- 4 tbsps. Dry white wine
- 1/2 cup Mayonnaise
- 1/2 cup Water

Intolerances:

- Gluten-Free
- Egg-Free
- Lactose-Free

Directions:

1. Add potatoes and water in a microwave-safe bowl and cook in the microwave for 15 minutes or until potatoes are tender.
2. Drain potatoes well and let them cool. In a large mixing bowl, stir together mayonnaise, garlic powder, rosemary, and wine.
3. Add potatoes and toss to coat. Cover bowl and place in the refrigerator for 1 hour.
4. Preheat the griddle to a high heat and oil grates. Remove potatoes from the marinade and thread onto the skewers.
5. Place potato skewers on a hot griddle, cover, and cook for 6-8 minutes. Turn skewers halfway through.
6. Serve.

Nutrition:

Calories: 135 Fat: 5g
Carbs: 20g
Protein: 2g

Curried Cauliflower Skewers

Preparation Time: 15 minutes
Cooking Time: 15 minutes **Servings:** 6
Ingredients:

- 1 cut into florets large cauliflower head
- 1 cut into wedges onion
- 1 cut into squares yellow bell pepper
- 1 fresh lemon juice
- 1/4 cup olive oil
- 1/2 tsp. garlic powder
- 1/2 tsp. ground ginger
- 3 tsps. curry powder
- 1/2 tsp. salt

Intolerances:

- Gluten-Free
- Egg-Free
- Lactose-Free

Directions:

1. In a large mixing bowl, whisk together oil, lemon juice, garlic, ginger, curry powder, and salt. Add cauliflower florets and toss until well coated.
2. Heat the griddle to medium heat.
3. Thread cauliflower florets, onion, and bell pepper onto the skewers.
4. Place skewers onto the hot griddle and cook for 6-7 minutes on each side.
5. Serve.

Nutrition:
Calories: 100
Fat: 8g
Carbs: 6g
Protein: 1g

Southwest Chicken Drumsticks

Preparation Time: 10 minutes
Cooking Time: 30 minutes
Servings: 8
Ingredients:

- 2 lbs. Chicken legs
- 2 tbsps. Taco seasoning
- 2 tbsps. Olive oil

Intolerances:

- Gluten-Free
- Egg-Free
- Lactose-Free

Directions:

1. Preheat the griddle to a medium-high heat and oil grates.
2. Brush chicken legs with oil and rub with taco seasoning.
3. Place chicken legs on the hot griddle and cook for 30 minutes.
4. Turn chicken legs after every 10 minutes.
5. Serve.

Nutrition:
Calories: 165 Fat: 12g Carbs: 1g Protein: 10g

Sweet Potato Fries

Preparation Time: 10 minutes
Cooking Time: 12 minutes **Servings:** 4
Ingredients:

- 2 lbs. peeled and cut into ½-inch wedges Sweet potatoes
- 2 tbsps. Olive oil
- Pepper and salt to taste

Intolerances:

- Gluten-Free Egg-Free
- Lactose-Free

Directions:

1. Preheat the griddle to medium-high heat.
2. Toss sweet potatoes with oil, pepper, and salt.
3. Place sweet potato wedges on a hot griddle and cook over a medium heat for 6 minutes.
4. Flip and cook for 6-8 minutes more. Serve.

Nutrition:
Calories: 230 Fat: 6g Carbs: 40g Protein: 4g

Balsamic Mushroom Skewers

Preparation Time: 10 minutes
Cooking Time: 10 minutes
Servings: 4
Ingredients:

- 2 lbs. sliced ¼-inch thick Mushrooms
- 1/2 tsp. chopped Thyme
- 3 chopped Garlic cloves
- 1 tbsp. Soy sauce
- 2 tbsps. Balsamic vinegar

- Pepper and salt to taste

Intolerances:

- Gluten-Free
- Egg-Free
- Lactose-Free

Directions:

1. Add mushrooms and remaining ingredients into the mixing bowl, cover, and place in the refrigerator for 30 minutes.
2. Thread marinated mushrooms onto the skewers.
3. Heat the griddle to medium-high heat. Place mushroom skewers onto the hot griddle and cook for 2-3 minutes per side.
4. Serve.

Nutrition:

Calories: 60
Fat: 1g
Carbs: 8g
Protein: 6g

CHAPTER 14
Dessert and Snacks Recipes

Spicy Sausage & Cheese Balls

Preparation Time: 20 minutes
Cooking Time: 40 minutes
Servings: 4
Ingredients:

- 1lb Hot Breakfast Sausage
- 2 cups Bisquick Baking Mix
- 8 ounces Cream Cheese
- 8 ounces Extra Sharp Cheddar Cheese
- 1/4 cup Fresno Peppers
- 1 tablespoon Dried Parsley
- 1 teaspoon Killer Hogs AP Rub
- 1/2 teaspoon Onion Powder

Directions:

1. Get ready griddle or flame broil for roundabout cooking at 400 degree F.
2. Blend Sausage, Baking Mix, destroyed cheddar, cream cheddar, and remaining fixings in a huge bowl until all-around fused.
3. Utilize a little scoop to parcel blend into chomp to estimate balls and roll tenderly fit as a fiddle.
4. Spot wiener and cheddar balls on a cast-iron container and cook for 15mins.
5. Present with your most loved plunging sauces.

Nutrition: Calories: 95 Carbs: 4g Fat: 7g Protein: 5g

White Chocolate Bread Pudding

Preparation Time: 20 minutes
Cooking Time: 1hr 15 minutes
Servings: 12
Ingredients:

- 1 loaf French bread
- 4 cups Heavy Cream
- 3 Large Eggs
- 2 cups White Sugar
- 1 package White Chocolate morsels
- ¼ cup Melted Butter
- 2 teaspoons Vanilla
- 1 teaspoon Ground Nutmeg
- 1 teaspoon Salt
- Bourbon White Chocolate Sauce
- 1 package White Chocolate morsels
- 1 cup Heavy Cream
- 2 tablespoons Melted Butter
- 2 tablespoons Bourbon
- ½ teaspoon Salt

Directions:

1. Preheat the griddle at 350 degree F.
2. Tear French bread into little portions and spot in a massive bowl. Pour four cups of Heavy Cream over Bread and douse for 30mins.
3. Join eggs, sugar, softened spread, and vanilla in a medium to estimate bowl. Include a package of white chocolate pieces and a delicate blend. Season with Nutmeg and Salt.
4. Pour egg combo over the splashed French bread and blend to sign up for.
5. Pour the combination right into a properly to buttered nine X 13 to dish inchmeal and spot it at the griddle.
6. Cook for 60Secs or until bread pudding has set and the top is darker.

7. For the sauce: Melt margarine in a saucepot over medium warm temperature. Add whiskey and hold on cooking for three to 4mins until liquor vanished and margarine begins to darkish-colored.
8. Include vast cream and heat till a mild stew. Take from the warmth and consist of white chocolate pieces a bit at a time continuously blending until the complete percent has softened. Season with a hint of salt and serve over bread pudding.

Nutrition: Calories: 372 Carbs: 31g Fat: 25g Protein: 5g

Cheesy Jalapeño Griddle Dip

Preparation Time: 10 minutes
Cooking Time: 15 minutes
Servings: 8
Ingredients:

- 8 ounces cream cheese
- 16 ounces shredded cheese
- 1/3 cup mayonnaise
- 4 ounces diced green chilies
- 3 fresh jalapeños
- 2 teaspoons Killer Hogs AP Rub
- 2 teaspoons Mexican Style Seasoning

For the topping:

- ¼ cup Mexican Blend Shredded Cheese
- Sliced jalapeños
- Mexican Style Seasoning
- 3 tablespoons Killer Hogs AP Rub
- 2 tablespoons Chili Powder
- 2 tablespoons Paprika
- 2 teaspoons Cumin
- ½ teaspoon Granulated Onion
- ¼ teaspoon Cayenne Pepper
- ¼ teaspoon Chipotle Chili Pepper ground
- ¼ teaspoon Oregano

Directions:

1. Preheat griddle or flame broil for roundabout cooking at 350 degree
2. Join fixings in a big bowl and spot in a cast to press griddle
3. Top with Mexican Blend destroyed cheddar and cuts of jalapeno's
4. Spot iron griddle on flame broil mesh and cook until cheddar hot and bubbly and the top has seared
5. Marginally about 25mins.
6. Serve warm with enormous corn chips (scoops), tortilla chips, or your preferred vegetables for plunging.

Nutrition: Calories: 150 Carbs: 22g Fat: 6g Protein: 3g

Cajun Turkey Club

Preparation Time: 5 Minutes
Cooking Time: 10 Minutes
Servings: 3
Ingredients:

- 1 3lbs Turkey Breast
- 1 stick Butter (melted)
- 8 ounces Chicken Broth
- 1 tablespoon Killer Hogs Hot Sauce
- 1/4 cup Malcolm's King Craw Seasoning
- 8 Pieces to Thick Sliced Bacon

- 1 cup Brown Sugar
- 1 head Green Leaf Lettuce
- 1 Tomato (sliced)
- 6 slices Toasted Bread
- ½ cup Cajun Mayo
- 1 cup Mayo
- 1 tablespoon Dijon Mustard
- 1 tablespoon Killer Hogs Sweet Fire Pickles (chopped)
- 1 tablespoon Horseradish
- ½ teaspoon Malcolm's King Craw Seasoning
- 1 teaspoon Killer Hogs Hot Sauce
- Pinch of Salt & Black Pepper to taste

Directions:

1. Preheat the griddle 325 degree F
2. Join dissolved margarine, chicken stock, hot sauce, and 1 tbsp of Cajun Seasoning in a blending bowl. Infuse the blend into the turkey bosom scattering the infusion destinations for even inclusion.
3. Shower the outside of the turkey bosom with a Vegetable cooking splash and season with Malcolm's King Craw Seasoning.
4. Spot the turkey bosom on the griddle and cook until the inside temperature arrives at 165 degree. Utilize a moment read thermometer to screen temp during the cooking procedure.
5. Consolidate darker sugar and 1 teaspoon of King Craw in a little bowl. Spread the bacon with the sugar blend and spot on a cooling rack.
6. Cook the bacon for 12 to 15mins or until darker. Make certain to turn the bacon part of the way through for cooking.
7. Toast the bread, cut the tomatoes dainty, and wash/dry the lettuce leaves.
8. At the point when the turkey bosom arrives at 165 take it from the flame broil and rest for 15mins. Take the netting out from around the bosom and cut into slender cuts.
9. To cause the sandwich: To slather Cajun Mayo* on the toast, stack on a few cuts of turkey bosom, lettuce, tomato, and bacon. Include another bit of toast and rehash a similar procedure. Include the top bit of toast slathered with more Cajun mayo, cut the sandwich into equal parts and appreciate.

Nutrition: Calories: 130 Carbs: 1g Fat: 4g Protein: 21g

Juicy Loosey Cheeseburger

Preparation Time: 10 minutes
Cooking Time: 10 minutes
Servings: 6
Ingredients:

- 2 lbs. ground beef
- 1 egg beaten
- 1 Cup dry bread crumbs
- 3 tablespoons evaporated milk
- 2 tablespoons Worcestershire sauce
- 1 tablespoons Griddlea Griddles All Purpose Rub
- 4 slices of cheddar cheese
- 4 buns

Directions:

1. Start by consolidating the hamburger, egg, dissipated milk, Worcestershire and focus on a bowl. Utilize your hands to blend well. Partition this blend into 4 equivalent parts. At that point take every one of the 4 sections and partition them into equal parts. Take every one of these little parts and smooth them. The objective is to have 8 equivalent level patties that you will at that point join into 4 burgers.
2. When you have your patties smoothed, place your cheddar in the center and afterward place the other patty over this and firmly squeeze the sides to seal. You may even need to push the meat back towards the inside a piece to shape a marginally thicker patty. The patties ought to be marginally bigger than a standard burger bun as they will recoil a bit of during cooking.
3. Preheat your Kong to 300 degree.
4. Keep in mind during flame broiling that you fundamentally have two meager patties, one on each side, so the cooking time ought not to have a place. You will cook these for 5 to 8mins per side—closer to 5mins on the off chance that you favor an uncommon burger or more towards 8mins in the event that you like a well to done burger.
5. At the point when you flip the burgers, take a toothpick and penetrate the focal point of the burger to permit steam to getaway. This will shield you from having a hit to out or having a visitor who gets a jaw consume from liquid cheddar as they take their first nibble.
6. Toss these on a pleasant roll and top with fixings that supplement whatever your burgers are loaded down with.

Nutrition: Calories: 300 Carbs: 33g Fat: 12g Protein: 15g

No Flip Burgers

Preparation Time: 30 minutes
Cooking Time: 30 minutes
Servings: 2
Ingredients:

- Ground Beef Patties
- Griddlea Griddles Beef Rub
- Choice of Cheese
- Choice of Toppings
- Pretzel Buns

Directions:

1. To start, you'll need to begin with freezing yet not solidified meat patties. This will help guarantee that you don't overcook your burgers. Liberally sprinkle on our Beef Rub or All to Purpose Rub and delicately knead into the two sides of the patty. As another option, you can likewise season with salt and pepper and some garlic salt.
2. Preheat your Silverbac to 250 degree Fahrenheit and cook for about 45mins. Contingent upon the thickness of your burgers you will need to keep an eye on

them after around 30 to 45mins, yet there's no compelling reason to flip. For a medium to uncommon burger, we recommend cooking to about 155 degree.

3. After the initial 30 to 40mins, in the event that you like liquefied cheddar on your burger feel free to mix it up. Close your barbecue back up and let them wrap up for another 10mins before evacuating. For an additional punch of flavor, finish your burger off with a sprinkle of Griddlea Griddle's Gold 'N Bold sauce. Appreciate.

Nutrition: Calories: 190 Carbs: 17g Fat: 9g Protein: 13g

Juicy Loosey Smokey Burger

Preparation Time: 30 minutes
Cooking Time: 30 minutes
Servings: 2
Ingredients:

- 1 pound Beef
- 1/3 pound per burger
- Cheddar cheese
- Griddlea AP Rub
- Salt
- Freshly Ground Black Pepper
- Hamburger Bun
- BBQ Sauce

Directions:

1. Split every 1/3 pound of meat, which is 2.66 ounces per half.
2. Level out one half to roughly six inches plate. Put wrecked of American cheddar, leaving 1/2 inch clear.
3. Put another portion of the meat on top, and seal edges. Rehash for all burgers.
4. Sprinkle with Griddlea AP rub, salt, and pepper flame broil seasonings.
5. Smoke at 250 for 50mins. No compelling reason to turn.
6. Apply Smokey Dokey BBQ sauce, ideally a mustard-based sauce like Griddlea Gold and Bold, or Sticky Fingers Carolina Classic. Cook for an extra 10 minutes, or to favored doneness.

Nutrition: Calories: 264 Carbs: 57g Fat: 2g Protein: 4g

Bread Pudding

Preparation Time: 15 minutes
Cooking Time: 45 minutes
Servings: 4
Ingredients:

- 8 stale donuts
- 3 eggs
- 1 cup milk
- 1 cup heavy cream
- ½ cup brown sugar
- 1 teaspoon vanilla
- 1 pinch salt
- Blueberry Compote
- 1 pint blueberries
- 2/3 cup granulated sugar
- ¼ cup water
- 1 lemon
- Oat Topping
- 1 cup quick oats
- ½ cup brown sugar
- 1 teaspoon flour
- 2 to 3 tablespoons room temperature butter

Directions:

1. Warmth your Griddlea Griddle to 350 degree.
2. Cut your doughnuts into 6 pieces for every doughnut and put it in a safe spot. Blend your eggs, milk, cream, darker sugar, vanilla, and salt in a bowl until it's everything fused. Spot your doughnuts in a lubed 9 by 13 container at that point pour your custard blend over the doughnuts. Press down on the doughnuts to guarantee they get covered well and absorb the juices.
3. In another bowl, consolidate your oats, dark colored sugar, flour and gradually join the spread with your hand until the blend begins to cluster up like sand. When that is **Prepa**red, sprinkle it over the highest point of the bread pudding and toss it on the barbecue around 40 to 45mins until it gets decent and brilliant dark-colored.
4. While the bread pudding is **Prepa**ring, place your blueberries into a griddle over medium-high warmth and begin to cook them down so the juices begin to stream. When that occurs, include your sugar and water and blend well. Diminish the warmth to drug low and let it cool down until it begins to thicken up. Right when the blend begins to thicken, pizzazz your lemon and add the get-up-and-go to the blueberry compote and afterward cut your lemon down the middle and squeeze it into the blend. What you're left with is a tasty, splendid compote that is ideal for the sweetness of the bread pudding.
5. Watch out for your bread pudding around the 40 to 50mins mark. The blend will, in any case, shake a piece in the middle however will solidify as it stands once you pull it off. You can pull it early on the off chance that you like your bread pudding more sodden however to me, the ideal bread pudding will be dimmer with some caramelization yet will at present have dampness too!
6. Presently this is the point at which I'd snatch an attractive bowl, toss a pleasant aiding of bread pudding in there then top it off with the compote and a stacking scoop of vanilla bean frozen yogurt at that point watch faces light up.
7. In addition to the fact that this is an amazingly beautiful dish, the flavor will take you out. Destined to be an enormous hit in your family unit. Give it a shot and express gratitude toward me.
8. What's more, as usual, ensure you snap a photo of your manifestations and label us in your dishes! We'd love to include your work.

Nutrition: Calories: 290 Carbs: 62g Fat: 4g Protein: 5g

Smoked Chocolate Bacon Pecan Pie

Preparation Time: 1hr 45 minutes
Cooking Time: 45 minutes **Servings:** 8
Ingredients:

- 4 eggs
- 1 cup chopped pecans
- 1 tablespoon of vanilla
- ½ cup semi to sweet chocolate chips - ½ cup dark corn syrup
- ½ cup light corn syrup
- ¾ cup bacon (crumbled)
- ¼ cup bourbon
- 4 tablespoons or ¼ cup of butter - ½ cup brown sugar
- ½ cup white sugar
- 1 tablespoon cornstarch
- 1 package refrigerated pie dough
- 16 ounces heavy cream
- ¾ cup white sugar
- ¼ cup bacon
- 1 tablespoon vanilla

Directions:

1. Pie:
2. Carry Griddle to 350 degree.
3. Blend 4 tablespoons spread, ½ cup darker sugar, and ½ cup white sugar in blending bowl.
4. In a different bowl, blend 4 eggs and 1 tablespoon cornstarch together and add to blender.
5. Include ½ cup dull corn syrup, ½ cup light corn syrup, ¼ cup whiskey, 1 cup slashed walnuts, 1 cup bacon, and 1 tablespoon vanilla to blend.
6. Spot pie batter in 9-inch pie griddle. Daintily flour mixture.
7. Uniformly place ½ cup chocolate contributes pie dish.
8. Take blend into the pie dish.
9. Smoke at 350 degree for 40mins or until the focus is firm.
10. Cool and top with bacon whipped cream.
11. Bacon whipped Cream:
12. Consolidate fixings (16 ounces substantial cream, ¾ cup white sugar, ¼ cup bacon to finely cleaved, and 1 tablespoon vanilla) and mix at rapid until blend thickens. This formula can be separated into 6mins pie container or custard dishes or filled in as one entire pie.

Nutrition: Calories: 200 Carbs: 18g Fat: 0g Protein: 3g

Bacon Sweet Potato Pie

Preparation Time: 15 minutes
Cooking Time: 50 minutes **Servings:** 8
Ingredients:

- 1 pound 3 ounces sweet potatoes - 1 ¼ cups plain yogurt
- ¾ cup packed, dark brown sugar
- ½ teaspoon of cinnamon
- ¼ teaspoon of nutmeg
- 5 egg yolks - ¼ teaspoon of salt
- 1 (up to 9 inch) deep dish, frozen pie shell
- 1 cup chopped pecans, toasted
- 4 strips of bacon, cooked and diced
- 1 tablespoon maple syrup
- Optional: Whipped topping

Directions:

1. In the first region, 3D shapes the potatoes right into a steamer crate and sees into a good-sized pot of stew water.

2. Ensure the water is not any nearer than creeps from the base of the bushel. When steamed for 20mins, pound with a potato masher and installed a safe spot.
3. While your flame broil is preheating, location the sweet potatoes within the bowl of a stand blender and beat with the oar connection.
4. Include yogurt, dark colored sugar, cinnamon, nutmeg, yolks, and salt, to flavor, and beat until very a whole lot joined. Take this hitter into the pie shell and see onto a sheet dish. Sprinkle walnuts and bacon on pinnacle and bathe with maple syrup.
5. Heat for 45 to 60mins or until the custard arrives at 165 to 180 degree. Take out from fish fry and funky. Keep refrigerated within the wake of cooling.

Nutrition: Calories: 270 Carbs: 39g Fat: 12g Protein: 4g

Griddle Fruit with Cream

Preparation Time: 15 minutes
Cooking Time: 10 minutes **Servings:** 6
Ingredients:

- 2 halved Apricot
- 1 halved Nectarine
- 2 halved peaches
- ¼ cup of Blueberries
- ½ cup of Raspberries
- 2 tablespoons of Honey
- 1 orange, the peel
- 2 cups of Cream
- ½ cup of Balsamic Vinegar

Directions:

1. Preheat the griddle to 400F with closed lid.
2. Griddle the peaches, nectarines and apricots for 4 minutes on each side.
3. Place a pan over the stove and turn on medium heat. Add 2 tablespoons of honey, vinegar, and orange peel. Simmer until medium thick.
4. In the meantime add honey and cream in a bowl. Whip until it reaches a soft form.
5. Place the fruits on a serving plate. Sprinkle with berries. Drizzle with balsamic reduction. Serve with cream and enjoy!

Nutrition: Calories: 230 Protein: 3g Carbs: 35g Fat: 3g

Apple Pie on the Griddle

Preparation Time: 15 minutes
Cooking Time: 30 minutes **Servings:** 6
Ingredients:

- ¼ cup of Sugar
- 4 Apples, sliced

- 1 tablespoon of Cornstarch
- 1 teaspoon Cinnamon, ground
- 1 Pie Crust, refrigerated, soften in according to the directions on the box
- ½ cup of Peach preserves

Directions:

1. Preheat the griddle to 375F with closed lid.
2. In a bowl combine the cinnamon, cornstarch, sugar, and apples. Set aside.
3. Place the piecrust in a pie pan. Spread the preserves and then place the apples. Fold the crust slightly.
4. Place a pan on the griddle (upside - down) so that you don't brill/bake the pie directly on the heat.
5. Cook 30 - 40 minutes. Once done, set aside to rest. Serve and enjoy

Nutrition: Calories: 160 Protein: 0.5g Carbs: 35g Fat: 1g

Griddle Layered Cake

Preparation Time: 10 minutes
Cooking Time: 20 minutes
Servings: 6
Ingredients:

- 2 x pound cake
- 3 cups of whipped cream
- ¼ cup melted butter
- 1 cup of blueberries
- 1 cup of raspberries
- 1 cup sliced strawberries

Directions:

1. Preheat the griddle to high with closed lid.
2. Slice the cake loaf (3/4 inch), about 10 per loaf. Brush both sides with butter.
3. Griddle for 7 minutes on each side. Set aside.
4. Once cooled completely start layering your cake. Place cake, berries then cream.
5. Sprinkle with berries and serve.

Nutrition: Calories: 160 Protein: 2.3g Carbs: 22g Fat: 6g

Coconut Chocolate Simple Brownies

Preparation Time: 15 minutes
Cooking Time: 25 minutes **Servings:** 6
Ingredients:

- 4 eggs
- 1 cup Cane Sugar
- ¾ cup of Coconut oil
- 4 ounces chocolate, chopped
- ½ teaspoon of Sea salt
- ¼ cup cocoa powder, unsweetened
- ½ cup flour
- 4 ounces Chocolate chips
- 1 teaspoon of Vanilla

Directions:

1. Preheat the griddle to 350F with closed lid.
2. Take a baking pan (9x9), grease it and line a parchment paper.
3. In a bowl combine the salt, cocoa powder and flour. Stir and set aside.
4. In the microwave or double boiler melt the coconut oil and chopped chocolate. Let it cool a bit.
5. Add the vanilla, eggs, and sugar. Whisk to combine.

6. Add into the flour, and add chocolate chips. Pour the mixture into a pan.
7. Place the pan on the grate. Bake for 20 minutes. If you want dryer brownies to bake for 5 - 10 minutes more. Let them cool before cutting. Cut the brownies into squares and serve.

Nutrition: Calories: 135 Protein: 2g Carbs: 16g Fat: 3g

Seasonal Fruit on the Griddle

Preparation Time: 5 minutes
Cooking Time: 10 minutes **Servings:** 4
Ingredients:

- 2 plums, peaches apricots, etc. (choose seasonally)
- 3 tablespoons Sugar, turbinate
- ¼ cup of Honey
- Gelato, as desired

Directions:

1. Preheat the griddle to 450F with closed lid.
2. Slice each fruit in halves and remove pits. Brush with honey. Sprinkle with some sugar.
3. Griddle on the grate until you see that there are griddle marks. Set aside.
4. Serve each with a scoop of gelato. Enjoy.

Nutrition: Calories: 120 Protein: 1g Carbs: 15g Fat: 3g

Bacon Chocolate Chip Cookies

Preparation Time: 30 minutes
Cooking Time: 30 minutes **Servings:** 6
Ingredients:

- 8 slices cooked and crumbled bacon
- 2 ½ teaspoon apple cider vinegar
- 1 teaspoon vanilla
- 2 cup semisweet chocolate chips
- 2 room temp eggs
- 1 ½ teaspoon baking soda
- 1 cup granulated sugar
- ½ teaspoon salt
- 2 ¾ cup all-purpose flour
- 1 cup light brown sugar
- 1 ½ stick softened butter

Directions:

1. Mix salt, baking soda and flour.
2. Cream the sugar and the butter together. Lower the speed. Add in the eggs, vinegar, and vanilla.
3. Put it on low fire, slowly add in the flour mixture, bacon pieces, and chocolate chips.
4. Preheat your griddle, with your lid closed, until it reaches 375.
5. Put a parchment paper on a baking sheet you are using and drop a teaspoonful of cookie batter on the baking sheet. Let them cook on the griddle, covered, for approximately 12 minutes or until they are browned.

Nutrition: Calories: 167 Carbs: 21g Fat: 9g Protein: 2g

Chocolate Chip Cookies

Preparation Time: 30 minutes
Cooking Time: 30 minutes
Servings: 8
Ingredients:

- 1 ½ cup chopped walnuts
- 1 teaspoon vanilla

- 2 cup chocolate chips
- 1 teaspoon baking soda
- 2 ½ cup plain flour
- ½ teaspoon salt
- 1 ½ stick softened butter
- 2 eggs
- 1 cup brown sugar
- ½ cup sugar

Directions:

1. Preheat your griddle, with your lid closed, until it reaches 350.
2. Mix the baking soda, salt, and flour.
3. Cream the brown sugar, sugar, and butter. Mix in the vanilla and eggs until it comes together.
4. Slowly add in the flour while continuing to beat. Once all flour has been incorporated, add in the chocolate chips and walnuts. Using a spoon, fold into batter.
5. Place an aluminum foil onto griddle. In an aluminum foil, drop spoonful of dough and bake for 17 minutes.

Nutrition: Calories: 150 Carbs: 18g Fat: 5g Protein: 10g

Apple Cobbler

Preparation Time: 30 minutes
Cooking Time: 1 hour 50 minutes
Servings: 8
Ingredients:

- 8 Granny Smith apples
- 1 cup sugar
- 1 stick melted butter
- 1 teaspoon cinnamon
- Pinch salt
- ½ cup brown sugar
- 2 eggs
- 2 teaspoons baking powder
- 2 cup plain flour
- 1 ½ cup sugar

Directions:

1. Peel and quarter apples, place into a bowl. Add in the cinnamon and one c. sugar. Stir well to coat and let it set for one hour.
2. Preheat your griddle, with your lid closed, until it reaches 350.
3. In a large bowl add the salt, baking powder, eggs, brown sugar, sugar, and flour. Mix until it forms crumbles.
4. Place apples into rack Add the crumble mixture on top and drizzle with melted butter.
5. Place on the griddle and cook for 50 minutes.

Nutrition: Calories: 152 Carbs: 26g Fat: 5g Protein: 1g

Caramel Bananas

Preparation Time: 15 minutes.
Cooking Time: 15 minutes.
Servings: 4
Ingredients:

- 1/3 cup chopped pecans
- ½ cup sweetened condensed milk
- 4 slightly green bananas
- ½ cup brown sugar
- 2 tablespoons corn syrup
- ½ cup butter

Directions:

1. Preheat your griddle, with the lid closed, until it reaches 350.

2. Place the milk, corn syrup, butter, and brown sugar into a heavy saucepan and bring to boil. For five minutes simmer the mixture in low heat. Stir frequently.
3. Place the bananas with their peels on, on the griddle and let them griddle for five minutes. Flip and cook for five minutes more. Peels will be dark and might split.
4. Place on serving platter. Cut the ends off the bananas and split peel down the middle. Take the peel off the bananas and spoon caramel on top. Sprinkle with pecans.

Nutrition: Calories: 152 Carbs: 36g Fat: 1g Protein: 1g

Cinnamon Sugar Pumpkin Seeds

Preparation Time: 15 minutes
Cooking Time: 30 minutes
Servings: 8
Ingredients:

- 2 tablespoons sugar
- Seeds from a pumpkin
- 1 teaspoon cinnamon
- 2 tablespoons melted butter

Directions:

1. Preheat your griddle, with your lid closed, until it reaches 350.
2. Clean the seeds and toss them in the melted butter. Add them to the sugar and cinnamon. Spread them out on a baking sheet, place on the griddle, and smoke for 25 minutes. Serve.

Nutrition: Calories: 127 Protein: 5g Carbs: 15g Fat: 21g

Blackberry Pie

Preparation Time: 15 minutes
Cooking Time: 40 minutes
Servings: 8
Ingredients:

- Butter, for greasing
- ½ cup all-purpose flour
- ½ cup milk
- 2 pints blackberries
- 2 cup sugar, divided
- 1 box refrigerated piecrusts
- 1 stick melted butter
- 1 stick of butter
- Vanilla ice cream

Directions:

1. Preheat your griddle, with your lid closed, until it reaches 375.
2. Butter a cast iron griddle.
3. Unroll a piecrust and lay it in the bottom and up the sides of the griddle. Use a fork to poke holes in the crust.
4. Lay the griddle on the griddle and smoke for five mins, or until the crust is browned. Set off the griddle.
5. Mix together 1 ½ c. of sugar, the flour, and the melted butter together. Add in the blackberries and toss everything together.
6. The berry mixture should be added to the griddle. The milk should be added on the top afterward. Sprinkle on half of the diced butter.
7. Unroll the second pie crust and lay it over the griddle. You can also slice it into strips and weave it on top to make it look like a lattice. Place the rest of the diced butter over the top.

8. Sprinkle the rest of the sugar over the crust and place it griddle back on the griddle.Lower the lid and smoke for 15 to 20 minutes or until it is browned and bubbly. You may want to cover with some foil to keep it from burning during the last few minutes of cooking. Serve the hot pie with some vanilla ice cream.

Nutrition: Calories: 393 Protein: 4.25g Carbs: 53.67g Fat: 18.75g

S'mores Dip

Preparation Time: 10 minutes
Cooking Time: 25 minutes **Servings:** 8
Ingredients:

- 12 ounces semisweet chocolate chips
- ¼ cup milk
- 2 tablespoons melted salted butter
- 16 ounces marshmallows
- Apple wedges
- Graham crackers

Directions:

1. Preheat your griddle, with your lid closed, until it reaches 450.
2. Put a cast iron griddle on your griddle and add in the milk and melted butter. Stir together for a minute.
3. Once it has heated up, top with the chocolate chips, making sure it makes a single layer. Place the marshmallows on top, standing them on their end and covering the chocolate.
4. Cover, and let it smoke for five to seven minutes. The marshmallows should be toasted lightly.
5. Take the griddle off the heat and serve with apple wedges and graham crackers.

Nutrition: Calories: 216.7 Protein: 2.7g Carbs: 41g Fat: 4.7g

Ice Cream Bread

Preparation Time: 10 minutes
Cooking Time: 1 hour
Servings: 6
Ingredients:

- 1 ½ quart full-fat butter pecan ice cream, softened
- 1 teaspoon salt
- 2 cups semisweet chocolate chips
- 1 cup sugar
- 1 stick melted butter
- Butter, for greasing
- 4 cups self-rising flour

Directions:

1. Preheat your griddle, with your lid closed, until it reaches 350.
2. Mix together the salt, sugar, flour, and ice cream with an electric mixer set to medium for two minutes.
3. As the mixer is still running, add in the chocolate chips, beating until everything is blended.
4. Spray a Bundt pan or tube pan with cooking spray. If you choose to use a pan that is solid, the center will take too long to cook. That's why a tube or Bundt pan works best.

5. Add the batter to your **Prepa**red pan.
6. Set the cake on the griddle, cover, and smoke for 50 minutes to an hour. A toothpick should come out clean.
7. Take the pan off of the griddle. For 10 minutes cool the bread. Remove carefully the bread from the pan and then drizzle it with some melted butter.

Nutrition: Calories: 148.7 Protein: 3.5g Carbs: 27g Fat: 3g

Conclusion

Thanks for making it to the end! This blackstone griddle cookbook has been written to be simple and easy to use. Its purpose is to make cooking on an outdoor griddle a simple task and to make the experience of cooking on an outdoor griddle an enjoyable one. The recipes are simple and easy to make, while producing attractive and delicious results. You have found a broad range of tasty recipes that are appropriate for a wide variety of tastes.

Happy Cooking!!!!

Made in the USA
Las Vegas, NV
17 December 2021